De Tocqueville

DE TOCQUEVILLE

Cheryl B. Welch

OXFORD
UNIVERSITY PRESS

OXFORD
UNIVERSITY PRESS

Great Clarendon Street, Oxford OX2 6DP

Oxford University Press is a department of the University of Oxford.
It furthers the University's objective of excellence in research, scholarship,
and education by publishing worldwide in

Oxford New York

Athens Auckland Bangkok Bogotá Buenos Aires Calcutta
Cape Town Chennai Dar es Salaam Delhi Florence Hong Kong Istanbul
Karachi Kuala Lumpur Madrid Melbourne Mexico City Mumbai
Nairobi Paris São Paulo Shanghai Singapore Taipei Tokyo Toronto Warsaw

with associated companies in Berlin Ibadan

Oxford is a registered trade mark of Oxford University Press
in the UK and in certain other countries

Published in the United States
by Oxford University Press Inc., New York

British Library Cataloguing in Publication Data

Data available

Library of Congress Cataloging in Publication Data

Data available

ISBN 0–19–878131–8

1 3 5 7 9 10 8 6 4 2

Typeset by RefineCatch Limited, Bungay, Suffolk
Printed in Great Britain by
Biddles Ltd., Guildford and King's Lynn

For John, Peter, and Jack

Acknowledgements

When Mark Philp and Tim Barton originally suggested several years ago that I should undertake this work on Tocqueville for the *Founders* series, I thought that it would be a relatively contained assignment. Having been teaching—and learning—about Tocqueville and nineteenth-century social theory for much of my academic career, I felt reasonably confident that I knew enough to write an introductory work that could both enlighten general readers and be of some interest to Tocqueville scholars. Alas, it did not prove to be such an easy task to explicate the importance of *M. de Tocqueville*! If, in the end, I have succeeded in doing him and my task some sort of justice, I owe that success to several people who have sustained me personally and intellectually along the way. When I have stumbled, of course, the responsibility is my own.

My husband, John, was as always my first and most exacting reader. I trust he knows how much I owe him, but it is my pleasure to acknowledge that debt here. My sons, Peter and Jack, tactfully refrained from asking how 'the Tocqueville' was going, and supplied my desk with some truly stunning statuary. To them, I dedicate this book.

For sparking my initial interest in Tocqueville, for providing an intellectual community for which I will always be grateful, and for so many sustaining conversations over the years, I thank several colleagues—now friends—whom I originally met in the Committee on Degrees in Social Studies at Harvard University: Robert Amdur, Michael Donnelly, Stanley Hoffmann, Stephen Holmes, David Landes, Murray Milgate, Anne Sa'adah, Shannon Stimson, and Judith Vichniac. To several cohorts of students in Social Studies 10, I can only say that I learned more from your penetrating questions than I probably ever taught you in tutorial.

Simmons College awarded me a faculty development grant to fund a research trip to Paris, and generously gave a semester of teaching relief that allowed me to launch this book project. For particularly helpful interactions at key points in the writing process itself, I am indebted to James Kloppenberg, Françoise Mélonio, Melvin Richter, and Shannon Stimson. For reading through several chapters with care and acuity, and for her encouragement throughout, I thank Nancy Rosenblum.

Finally, Mark Philp was a superb editor, whose fine judgements about forests and trees I much appreciated and tried to honour. Matthew Cotton shepherded the book through production with dispatch and tact, and Sarah Barrett's sharp editorial eye and sense of style saved me many errors.

Contents

Introduction

Alexis de Tocqueville was born nearly two centuries ago into what he himself characterized as a dying breed of anachronistic aristocrats. Yet his work seems to retain a greater measure of normative and explanatory power—and intellectual provocation—than that of many other nineteenth-century thinkers who are read today only to illuminate the historical genealogy of ideas. Tocqueville's readers still turn to him for more direct intellectual sustenance, and they are both many and surprisingly varied.[1] It is the underlying purpose of this book to explore this paradox, to probe the appeal of 'M. de Tocqueville' and the ability of his texts to shape our awareness of some of the central tensions of political life as it has been lived in the late twentieth century.

The timeless quality of a theorist's work might be thought to stem from its generality: the more universal the formulations, the more readily one may fill in a particular content and make the work one's own. In the case of Tocqueville, however, the opposite is true. Despite the fact that Tocqueville rhetorically set his sights on a general account of the nature of modern democracy, a 'new political science for a world quite new' (DAI, 8), the very character of his insight feeds on detail and context and resists too great an abstraction from that context. Without a sense of the particular problems with which he was engaged—largely problems associated with the constraints, opportunities, and complexities of political culture after the French Revolution—the power of his observations and the appeal of his method are less compelling. Tocqueville, as many commentators have noticed, examined social life through the lenses of 'ideal types'. He created from history and from his own observations certain hypothetical models of social and political action in order to make comparisons among societies and cultures and to create hypotheses about larger social patterns. In Tocqueville's case, these abstract sketches—for example, 'individualism' or 'the revolutionary spirit' or even 'democracy itself'—are particularly closely linked to the materials from which they are drawn and to his own heuristic purposes. Though some have tried to reconstruct a larger vision of Tocquevillian sociology, his contributions do not seem to me to lend themselves to the creation of grand theory. Rather, his particular mix of sociology, history, politics, and moral concern points to the inevitable limits of any overarching theoretical perspective—social scientific or philosophical—in illuminating matters of social and political choice that are necessarily grounded in unique cultural contexts. To understand what Tocqueville's intellectual project really is, then, one needs to read his texts, even more than those of many others, against the backdrop of what used to be called unselfconsciously his 'life and times.' Indeed, Tocqueville is important less as a general theorist of democracy than as a perceptive practitioner of 'culture studies' who focused his attention on certain key issues in his own political world that have since turned out to present intractable tensions in democratic politics and culture.

For much of the latter part of the twentieth century, Tocqueville has manifested a unique power to bring certain political anxieties into sharper focus, anxieties stemming from efforts to sustain civic cultures that will support the practices of self-government, from historical attempts to create liberal democracies without violence in unpropitious historical circumstances, and, finally, from troubling questions about the need for unifying moral beliefs as the basis for democratic viability. In shaping my own portrait of Tocqueville's historical context, I have consciously kept this provocative legacy in mind. The goal of Chapter 1 is to situate Tocqueville among a specific set of problems and writers in post-revolutionary France in order to give the reader a sense both of the idiosyncrasy of Tocqueville's project in his own milieu and its potential relevance to our own. Not only a theorist and writer, but a political man with a cause, Alexis de Tocqueville wished to write the sort of books that would inspire leaders to direct French political culture along new paths. But his characteristic manner of argument fell outside certain patterns that would define not only the discourse of his own time but much of French intellectual life in the nineteenth century. Though his books brought him fame, he found himself bitterly disappointed in his political hopes. But the very reasons for his failure to found a liberal 'movement' in his own time paradoxically help to explain his success in our own. Chapter 1 ('Tocqueville in His Time') and Chapter 5 ('Tocqueville in Our Time') are thus linked in particular ways. I have deliberately called attention to his avoidance of certain nineteenth-century orthodoxies in order to suggest that this avoidance has given him greater authority in a time when those orthodoxies have lost much of their theoretical purchase.

Chapters 2 and 3 explore the contributions to social and political analysis of Tocqueville's major published texts: *Democracy in America I* (1835), *Democracy in America II* (1840), and *The Old Regime and the Revolution* (1856).[2] In a certain sense Tocqueville had the same purpose in each of his works: to create in his readers a sense of the creative and destructive affinities between an inevitable social equality and an elusive political liberty. He was a thinker with one overriding preoccupation, filtering everything that he read or observed—about France, America, England, Ireland, Algeria, India, or Germany—through the lens of the potential connections between the increasing dominance of equality and the fragile practices of freedom. There were, nevertheless, important shifts of emphasis and concern in his work. In this brief introduction I want to signal two kinds of shiftiness with which any student of Tocqueville must reckon, and to which I will return below: his careless use of key terms and the seeming displacement of concern over time from democracy 'itself' to democracy in France.

The more attentively one reads Tocqueville, the more he disconcerts by his apparent disregard for terminological consistency. Certain phrases and words recur continually: for example 'liberty', 'equality', 'democracy', 'aristocracy', 'despotism', 'revolution', and 'centralization'. These words do not carry a completely stable set of meanings: they are context-dependent constructs designed to present some new insight in a particularly striking way. While Tocqueville was sometimes aware of the difficulties that resulted from his use of terms in new ways, he wished to avoid an overly technical vocabulary, and trusted his readers to glean his meaning from the context. Moreover, he loved contrast and paradox, often deliberately leaving his readers the task of inferring how some new discussion of the unexpected affinity between two concepts might relate to a previous discussion of the tensions between those same concepts. There is a powerful singularity of vision behind his work, but no systematic elaboration of interrelated theoretical categories. Especially in Chapter 2, which examines Tocqueville's initial elaboration of his social and political thought in the two volumes of *Democracy in America*, I shall consider how his loose terminology forces the reader to attend carefully to his specific intentions and to the relevant context of a discussion. I try to keep intention and context in the foreground, then, not for reasons of putative historical accuracy, but because without this context it would be difficult to recognize the quality and character of Tocqueville's thought. He often complained that he was misunderstood or read only superficially, and that in consequence people missed the true significance of his work. Yet due to his own desire to find the right phrase to capture his immediate insights, or perhaps to capture his audience, and to his failure to revisit old discussions in light of new ones, he bears some responsibility for this ease in misapprehension.

Tocqueville's writing over time reveals a second kind of shift. While his lack of attention to precision in the use of important concepts is a permanent feature of his style, more marked differences among his major works raise the question of whether he fundamentally changed his mind over the course of his lifetime. Is there, for example, an early Tocqueville and a late Tocqueville in the way that there is sometimes alleged to be an early Marx and a late Marx? The question of the relationship between the two *Democracies* has long been a contentious one among Tocqueville scholars. My decision to treat them together as one work reflects a conviction that there is a substantial unity of method and theme between the works, despite some obvious differences.[3] A more significant shift emerges, however, between *Democracy in America* and *The Old Regime*, a text that forms the basis of Chapter 3. Tocqueville's discussion of American democracy was always intended to address European problems for a European audience. But when he turns specifically to the significance of the French Revolution in *The Old Regime*, he leaves behind not only America but also a kind of theoretical comparative experiment based on the notion that there are at least two approximate instantiations of the ideal-typical construction that he sometimes called 'the shape of democracy itself'. Tocqueville does not abandon either comparative analysis or his central concern with the potential for freedom in an egalitarian world, but he turns his attention to the emergence (in time) of a unique historical formation —modern French democratic culture—rather than considering the generic concept of the shape of democracy. Thus he retreats from the overtly generalizing bent of *Democracy in America* to focus more closely on the underlying concern of all his work: the destiny of France.

Finally, I wish to say something in this introduction about the particular way in which Tocqueville connects his moral concerns to what we would today describe as his political science and historical sociology. In the first half of the nineteenth century, before the boundaries that now delineate academic canons were drawn, many social thinkers and historians demarcated their subjects in ways that today would cross disciplinary boundaries. That Tocqueville's work should be 'pre-' or 'inter-' disciplinary in this sense is not surprising. What is unusual is that he both wears his heart on his sleeve—in his references to eternal values or to divine purposes in history—and yet urges us to consider social matters purely from 'the human point of view', i.e. from the point of view of sober secular history or functionalist sociology. Chapter 4 specifically considers the relationship of Tocqueville's moral beliefs and spiritual anxieties to his social science, a relationship at the very core of the irony and detachment that permeate all of his work, and that—ironically—still compel in an age tormented by different social demons and fears.

Notes

1 For example, in January 2000 the *Journal of Democracy* chose to devote its special tenth anniversary issue on 'Democracy in the World' to commissioned articles discussing Tocqueville's *Democracy in America*. Authors as varied as Francis Fukuyama, William Galston, Philippe Schmitter, Nathan Glazer, Adam Michnik, Zbigniew Brzezinski, Terry Karl, Jean Elshtain, and Paul Cantor use Tocqueville to discuss the end of history, civil society, European federalism, race and ethnicity, the collapse of communism, war and foreign policy, international inequality, women and the family, and the democratic aesthetics of postmodernism. As the editors comment, 'as we enter the millennium one may say with little exaggeration: *We are all Tocquevilleans now*': *Journal of Democracy*, 11(1)(2000), 9.

2 I also rely, of course, on Tocqueville's *Recollections*, first published in France in 1893, and on a wide range of his work now available in the meticulously edited *Œuvres complètes*. But the organizing principle of Chaps. 2 and 3 is the impact of each major work.

3 See below, p. 116.

I

Tocqueville
in His Time

Contextualizing Tocqueville

The distinctive voice of Alexis de Tocqueville—analytical but not arid, detached but not disengaged, passionate but not partisan—has spoken directly to many audiences, and not only to French ones. Thus Tocqueville has many contexts, including a rather astonishing centrality in current debates about the past and future of democracy as a modern regime. Tocqueville's presence in our time will be the subject of the conclusion of this book. It is the purpose of this chapter to locate him in his own. Historical contextualization, of course, is an intellectual practice filled with hidden assumptions and value-laden choices about the ultimate significance of a writer's work. Is Tocqueville to be placed among the builders of the western social science canon? Among the French Romantics? Among the guardians of the liberal spirit? Among the European conservatives? Among the nineteenth-century historians of grand narrative? Or perhaps among the great travel writers?

My efforts at location are no exception to the rule that contexts are made, not found. The questions that motivate this book—how has Tocqueville's work, chameleon-like, been able so easily to take on new theoretical colourings in new settings? and why does this body of work seem to retain a greater measure of normative and explanatory power than that of his nineteenth-century rivals?—have guided my particular location of Tocqueville in the landscape of nineteenth-century French thought. Since I believe that his ability to provoke us today is linked to his original exoticism in that landscape, I structure this chapter around certain characteristic intellectual idioms that Tocqueville largely avoided or eluded.

This introductory chapter, then, situates Tocqueville's work among three changing patterns in sensibilities that transformed how people argued about social and political issues after the French Revolution: first, the search for a science of the social that would save the French from the results of their apparently disastrous experiments in revolutionary politics; second, the pull of the past, or what has sometimes been termed the 'rise of historical consciousness'; and, finally, the widespread yearning to validate a spiritualized version of human reason to stand against the dark forces unleashed by the Revolution. These altered intellectual horizons inevitably marked Tocqueville's thought, no less than that of his contemporaries. He responded, however, by taking an original and sometimes solitary path that disregarded the markers and signs constructed by others. For that very reason his work engages those who dispute the validity of that nineteenth-century intellectual map: the many who question disciplinary canons, deconstruct historical narratives, or distrust liberal 'universalism'. My aim here is not to describe fully the political and social discourse of a period so complex and volatile as early nineteenth-century France—that would be a daunting and perhaps pointless task—but rather to suggest a particular way to think about Tocqueville by distancing him from his contemporaries. Because he attributed his estrangement to the peculiarity of his having lived suspended between two worlds, I begin with a brief sketch of the circumstances of his life.

Tocqueville's 'Life and Times'

Born in 1805 under the empire of Napoleon Bonaparte, Alexis de Tocqueville outlived two monarchies and a republic and died in 1859 under the empire of Napoleon's nephew. Thus he belonged to the first generation with no personal memory of the French Revolution, but with an intense consciousness of existing in its unruly political wake. This time may have been no more turbulent than others in French political history, but its ideological confusions and sense of social crisis marked an entire generation. Exceptional in other ways, Tocqueville was nevertheless completely the child of his time in his consciousness of living in a 'world quite new' (DAI, 8).

Alexis was the third son of Hervé de Tocqueville, of the ancient Norman nobility, and Louise de Rosanbo, granddaughter of Malesherbes, defender of Louis XVI before the revolutionary tribunal. The guillotine claimed many of his relatives. His parents, imprisoned shortly after their marriage, were spared only by Thermidor. Tocqueville's father became a dedicated and respected royal prefect under the Bourbon Restoration, and his two brothers took up military careers and reactionary opinions. His mother, always prone to periods of melancholy and depression, mourned the Old Regime and believed that the legitimists could reconquer France and restore both the royal line and true religion. Tocqueville, then, was born into a tight cocoon of aristocratic reaction. He remained all his life an aristocrat, as he phrased it, 'by instinct', and the most intimate of his lifelong friends were fellow nobles. Unlike his family and closest associates, however, he decisively broke with his caste and chose the new France on 'principle'.[1] How was this transformation accomplished?

Tocqueville grew up near Paris, educated like his two older brothers by a pious abbé who instructed the Tocqueville *fils* out of Jansenist-inspired Catholic texts.[2] At 15, Tocqueville accompanied his father to Metz, where he entered the lycée and a wider social world than his restricted family circle. This was, by most accounts, a crucial period in his life. At 16, he lost his religious faith and began a lifelong struggle with doubt, 'not only doubt about one thing or another in particular, but an all-embracing doubt'.[3] According to his biographer, he began also to question the social values revered by his family and by the closed world of the aristocracy.[4] From his studies and his middle-class acquaintances at Metz, he learned that this world was scorned as anachronistic and inimical to the values of post-revolutionary society. Very early he seems to have come to the unshakeable conviction that the world of the French nobility— with its norms of hierarchy, ascriptive privilege, honour, exclusivity, and loyalty—was destined to be replaced completely by an egalitarian social order, and that he would need to make his way under this new dispensation.

During the remaining years before his departure for America, as a law student and then as *juge auditeur* in the Versailles courts, Tocqueville struggled both with his identity as a member of an anachronistic caste and with his potential vocation in the new France. Indeed, the roots of the particular estrangement between sense and sensibility in all his writings are inevitably entangled in this early awareness of being a displaced person, an aristocrat who had never lived and would never live in an aristocracy. His intellectual reworking of this fractured social identity—rather than, as for Mill or Comte or Marx, a particular intellectual tradition or milieu—would be the greatest single influence on his thinking about society and politics. If he was not to abandon either his country or his time, he needed to understand the alien norms and passions of the larger society in which he found himself. As he said later in a letter to his English translator, 'one can be powerfully interested only in the living'.[5] His appetite for history and comparative study, which was whetted by François Guizot's lectures on European and French history and civilization, remained a passion with a single object: how could one grasp the new logic and psychology of what he would eventually call the democratic social condition?

The Revolution of 1830 precipitated a reluctant declaration of allegiance to the new dynasty, but Tocqueville had no real moral qualms about ratifying a commitment to liberal constitutional government at which he had arrived much earlier. 'I have at last sworn the oath. My conscience does not reproach me, but I am still deeply wounded. . . . '[6] Nevertheless, the future of a young magistrate with impeccable legitimist connections must have looked quite unpromising in 1830. The trip to the United States that he undertook with his friend Gustave de Beaumont in 1831–2, allegedly to examine its penal system, was in part an expedient escape from an uncertain personal and political situation. But it was more than that. French liberals of many varieties had long perceived America as that 'other' republic which had sought political equality but had escaped the taint of Jacobinism or tyranny. Moreover, there were many links between public-spirited French nobles and the fledgling democracy. It would be natural for Tocqueville to think that America had much to teach him about the culture of democracy. It is clear that this belief, and the optimistic hope of using what he would learn to make a stir on his return, helped to precipitate his decision to visit the United States.

Tocqueville and Beaumont spent nine months in America.[7] The pretext for their trip was satisfied by the 1833 *Du système pénitentiaire aux États-unis et de son application en France*, written almost entirely by Beaumont.[8] On his return, Tocqueville resigned his legal position and for the next decade devoted himself totally to writing the two volumes of *De la démocratie en Amérique* (published in 1835 and 1840). An instant success in Europe and America, the first volume gained him official recognition by the Académie Française and election to membership in the Académie des Sciences Morales et Politiques. The obscure magistrate had become a famous author at the age of 30. He visited England and Ireland in 1835 as a fêted *homme de lettres*, with immediate access to influential intellectual and political figures, with whom he remained in contact for the rest of his life.[9] Also in 1835 he married, against the wishes of his family, a middle-class English woman of limited means several years his senior. This marriage to Mary Mottley, whatever its difficulties, apparently brought Tocqueville a certain equilibrium that was necessary to his life as a writer and public figure.[10] While still taken up with composing the second volume of *Democracy*, Tocqueville ran unsuccessfully for a seat in the Chambre de Deputés from his native Normandy. He stood again for election in 1839, won his seat, and remained in the Chamber until the Revolution of 1848. When the second volume of *Democracy* appeared in 1840, he was already launched on a career of active participation in French public life.

From his early 20s Tocqueville had believed that his calling was not merely for the study of politics, but, like his noble forebears who had long dominated the affairs of the Cotentin region, for public service. The voyage to America had in part been a rigorous intellectual preparation for such an active role, and the success of *Democracy in America*, as well as the lowering of the age requirement for deputy, made it possible for him to begin his political career sooner than he had hoped. This career, all things considered, was a disappointment. Tocqueville possessed the intellect, but not the temperament, for political life. He was a mediocre speaker, uncomfortable in circumstances of political manoeuvre, often either too hesitant or too precipitate in action, and wedded to a proud independence that interfered with the building of successful alliances. Moreover, his nuanced political positions made him less than comfortable in the ranks of the opposition, which he occupied for most of the July Monarchy. During his time in the Chamber of Deputies, he was associated most closely with the work of certain expert committees dealing with the abolition of slavery in the French colonies and with social and prison reform. He also followed foreign affairs closely, particularly the colonization of Algeria, which he visited in 1841 and 1845 and on which he wrote a memoir and several long parliamentary reports.[11]

Elected by universal suffrage to the Constitutent Assembly in 1848, Tocqueville helped to draft the constitution of the Second Republic. The next year he was elected to the Legislative Assembly, serving as its vice-president. After Louis-Napoleon Bonaparte's election as president of the Republic—Tocqueville had supported Cavaignac—Tocqueville joined the Barrot cabinet as Minister of Foreign Affairs, a post that he held for five months until the entire ministry was dismissed. During the summer of 1850, Tocqueville, always in frail health, fell ill with pulmonary tuberculosis and took an extended leave of absence from the Assembly. He returned in time to be arrested and briefly imprisoned along with other parliamentary leaders after Louis-Napoléon's *coup d'état* on December 2, 1851. Tocqueville then withdrew completely from public life. He completed a personal memoir of the Revolution of 1848 that would eventually be published as the *Souvenirs*, and spent his final years, plagued by deteriorating health, writing *L'Ancien Régime et la Révolution*. It was published in 1856 to immediate acclaim in England, Germany, and Russia, as well as in France.

Alexis de Tocqueville, then, was a prominent man of letters and a deputy in the July Monarchy, an important participant in the turbulent Second Republic, and a public figure of great prestige under the Second Empire. Moreover, from the beginning he addressed his work deliberately to his fellow *notables* with the explicit aim of influencing their political practice. Yet his writings, more than most, have escaped the confines of their intended audience. His success in reaching beyond his original readers is partly related to his failure to connect to their most characteristic patterns of thought. Quintessentially French, Tocqueville's writings on society and politics nevertheless fell outside the prevailing terms and references of debate in postrevolutionary France. The rest of this chapter will discuss three of those emerging patterns of thought, patterns that underlie debates over the claims of social science, the uses of history, and the imperatives of morality. In each case I will attempt in a preliminary way to contrast Tocqueville's approach to those of key contemporaries in order to throw into relief the substantive 'Tocquevillian' contributions discussed in subsequent chapters.

Social Science and 'the Shape of Democracy Itself'

In one of his famous phrases from *Democracy in America* Tocqueville proclaimed that what was needed by his generation was 'a new political science for a world quite new' (DAI, 8). This invocation of a 'new science' has provoked many debates over what sort of science he can be said to have introduced, but the phrase was in some ways *de rigueur* for a young man who wished to make a name for himself by analysing post-revolutionary Europe. Indeed, a host of early nineteenth-century thinkers were busy sketching 'new' social scientific utopias that would in some way both encompass and transcend the legacy of the Enlightenment.

Tocqueville, like those contemporaries, ultimately failed to found a new science for a new age. Nevertheless, the analytical structure underlying the two volumes of *Democracy in America* did break away not only from the eighteenth century but also from contemporary ways of thinking about how to study human society scientifically. In a very fundamental sense Tocqueville's particular conjoining of 'science' directly with 'politics' contradicted tendencies that had long been developing in French thought and that greatly accelerated after the Revolution. For many, the proper object of scientific study was not the body politic at all, but the social body, an entity conceived as separate from, and superior to, political agency. Hence the term of art was increasingly 'la science sociale', though there was little agreement on either the meaning of the 'social' or the methods of its particular science. Reviewing the post-revolutionary fate of what eighteenth-century *philosophes* had usually termed the 'science of man' reveals both a growing preoccupation with 'social science' and the freshness of Tocqueville's approach against this background.

Revolutionary legacies: the science of man and the rights of man

It was during the French Revolution itself that the Enlightenment project of a 'science of man' began to be transformed into the nineteenth-century search for a meta-social science. The term 'science sociale' was first heard in the salons and clubs of the moderate republicans in the early 1790s.[12] It referred to a body of knowledge that would allow one to identify the natural needs of society—for freedom or equality or rights or property—that had been ignored or despised by allegedly unnatural aristocratic governments. This explosive ideological charge underlay the use of the term 'social science' in the important pamphlet literature of the early phases of the Revolution, including the writings of Siéyès and Condorcet. Their initial attempts to ground revolutionary political action scientifically were swept up in a general glorification of the Declaration of the Rights of Man and Citizen, viewed as a kind of rallying-cry for the social and political truths revealed by clear analytical thinking.

Although never explicitly stated, the logic of the connection between a universal set of truths about human psychology and the desirability of universal equality in rights seemed obvious from the very definition of all people as sensate creatures endowed with reason.[13] During the early phase of the Revolution, then, the terms 'social science' or 'political science' were quite often spoken in the same breath as the 'rights of man'; they connoted a set of principles that would free society from the grip of a barbaric political absolutism. It is this meaning to which Tocqueville refers in the following passage from a sketch of the history of France that he published in 1836: 'grasping in passing the principal ideas that had been running through the world for five centuries, France was suddenly the first on the continent of Europe to formulate the new science whose elements had been assembled with great effort by her neighbors.'[14]

As the Revolution progressed, however, the rhetoric of rights seemed to take on its own frantic momentum and to break through the unspoken economic and social assumptions of the moderates. Frightened at the course of the Revolution under the Jacobins and the Terror, and uneasy about their own earlier embrace of revolutionary slogans, many moderates abandoned talk of rights.[15] During the Thermidorian reaction and the rule of the Directory, Condorcet's younger associates from the early liberal phase of the Revolution, who emerged as a distinct group of thinkers known as the Idéologues, began to seek a new conception of social science distinguished from revolutionary rhetoric. Like the English utilitarians, whom they greatly resembled, the Idéologues self-consciously developed the theme of social utility, in the process separating it sharply from the notions of natural right with which it had been conflated in the works of earlier theorists. They also resolved to be more positive—i.e. more exact, careful, and attentive to facts—deliberately following the lead of the physical scientists in the newly formed Institut National. The Idéologues did not abandon the hope that their philosophical method would lead to knowledge that could foster a regeneration of the French polity, but they began to draw directly on a notion of scientific legitimacy that was distinct from revolutionary ideology.

Idéologue social science

For the Idéologues, the scientific method underlying both research and public instruction was still to be *analysis*, i.e. the decomposition of all ideas into basic elements of individual sense perception and the lucid recomposition of these elements into complex ideas that could then be used to clarify the misguided practices of their contemporaries. Inherited from the *philosophes* and especially from Condillac, this method was invoked universally as the way to achieve progress in the physical and social sciences. Among the most influential articulations of the passion for analysis were the lectures in the Institute's second class (Moral and Political Sciences) delivered concurrently by Pierre Cabanis and Destutt de Tracy. Later published, these works were widely disseminated in the next thirty years.

The Idéologues rather grandly hoped to launch the French era in world history: a union of peaceful democratic republics filled with individuals pursuing their own and society's interests in a symbiosis guided by the utilitarian dictates of Idéologue social science. The fate of this vision in Restoration France, however, was quite other than its authors intended. For many writers, including Alexis de Tocqueville, it was to become an object lesson in methodological failure rather than a model of the way to connect political action to a scientific analysis of society. The work of the Idéologues is important precisely because it became a negative symbol of a whole school of social analysis, a school that was thought to be both dangerous (because associated with revolution) and bankrupt (because it had failed to found a lasting regime). Increasingly, critics traced the flaw in Idéologue theory—and by extension in the Enlightenment theories on which it drew—to its false starting point in the needs of abstract individuals.

Often the works of the Idéologues themselves foreshadowed their supersedence by more organic or collectivist models. Pierre Cabanis, for example, was a doctor whose research into human physiology proved particularly subversive of the universalistic ideal of the *bon citoyen* that he himself continued to uphold. Presenting himself as a methodical collector of physiological facts for a history of human nature, he catalogued various influences (including temperament, age, sex, disease, climate, and diet) upon individual sensibility: a necessary tilling of the intellectual fields in preparation for producing a generation of more equal individuals who could shoulder the duties of republican citizenship.[16] Cabanis, however, left those fields sown with the seeds of an entirely new crop of organic metaphors: biology as the primary context of social theorizing, a physiological proof of innate differences among humans, and a profoundly gendered view of the social passions. This crop would be harvested by a new generation of social thinkers who abandoned Cabanis's attachment to methodological individualism.

Like the physiological *idéologie* of Cabanis, the rational *idéologie* of Destutt de Tracy had the paradoxical result of providing the basis for an attack on his own political ideals, and of further detaching French notions of social science from sensationalism and individualistic empiricism. In the case of Tracy, however, the instrument of this detachment was not a turn to biology, but to economics. He applied the method of analysis to political economy, which put a 'logic of the human will' at the centre of social science. Heavily dependent on the work of J. B. Say, the most important interpreter and popularizer of Adam Smith on the Continent, Tracy restated Smithian economics in a way that idealized the vision of society as self-interested exchange. This orderly rational substratum, which he was among the first to term the realm of 'social' economy, was separate from politics but could provide normative guidance to it. Tracy's logic of the will and its effects exalted the scientific laws of production and largely equated these laws with the laws of social happiness. Moreover, he prefaced his discussion of production with a series of definitions—of personality, property, wealth, and value—that pointedly exaggerated this utopian vision based on self-interested individuals.

Tracy's discussion of the individualistic method of analysis as the basis of social science, however, also called attention to its philosophically weakest points. He recognized radical defects in memory and language that told against the historical emergence of an ideal model of social commerce in which everyone would gain. More important, his chapters on the distribution of the social product heightened the sense of a radical disjuncture between the rational theory and irrational practice of commercial societies. Adopting a pessimistic Malthusian perspective on the population problem, he argued that population would outstrip the productive capacities of the economy. Indeed, from the point of view of the actual distribution of the social product, Tracy could conclude only that the optimistic promises of production remained tragically unfulfilled; one had to 'recognize everywhere the superiority of needs over means, the weakness of the individual, and his inevitable suffering'.[17] He thus painted a bleak picture of an unequally distributed social product that caused misery and suffering among the wage-earning 'people', even as he reiterated that justice required an equal weighting of every individual's pleasure and pain. Despite this unsettling presentation of inevitable inequality and suffering, Tracy's solutions did not go beyond the classical economists' pleas for education, complete liberty of trade, and freedom to emigrate. Hence he left the distinct impression that the new science of the social—i.e. Smith's theory of production and distribution as popularized and philosophized by his French followers—was radically wanting in its ability to deliver on its theoretical and normative promises.

The Idéologues' recoil from years of political instability, terror, and dictatorship led them to yearn for a substratum of social laws that would provide a scientific grounding for politics. They were attracted to the newly emerging sciences of biology and economics because both were apparently rooted in the reality of everyday life. After what seemed to them the psychotic delusions of revolutionary and imperialistic politics, they longed for the comforting touchstone of mundane need. Although their formulations of social science proved to be transitional, the Idéologues were highly successful in publicizing the notion that 'the social'—a realm of human experience with its own laws and regulating principles—was superior to 'the political'—a realm of application in which things might go radically awry if leaders departed from science and reason and succumbed to the lure of ambition or the mob. They were to have a few faithful disciples among economists and a small sect of free-trade liberals, but their more important legacy lay elsewhere. The superiority of the 'social' to the 'political' was taken up both by their radical followers, who eventually abandoned liberal politics in favour of social utopias, and by their conservative antagonists, who ignored liberal politics in favour of a social economy flavoured with nostalgia for functional feudal interdependence. Tocqueville had certain affinities with both of these groups, but he never followed them down the path of privileging social laws as guides to political action.

Socialist democrats and social economists

The largely individualist conceptions of the social found in the works of the Idéologues during the early years of the nineteenth century rapidly gave way to more explicitly collectivist conceptions. We can follow this development in two very different groups: post-revolutionary democratic and socialist writers (largely radical and secular) and writers interested in issues of public charity, prison reform, and public health (largely conservative and Catholic). Among these writers, though for different reasons, one finds the same confidence that a science of the social should guide politics, and a similar hostility towards Enlightenment and revolutionary versions of that science. Though he shared some of their ideas, including admiration for the American republic and for 'self-interest well understood', Tocqueville came to believe that the former were irresponsible and even psychologically unbalanced radicals; similarly, while he agreed with the latter about the need for certain social reforms, he opposed their attempts to make politics reflect a new vision of hierarchical interdependence. This refusal to adopt a privileged view of the 'social' placed Tocqueville outside a peculiar consensus that bridged fundamental political differences in France. Let me rehearse briefly the emergence of this agreement among important portions of both left and right, an agreement that politics was a derivative activity.

The initial followers of the Idéologues, whose tortured personal odysseys would eventually lead to sectarian withdrawal or alienated dissent, often began their political involvement in the 1820s by joining illegal political movements or by participating in inchoate reading circles on the fringes of university life. Steeped in authors like Rousseau, Kant, Tracy, and Bentham, these young radicals called themselves *individualistes*, a term adopted to signify the search for a scientific basis for individual rights in human organization.[18] The term would eventually pass into French usage as an epithet; Tocqueville's important concept of *individualisme* is a distinctive variation on a range of pejorative meanings. In any case, for the most passionate and committed of these young radicals, their particular method of 'individualism' proved to be a way-station rather than a destination. They began to fault eighteenth-century writers—and their nineteenth-century followers—for a flawed understanding of physiology or history and a blind acceptance of individualist economic dogmas. Increasingly, they turned to alternative versions of social science, such as that of Saint-Simon or other utopian socialists.[19]

In France many thinkers would eventually follow this path and claim to have privileged scientific access to the social. The development of sociology as a discipline—from Saint-Simon to Auguste Comte to Emile Durkheim—was premissed on the independent reality of the 'social' and the need for a new positive methodology to analyse social facts. This conception of subordinating politics to a positivist science of society was to come into its own with the founding of the Third Republic, and was eventually to mark French conceptions of republicanism very deeply.[20] There were in fact powerful reasons to concentrate one's intellectual and reformist energies outside the established arena of politics in nineteenth-century France, since the dynastic and religious divisions that plagued representative politics continually frustrated the creation of a regime with broad-based legitimacy. The resulting temptation to defer to the demands of something called the 'social' that would supersede politics was not limited to those scattered on the republican and socialist left. The group of conservative social reformers who became known as social economists objectified the needs of society and the priority of these needs in a similar way.

Interested in issues of charity and public welfare from a traditional Catholic perspective, the social economists agreed with the nascent socialists that unemployment and poverty, with their attendant problems of disease and crime, were evils that ought to be addressed by social policy.[21] More important, they also came to view these ills as specifically modern diseases, caused neither by individual sinfulness nor by governmental corruption or neglect, but by particular laws of social development. Unlike the socialists, however, these writers feared rather than glorified the victims of modern poverty. They saw the newly pauperized classes as a frightening social threat: ignorant, immoral, insubordinate, and imbued with a false sentiment of honour and confidence that was the legacy of popular politicization during the Revolution. The anxiety and tension generated by this conjunction—belief in the objective causation of poverty and fear of its effects—led these thinkers to seek to remedy the deficiencies of earlier economic versions of social science. Those earlier theories, they thought, had not only assumed but glorified selfishness. And selfishness—of employers and workers alike—had exacerbated the emergence of rootless revolutionary mobs. The social economists could not accept an economic science that seemed predicated on the emergence of menacing hordes who 'made one tremble for the whole order of society'.[22] Their instinct was to shoot the messenger, that is, to reject the science of political economy itself. Its methodological focus on the needs and desires of the abstract individual, they thought, interacted perniciously with the legal individualism that had been introduced in the Revolution and consolidated in the Napoleonic Code. They argued that legal individualism aggravated the inevitable condition of being poor and created an abnormal social condition called pauperism. By destroying intermediary associations (guilds and corporations) that had formerly served to contain the social perversions associated with poverty, exclusive economic 'rights' were among the causes of modern pauperism. Solutions that depended on further recognition of such individual rights—whether exclusive rights to property or to work or to state aid—would intensify individualism and deepen the void between state and citizen.[23]

These conservative writers took on the task of reforming the science of political economy, which they renamed 'social economy', but accepted the notion that their reformed social science had a special relationship to public policy. The aim of this social science should be not only to maximize production, but also to provide adequate food, clothing, and shelter for the pauperized classes, and moral education and discipline for the entire population. If social development had loosened moral ties and taken away traditional associations, then the science of society must lead the way in fashioning a new moral and social integument. As conservative Catholics, many of the social economists adopted a notion of social obligation with clear affinities to a religious conception of the reciprocal duties that bound Christians together within a Catholic community. Their specific recommendations ranged from creating an infrastructure of worker self-help, to infusing new economic elites with a sense of social responsibility, to individual moral therapy. Yet their idea of the social community—a functional replacement for the community of the faithful—was not itself religious; it had no specific theology or clerisy to give it determinate shape. Rather, what gave their conception of the social realm a certain coherence was their determination to avoid legal and political vocabularies in favour of a different legitimizing mantle: social science. Indeed, to call an issue such as prison reform, child labour, or poor relief 'social' in the elite political culture of the Restoration and the July Monarchy was to signal that positions on the issue would not be discussed in political or legal terms, but rather would be determined by an impartial analysis of social facts as manifested in a consensus of expert opinion.[24] Society, these reformers began to argue, had its own logic and regulating force, different from that of merely economic laws. This logic ought to rule the arena of political interaction.

We are now in a position to see more distinctly some characteristic patterns of thinking about the relationship between 'science', 'society', and 'politics' in early nineteenth-century France. Two groups in particular concerned themselves with the notion of a science of society: utopian thinkers and conservative social reformers. Both groups, although they defined themselves in distinct opposition to liberal individualistic versions of social science, were at the same time deepening and sharpening earlier assumptions of an antagonism between the realm of politics and the distinctive realm of the 'social'. Their increasing resort to the term 'social science' signalled a distancing or disaffection from contemporary political practice within France's new representative institutions. Either the term was appropriated to a utopian sensibility (separatist or revolutionary) or it was used to avoid ideological divisions by validating a separate realm of expertise, namely an expertise in diagnosing the spiritual pathologies inherent in modernity. In both cases, however, social science was thought to provide both an explanation for why things were as they were and an explicit normative direction for reform.

Against this background Tocqueville's call for a new political science, and his own efforts to develop and practise an alternative rhetorical approach to guiding political practice, emerges as distinctly original.[25] Tocqueville shared some of the sensibility and concerns of both republican socialists and social economists. Like the socialists he believed that one could not transcend 'individualism' by going back to the Old Regime. Like the social economists he worried about the moral debasement associated with pauperism and the 'dangerous' social question.[26] In a fundamental way, however, he would violate the understanding of the relationship between social and political that these early proponents of 'social science' implicitly endorsed. Tocqueville did not take as his special subject the regulating principles of the 'social', principles at once normative and scientific that should either enlist or trump state action. Rather he sought to analyse the complex links—institutional, intellectual, and above all psychological—*between* social and political institutions.

21

Democracy in America focuses above all on *mœurs* or mores, patterns of behaviour that reinforce each other—or pull against one another—and settle into cultural practices. The world of politics itself turns out to have a culture and a history and sustaining *mœurs*. Tocqueville, then, attempted to fathom the intricate psychological mechanisms that sustain a political culture and to assess the weight of these practices on contemporary action. This is not to say that his conception of political science is primarily empirical rather than normative. Indeed, his purpose was always to understand and recommend particular social and political patterns of behaviour because those patterns reinforced a 'free' way of life that he thought transcendently valuable. It is only to say that his norms were not implicit in any notion of the 'social'. His conception of the proper fit between society and politics gave primary place to the potentially creative activity of citizens, not to the constraining or directive laws of society. Democratic individuals could intervene successfully to create free institutions only if they first understood the 'tendencies' shaping their world, but tendencies and instincts were not social laws.

What made possible Tocqueville's particular rearrangement of conceptual space, and his reversion to a concept of political science that owes more to Montesquieu than to any of his contemporaries, was in large part the power of his imaginative encounter with America. Part acute observation, part projection, part aesthetic intuition, Tocqueville's brilliant portrait of democracy in America would bypass the developing polarities in French intellectual life. He was of course not alone among his contemporaries in noticing that institutions, attitudes, and beliefs connect what we now call civil society to politics. Nevertheless, he was unique in focusing all his intellectual energies on elucidating these connections in a manner that was largely comparative and non-teleological. In America he thought he had found a laboratory where the social was so saturated with the political that democratic society was in effect self-activated. There, a set of intimate connections between the social and the political instincts of democracy could be dissected and described. 'There are countries in which some authority, in a sense outside the body social, influences it and forces it to progress in a certain direction. There are others in which power is divided, being at the same time within the society and outside it. Nothing like that is to be seen in the United States; there society acts by and for itself.'[27]

Like his contemporaries, Tocqueville would conceptually separate the social from the political; unlike them, he did so not to grant the former a special normative status, but only to analyse the interlocking ideas and sentiments that connected the two in a dense web of mutually reinforcing practice. He would develop a number of powerful intuitions about the dominant patterns of interaction in a new society that was purely 'democratic'. And these intuitions, or *idées mères*, imposed a certain pattern on his interpretation of what he observed in both America and Europe, a pattern that will be the subject of Chapter 2. But these leading ideas never rose to the level of social 'laws' and did not constitute a species of grand 'social' theory.

History and 'the Natural Destiny of a People'

Tocqueville's original American journey, and the second intellectual journey that occurred as he reworked his thoughts and observations into the text of *Democracy in America*, effected a radical displacement of his analytical focus onto a subject that was anomalous within developing French discussions of social science.[28] This subject—the interpenetrations of society and politics that create a particular public culture—was Montesquieuian in inspiration but would be original in execution. One might argue, however, that it is quite premature to conclude from Tocqueville's distance from the project of creating 'social science' that his approach to political science stood outside the major theoretical *problématiques* of his time. There were other genres of writing about politics and society that may provide a more illuminating context for his particular concerns. Indeed, Tocqueville's contemporary reputation in France has until recently rested more on *The Old Regime and the Revolution* than on *Democracy in America*. Although *Democracy* made him famous, it was as historian rather than sociologist that he would enter the pantheon of French writers.

The purpose of both of Tocqueville's major works is ultimately the illumination of France's political destiny. America—like England, Canada, Ireland, and Germany—serves heuristically only as a way of shedding light on France's particular historical situation. Perhaps, then, we should measure Tocqueville's intellectual project primarily against the standard of post-revolutionary histories, many of which took as their particular subject the relationships among social, economic, and political development in France. François Guizot, for example, emerged from the shadow of the Revolution with the clear view that the new generation could be successful only if it recognized the interpenetration of the new social and political orders.

In a striking image of the way a traumatic event can transform a person's or a nation's perception of its past, Guizot compares the French Revolution to a seismic disturbance that turns a familiar landscape into alien territory. Such events

take possession of all that exists in society, transform it, and place everything in an entirely new position; so that if, after such a shock, man looks back upon the history of the past, he can scarcely recognise it. That which he sees, he had never seen before; what he saw once, no longer exists as he saw it; facts rise up before him with unknown faces, and speak to him in a strange language . . . The actual spectacle remains the same, but it is viewed by another spectator occupying a different place; to his eyes all is changed.[29]

We can complicate Guizot's image even further by multiplying the spectators of the revolutionary earthquake and placing them at different topological lookout points. From the fall of Napoleon to the consolidation of the Third Republic, French historian/ spectators in fact disagreed bitterly about what they saw when they gazed at their collective past. The initial sights, recorded in the Bourbon Restoration, were constantly redrawn and refined as each faction strove to promote its own politics as the realization of France's national destiny. New generations would tell and retell the story of the Revolution itself, with different accounts of the rising action, climax, and dénouement, and with different heroes and villains.

The reconstructions of the French past with the strongest claim to have formed Tocqueville's historical sensibilities are the jeremiads on the Revolution of writers like Burke and DeMaistre and the 'new' history of the so-called Doctrinaires. Among the latter, the most important was François Guizot himself. From 1828 to 1830, Tocqueville attended his seminal course of lectures on the history of civilization in Europe and on the history of France. For all this undoubted influence, however, Tocqueville's account of the significance of the French Revolution has outlasted its sources; it is both subtly original and a continuing inspiration to those who practise the craft of political and cultural history. Neither reactionary nor Doctrinaire, Tocqueville's view of the destiny of France combines history and politics in a way that challenges many of the assumptions of his teachers.

The conservatives were among the first to claim history as the basis of post-revolutionary politics, largely inventing the notion of an *ancien régime* as they looked back in grief and anger. There were important differences among conservative writers from the émigré generation, but certain themes surface again and again in their writings: a new realism about the fragile bases of political authority and the need for legitimizing beliefs; a perception of the religious significance of the Revolution, whether as divine punishment for eighteenth-century hubris or as the work of the Anti-Christ; a tendency to equate revolution with crime and conspiracy; and finally, a view of the Old Regime as an aristocratic monarchy that represented the full flowering of the French political spirit, even if it had inevitably made mistakes or mis-steps.

Tocqueville understood this milieu in his bones. His mother could bring tears to the eyes of a family gathering by singing a lament for Louis XVI.[30] With these aristocratic reactionaries, Tocqueville shared a painful sense of dislocation and loss. Moreover, an awareness of legitimist sensibilities and a desire to remind the nobility of what were in his view their historical responsibilities would underlie much of his rhetoric.[31] Yet, although a vestigial nostalgia surfaces in his published portraits of the feudal nobility, and even more frequently in his private correspondence, what is surely more remarkable is the extent to which he was able to free himself from reactionary refrains. He departed from his legitimist friends and relatives in his unwavering disengagement from the past, and in his steady recognition of a French future in which his own class should not expect to play any part as a collective entity, but rather must enter the political game as individuals on terms dictated by the victors.[32] He understood the sensibilities of De Maistre and Bonald, but his intellectual mentors lay elsewhere. From his earliest days as a student, he wished to use the past to take the measure of his contemporaries and the nature of the challenges they faced. In this quest it is undeniable that '[h]e found his guide and teacher in the person of Guizot'.[33] Indeed, Tocqueville learned so much from liberal historical arguments in the Restoration that it has recently been argued that the great debates of the 1820s supplied the questions that led him to America and that governed his observations there.[34]

The milieu of moderate liberalism certainly shaped Tocqueville's views on the inevitability of the democratic revolution, and hence his decisive break with legitimism and his family. Guizot's lectures and writings are the proximate source for Tocqueville's notion of advancing 'civilization', and they also stimulated him to think comparatively about the different historical trajectories of political liberty, particularly in France and England. The categories of analysis developed by Guizot and others, then, formed an important lens through which Tocqueville would view American institutions. Moreover, he could easily have encountered the phrase 'political science' among Doctrinaire writers.[35] It may indeed seem that the influential historical and political writings of Guizot contradict my claim that French writers increasingly privileged the realm of the social (susceptible of elaboration by laws) over the political (a derivative activity dependent on those laws). As the historian and chronicler *par excellence* of 'bourgeois society', Guizot tirelessly promoted embedding the political in the social, rethinking the relations between the two realms, and creating political institutions that would reflect and organize the new social powers that history had created.[36] But his fusion of the social and political was more apparent than real. His plea for rational government or 'political science', while not completely abandoning politics to mere administration as did Saint-Simon or Comte, nevertheless shares more with Comte's perspective than it does with Tocqueville's.

Guizot's political programme and rhetoric aimed to create a consensus on the inevitability of middle-class ascendance and on the necessity of refining representative institutions to express the needs and desires of that class. The task of his generation was to convince those who wished either to turn back the clock (the reactionaries) or to rush beyond history (the radical republicans and socialists) that historical realities severely limited the political moves they might make. His vision of politics tended to exclude the possibility that people could define themselves collectively or construct a new future for themselves. Indeed, he believed that in general 'we give to politics too large a part'.[37] In contrast, Tocqueville's concern was precisely to exhort his fellow men (and women) to redefine themselves as a democratic people and to build an alternative future. Although Tocqueville too deplored republican excesses and 'feared and detested the mob', and although he believed that reform must be slow and cautious, his aim was not adjustment but transformation. These different views of the tasks of politics flowed from the contrasting ways in which Guizot and Tocqueville described the historical landscape that revolutionary eruptions had so sharply revealed.

Guizot saw in that history the inexorable rise of representative institutions, fruits of a European society that had become increasingly complex and interdependent, and that now needed to be made conscious of itself through the creation of a politically aware bourgeois class.[38] The economic, political, intellectual, and moral aspects of this society were linked in a web of reciprocal causality, but Guizot's inclination was not so much to explore these circular mechanisms of connection as to underscore the conclusion that progress in all spheres was steady and unstoppable. In his account, despite lags and surges, these spheres of human activity are never more than a short distance apart. Political science should fine-tune the balance among these different manifestations of human progress; it should aim to 'reform, to perfect, to regulate' what is immanent in history.[39] His underlying themes, then, are the flowering of civilization and the inevitable intermeshing of 'material' history with 'moral' history, economic and social history with the history of general ideas. In this account of the rise of Europe, the role of France stands out as universal exemplar. 'Her civilization has reproduced more faithfully than any other the general type, and the fundamental idea of civilization. It is the most complete, the most veritable, and so to speak, the most civilized of civilizations.'[40]

Fundamental to this French genius for civilization, on Guizot's account, was the particular historical conjunction of the free play of intelligence with the centralization of the powers of the nation.[41] The middle classes took the intellectual lead in creating the nation. Their rise hence appeared as both fated and heroic. Beginning with the Crusades, Guizot argues, the localization that had fostered a regime of feudal privilege throughout Europe gave way in France to a movement of centralization in which a coalition of monarchs and municipal powers fought against the aristocracy. To consolidate the fruits of these historical class struggles and to make the middle classes into the political as well as the social heart of the nation was the challenge of his generation. Here Guizot also pointed to the darker side of the legacy of alliances between king and commons. Because of the success of monarchical centralization and the continued presence of aristocratic privileges, municipal freedoms had languished.[42] For the middle classes to take their rightful place, political and municipal authorities needed to be 'included in each other', a process that unfortunately was frustrated by complete centralization of state power by the monarchy.[43]

The writings of Guizot and his school have always fascinated Marxists, who easily perceive in them a prescient anticipation of historical materialism. As in Marxism, the historical trajectory of class conflict directs political action and produces a sense of necessity at odds with the notion of politics as an indeterminate process or as a particular way of life. Although Guizot attempted to awaken the French middle classes to the need for consolidating representative institutions by locating this unfinished task within a long and recurrent fight for liberty, his politics were ultimately based on the view that the most difficult choices had already been made by history. What was necessary was decisive action on the part of the middle class to consolidate its historical victory. Pierre Rosanvallon nicely captures this aspect of Guizot's otherwise sober politics in calling him a 'Lenin of the bourgeoisie'.[44]

When Tocqueville came to survey French history from a post-revolutionary vantage-point, he perceived a similar outline but took its measure differently. Although he accepted the idea of the irreversible transition to democratic society, the dominance of centralization, and the dearth of political institutions that could organize the energies of the new France, he invested this story with a very different significance. Most important, his would not be a story about the inevitable rise of free institutions. Tocqueville's historical accounts of the coming of democracy in France in both *Democracy in America* and *The Old Regime and the Revolution* emphasize jagged breaks, unintended consequences, and disastrous wrong turns in the progress of freedom. History demonstrates the inevitable emergence of democratic social conditions, but does not provide in any straightforward way an engine to which contemporary actors may hitch their political wagons. While the impulse to be free may spring eternal in the human breast, it is not always possible to reattach this contemporary impulse to a clear historical trajectory. Guizot tried to create an indigenous tradition of freedom for the French middle classes and to call on them to assume the burden of their history. Tocqueville, in contrast, believed that France's feudal regime was the ancient source of French liberty. But it was this very regime that history had destroyed beyond repair. Therefore, although his deepest longing was to create functional equivalents for the institutions that had formerly sustained French liberties, Tocqueville viewed the materials bequeathed by history as unpromising. The demanding project of creating liberty under democracy would in many ways be unprecedented. Indeed, rather than looking to history for a programme, one must begin with an almost cathartic recognition of the ruins of the past (DAI, 16).

Tocqueville's historical narratives lack precisely the combination of internal necessity and moral coercion that characterize the writings not only of Guizot and Marx, but of so many other chroniclers of the rise of civil society or democracy. Indeed, for Tocqueville, determinism is what history must be defined against, and the steadfast will to build a free political culture is what must be elicited from its human protagonists against all odds.[45] Tocqueville's discussion of democratic historians in the second *Democracy* criticizes them on just this point. Historians who write in democratic ages (among whom he implicitly includes himself) quite rightly slight the contributions of individuals, because no one individual exercises enough influence over democratic society to achieve a powerful and lasting effect. A name index of Tocqueville's own works, including the *Old Regime*, would in fact turn up a surprisingly tiny number of references to individuals.[46] Because society seems to progress on its own, the democratic historian is naturally drawn 'to look for the general reason which acts on so many men's faculties at once and turns them all simultaneously in the same direction' (DAII, 494). The temptation besetting these historians, however, is to give up altogether the effort to analyse the labyrinthine contributions of real historical individuals. Those who give in to this weakness present a world moving without anyone in it, and may even deny that people can escape a 'blind fatality' (DAII, 496).

Hovering on the brink of methodological self-consciousness in these passages, Tocqueville is trying to articulate his own historical method. Like all historians in democratic ages, his intellect and curiosity quite rightly drive him to seek general causes, for 'general causes explain more, and particular influences less, in democratic than in aristocratic ages' (DAII, 495). He scorns narration as a mere 'knack' that has little to do with the democratic historian's difficult task.[47] And Tocqueville himself will freely use the language of providence and inevitability to make general patterns (such as the coming of democracy or the advance of centralization) appear more compelling. But what he wishes to identify above all are not these 'fated' patterns, but rather the historical windows of opportunity for political intervention that remain.

The value of history for the democratic political actor—and here Tocqueville is directly in the line of Polybius and Machiavelli—is to reveal the interplay of necessity and contingency. In Tocqueville's case, this revelation takes the form of determining the cumulative weight and varying strengths of intersecting social and political practices in order to assess the opportunities for present action. It also takes the form of identifying past moral lapses and failings, opportunities lost to human fumbling. The need to gain a clear view of discrete patterns of human behaviour pushes him to constant comparisons. Comparison is indeed the only tool at hand with which to create any lucidity out of the overwhelming complexity of historical events. Tocqueville's most arresting insights, then, will come not from his occasional sweeping statements about universal human development but rather from his attempts to isolate and compare historical processes: the role of the nobility in England versus France; the mentality of serfs in France versus Germany; the intricate relationships between centralization in one sphere of human activity and others; Catholicism's different historical trajectories in Ireland, Baltimore, Quebec, and France; the effects of national character in different social milieus; the effects of becoming equal versus being born so. From these partial threads and pieces, he loosely weaves a larger fabric, namely a picture of the emergence of a society, premised on equal social conditions, that contains the seeds of new forms of despotism. He does not, however, discipline his intuitions with anything like the precision needed for grand historical theory. Perceptive nineteenth-century commentators judged him to be an outsider to the main schools of thought in France precisely because of his lack of zest for broad generalizations about all of human history.[48]

Finally, unlike Guizot's history of France or those of his many democratic successors, Tocqueville's history lacks a heroic class or group that implicitly holds victory in its grasp: not French aristocrats, who naively lost their birthright and have since lived in a fog of self-delusion; not the middle classes, who fight a losing battle with their materialistic and cowardly instincts; not the republicans' peasantry or the socialists' urban workers, who risk becoming a mindless mob; not even his own lucky Americans, whose success in creating and sustaining liberty comes from factors that they did not create, do not fully understand, and perhaps cannot reproduce. Rather, Tocqueville writes history for unsung future heroes and heroines. He addresses those who, like himself, strive to create a rare and valuable social good—democratic liberty—in unpropitious circumstances. 'After the battle comes the lawgiver' (DAI, xiv, preface to 1848 edn.). Tocqueville writes for the hypothetical citizen-lawgivers who inherit both the destruction and the desolation bequeathed by history's battles. This rhetorical stance perhaps accounts partially for his trans-historical and trans-cultural appeal to political actors who find themselves in just such positions of existential choice.

Tocqueville's particular understanding of the larger significance of French history for humanity as a whole intensifies this transnational appeal. Unlike Guizot, Thierry, Michelet, or even Marx, Tocqueville does not view the history of France primarily as a template of either universal social development or universal human aspiration. If French history is exemplary, it is because it tells a cautionary and potentially tragic tale whose dénouement is uncertain. His increasing pessimism about the ability of the French to create free institutions after mid-century is well known, but this more fundamental attitude towards French history was present much earlier. Tocqueville was a patriot; he felt strongly, if somewhat obscurely, that his line of descent from the eleventh-century Norman conquerors made public service a familial duty. The personification of France that lurks in his works, however, is ultimately closer to the Greek hero brought down by a tragic human flaw than to the conquering mythical hero who comes home in triumph.

Despite strenuous attempts to divine the course of French history —by contrasting it to America, by Europeanizing it, by investigating its moral lapses and triumphs and delusions—Tocqueville does not place France at the centre of a world-historical drama. His refusal to be swallowed up in history and his consequent attention to the complicated processes that create historical trends draw his readers into a conceptual space of criticism that is both inside and outside French culture. And his example invites them to create such spaces to examine and judge their own historical situations. I shall turn to Tocqueville's effort to wrest both meaning and a certain guidance from French history in Chapter 3.

Moralism and 'the Secrets of the Heart'

Thus far I have argued that Tocqueville sits uneasily in the company of the dominant writers about social science and history in nineteenth-century France. Though he spoke out of an exquisite sense of the problems of his time, and spoke directly to those who faced them, he theorized as a prescient outsider—not only in America but also in France. I now want to consider in a preliminary way the moral and religious grounding of Tocqueville's thought and to anticipate a different judgement on the fit between Tocqueville and his time. If his views on the relationships among society, history, and political praxis are outside the mainstream, his ethical assumptions and sense of urgency about connecting morality to politics are deeply rooted in his particular time and place.

Tocqueville's view that politics must be anchored in morality, and his assumptions about the content of that morality, do not appear remarkable or exceptional among post-revolutionary liberal thinkers. What is distinctive about Tocqueville's moral sensibility is the abrupt juxtaposition of exhortation 'from the heart' with analysis from the head. For all his apparent frankness about his underlying convictions, he was less likely than other writers of his time to analyse his assumptions or to worry over them openly. He devotes so little attention to the ethical grounding of his thought that some subsequent commentators, attracted to his comparative method or to his political conclusions, have assumed that these conclusions are not linked in any important way to specific moral or religious beliefs. For example, otherwise astute scholars have argued quite wrongly that Tocqueville's interest in religion was purely sociological and based on the usefulness of belief.[49] I will argue in Chapter 4 that Tocqueville's convictions about the need for Christian religious belief and his dread of social and sexual transgression both shape and limit his ability to analyse society and politics. Because these assumptions and associations, to some extent the common property of his generation and milieu, were both important and unacknowledged, I want to spend some time reconstructing them here. It is a shared moral terrain that at first glance exhibits some peculiar features.

Moral argument and liberal rhetoric

The first half of the nineteenth century in France has often been painted as a triumph of self-interest and place-seeking in politics and greed and materialism in private life. Yet rarely have writers and politicians trumpeted more boldly their devotion to pure reason and sacred values. Although soaring political rhetoric and sordid motives often coexist in political life, the intimate union of sanctimony and self-interest during these years seems to call for some explanation. One has only to read Balzac or Marx to appreciate the contempt that this public moralizing could induce in contemporaries.

The question of why French political elites, at least that significant portion who saw themselves somewhere in the middle of the polarized extremes of reaction and continuing revolution, proclaimed so insistently that politics must have unbreachable moral limits proves to be, like so much else during these years, answerable only in light of the Revolution's legacy. A particular set of questions haunted the post-revolutionary generations: what crimes had the French Revolution committed and who was responsible? Why were liberal expectations so brutally quashed? How could the positive legacy of the Revolution be claimed even as its destructive aspects were disavowed?

Responses to these questions usually involved some reference to a distorted relationship between political will and human reason that had mysteriously come to dominate revolutionary politics. Amidst the conflicting interpretations of the political and social legacies of the Revolution, many liberals and conservatives had come to a rough substratum of agreement about how this relationship between will and reason had been played out in the years from 1789 to 1815. On this view of things, exercises of raw unfettered will (by either lawless mobs, a despotic minority, a dictator, or some combination of the three) had ignored or trampled basic human rights and duties. Tocqueville, for example, explicitly contrasts republican regimes in Europe, which allowed 'rulers to act in the nation's name without consulting it and to claim its gratitude while trampling it under foot', to the American republic, in which '[h]umanity, justice, and reason stand above [the majority] in the moral order'.[50] The consensus was that unbreachable moral laws had been breached; unnatural acts had been performed; and the moral world had been turned upside-down during the revolutionary and imperial years. Although there might be conflicting judgements about individual actors and deeds, there was a generalized sense that the 'Terror' had unleashed grave disturbances. Thus the Terror bred not just political trials and the guillotine, but deep transgressions against the norms of propriety and family life.

For conservatives of the stamp of DeMaistre, this unnatural dynamic could be understood only in biblical terms as the scourge of an angry God who had punished a sinful France for abandoning traditional ways, just as He had earlier annihilated Sodom and

Gomorrah. Some radical democrats and socialists, on the other hand, came to embrace this powerful revolutionary force, in the process purging it of, or excusing it from, evil and transforming it into the means for creating an earthly paradise: *La République*. Both total repudiation and total embrace of the wilful dynamic of revolution seem to have freed their respective adherents from the need for an explicitly moralistic political discourse. The idioms of social science and the new discipline of sociology in France were fuelled more by the stark realism of the conservatives and the historical messianism of the socialists than by the moral angst of the liberals. For those, however, who wished to claim an affinity with revolutionary aspirations but to disclaim responsibility for the Revolution's excesses or connection to its contemporary adherents—and who, moreover, positioned themselves in a line of descent from a morally compromised Enlightenment—an establishment of moral bona fides was a necessity. These heirs of the 'godless' Revolution needed to occupy the moral high ground while divorcing themselves both from eighteenth-century philosophical hubris and from the claims of popular will.

Liberal arguments about reason and faith

Liberals in fact believed that revolutionary attacks on religious faith, prepared by a century of philosophical criticism, had produced devastating effects, and not only on the masses. Detachment from an underlying faith had in some fashion loosened the general human grip on the moral notions that allowed a community to function. On this view, eighteenth-century writers had been psychologically naïve in believing that moral norms would blossom spontaneously in the human heart once the weeds of superstition had been uprooted. Revolutionary experience seemed to have proved them wrong. Hence liberals expressed almost ritually the need for new accommodations between faith and reason.

There were many accents in which one could proclaim allegiance to pure reason and sacred values, but it was simply not possible to refuse to speak some version of this language if one wished to participate in politics without standing accused (by others and one's own conscience) of unleashing destabilizing violence. Unlike the 'reason' of the Enlightenment, the 'reason' invoked by post-revolutionary liberals carried the burden of overtly supporting certain bulwarks of established society like religion, family, and property. Alexis de Tocqueville, no less than others, adhered to these fixed moral points. His defences of spiritual discipline, of women's place, and of property rights and civilization are incomprehensible outside this context. Rarely, however, did he try to justify his allegiances. It may be useful, then, to focus briefly on others who more directly convey the set of issues involved in the spiritualizing of political argument after the Revolution.

For the purpose of illustrating patterns of liberal moralizing, two figures are particularly illuminating: Pierre-Paul Royer-Collard and Charles de Rémusat.[51] Both were active in politics under several regimes, both moved in the same *bonne société* as did Tocqueville, and both were particularly attuned to the need for a transcendent morality that would stabilize self-government. Beyond these shared characteristics are some useful differences. Royer-Collard is most vividly revealed to us through the eyes of others, although he has also left lectures, letters, and speeches. Greatly admired by Tocqueville, as well as by a fairly large swathe of public opinion, his unswerving rectitude was thought to exemplify the conscience of French liberal politics in the Restoration. In contrast, Rémusat, himself one of Royer-Collard's admiring portraitists, has left thousands of pages of somewhat inconclusive commentary on philosophy, religion, and politics in which he seems always to be seeking but never finding a moral anchor for his opinions. His works chronicle an obsessive need to reconcile reason and faith in the face of his own scepticism. Together the moral paragon and the dissatisfied pilgrim form a particularly useful guide to the spiritual aspirations of these years, aspirations that lay just beneath the surface of much of Tocqueville's writing as well.

A professor of philosophy and a politician of some eminence in successive legislative bodies, Royer-Collard was judged by Tocqueville to be 'a great soul' and an exemplar of the kind of independent politics that Tocqueville himself wished to emulate.[52] Indeed, the most striking aspect of Royer-Collard's political career, attested to by many of his contemporaries, was his apparent personal incorruptibility. He became an object of veneration to his contemporaries because he symbolized a fusion of moral conviction and reasonable politics for which the new generation yearned. If he had not existed, it would probably have been necessary to invent him. In 1836 Royer-Collard wrote to Tocqueville that 'politics without morality is only a game of knaves and fools, or the oppression of the weak by the strong'.[53] He had practised his own brand of 'ethical' politics since the end of the Empire, when he circumspectly negotiated for a return of the Bourbons, and during the Restoration, when he manoeuvred continually to limit Bourbon power and diversify its support. He fought above all for the Charter, an uneasy compromise between legitimism and liberalism that failed to take root in the new France and was discarded in the July Days of 1830.

Royer-Collard was the most influential spokesman for the Doctrinaires, who formed the heart of the loyal liberal opposition during the Restoration. They tried to recall the monarch to what they saw as the real needs of the new France: balanced government and the rule of law. For Royer-Collard, these needs were less explicitly equated with the universal interests of the bourgeoisie than they were for Guizot, who would lead the Doctrinaires into the July Monarchy. Nevertheless, he shared Guizot's recoil from the notion of popular sovereignty, which connoted an attachment to 'persons and wills' rather than to 'rights and interests'; he favored the expression 'organized sovereignty of free governments', an expression akin to Guizot's 'sovereignty of reason'.[54]

Royer-Collard's self-imposed duty, then, was to help establish representative monarchical institutions in France. For this task he needed a strong moral compass to avoid the perilous temptations of representative politics, which he increasingly perceived as the devil's work. Whereas politics should be the disinterested pursuit of 'true prosperity and solid glory', it seemed increasingly to consist of wilful self-serving lies and corrupting compromises.[55] Only unshakeable personal convictions could provide the politician with the strength to act effectively without becoming contaminated by his surroundings. In Royer-Collard's case, this personal rectitude was apparently the result of a severe religious upbringing, filtered through the moral theories of the Scottish common-sense school. In his eulogy of Royer-Collard, Rémusat recalled the village in which the statesman was born, which offered, he said, the rare spectacle of a moderate Jansenism, a population regenerated by the kind of religious teaching that confirmed faith by intelligence.[56] Indeed, references to Jansenism, that Puritan-like strain in French Catholicism associated with the famous convent of Port-Royal and connected with notions both of a purifying faith and of a clarifying reason, enjoyed a remarkable renaissance during this period, even among writers who were notably secular.

Jansenism had a complicated social and political history in France, from its initial awakening of the hostility of Richelieu, who distrusted its notion of a self-sufficient community of saints, through its long association with oppositional politics in both church and state.[57] By the nineteenth century, it existed only as a moral attitude or habit rather than as a living current within Catholicism. Despite, or perhaps because of, its demise as a significant religious force, the language and images of Port-Royal fascinated those members of the post-revolutionary generation who longed for a spiritual validation different from the religious romanticism of the ultra-royalists. Reactionary Catholicism taught blind submission to hierarchy, while these adherents of the new France sought some means of inner self-restraint, an internal tether that would allow them to negotiate the treacherous waters of post-revolutionary politics in safety.

Not a few liberals traced France's political problems to the failure of the Protestant Reformation in France, and yearned for the contribution that an essentially Protestant sensibility could make to liberal culture.[58] But Protestantism was not a viable cultural symbol in France; hence, many used the example of Jansenism to evoke the possibility of a responsible free society composed of citizens who possessed a set of internalized moral convictions that would anchor their restless imaginations and activities. This anachronistic religious sensibility, without any real social existence in nineteenth-century France, had in fact become a paradoxical symbol of the discipline necessary for modern liberal politics. Royer-Collard's great appeal, to Tocqueville as well as to other liberals, was as a living personification of the efficacy of this discipline. In Royer-Collard, moral rectitude was combined not with uncompromising rigidity but with political flexibility. Rémusat wrote of him, 'I have never known a man so mobile and so unshakeable at the same time.'[59]

If the attraction to Jansenism, embodied in a public figure like Royer-Collard, was a barometer of the spiritual longings of the liberal post-Revolutionary generation, nevertheless Jansenism itself could not really satisfy those longings. Praising Jansenism or the products of its teaching remained an allusive way to proclaim the need for an animating conviction to invigorate liberal principles. The difficulty, of course, was that the source of Jansenism's power to produce moral certainty was privileged truth linked to Christian revelation. But for most nineteenth-century thinkers, Christian revelation had become an exhausted source of spiritual capital.

Charles de Rémusat's restless spiritual odyssey reveals some of the quandaries of this liberal milieu. In his writings during the July

Monarchy, he constantly returned to a consideration of the scepticism that characterized his age: not the aggressive reforming scepticism of the Enlightenment, but the exhausted, indifferent scepticism following an apparently successful revolution—he is thinking of 1830—that could not find a way to believe in its own virtues.[60] Despite real progress in the efficiency and moderation of government, and a middle-class elite that was careful, apparently intelligent, and enlightened as to its interests, political life had become completely enervated. The regime had lost the ability to justify itself. Rémusat concludes that prudent egoism is not enough to sustain the spirit of a self-governing regime. A *société régulière* is inherently unstable because interactions based only on individual interests and values do not anchor the imagination; they leave the mind prey to unsatisfied yearnings. Faith in revealed dogma once provided such an anchor. But in a society in which faith had fled, only rational principles could fill the deficit. A moral paragon like Royer-Collard could be admired, but not replicated, since the well of spiritualism that had produced him had run dry. Rémusat, like other proponents of a middle way in French politics, turned to philosophy, and in particular to the Eclecticism of Victor Cousin, as a guide out of this morass. Though he would prove a discontented disciple, Rémusat's initial attraction to Ecleticism was typical of his generation.[61]

French Eclecticism tried to recreate in moral philosophy a new spiritual and psychological anchor for politics, and to defend the notion of intuitive moral truth from the assaults of scepticism. Cousin performed this operation in a manner similar to that of the common-sense school in England. From the Scottish philosophers, the Eclectics took the notion that the human conscience was both an intellectual and active power, whose authority over action was a self-evident fact. The dictates of conscience in this way became intellectual instincts that required no independent confirmation from experience. This conception of conscience provided a bridge to reconnect religion, which had always taught that moral truths were intuitive, to philosophy. Influenced also by German philosophy, Cousin likened this moral intuition to *vernunft*, an impersonal spiritual and rational force working through individuals. Hegel commented, not without reason, 'It is my fish, served up with his sauce.'[62]

First served up with mesmerizing authority in Cousin's public lectures, this philosophy was to hold sway in France from the early years of the nineteenth century to the consolidation of the Third Republic and even beyond. Much of this influence has to do with Cousin's prominence not only as an academic philosopher but as an empire-builder who has been called the generalissimo of French higher education.[63] But the attractions of what he had on offer were real enough. Eclecticism seemed to avoid the dangers of atheistic sensationalist philosophy and to recognize the positive contributions of religious faith. 'Christianity ought to be the basis of the instruction of the people; we must not flinch from the open profession of this maxim; it is no less politic than it is honest.'[64] Eclectic philosophy recreated familial duties—the complex of individual duties inherent in the relations of husband, wife, and children—as intuitive ethical truths that were the basis of all civilization. Property rights were not simply useful, but were sacred and inherent in the personality. Furthermore, they enhanced the security and independence of the family and thus did ethical double duty.[65] Just as Royer-Collard was a living exemplar of the kind of fusion of faith and reason that could equip citizens to resist the potential chaos of their own democratic desires, so Eclecticism's equation of divine spirit and the dictates of individual conscience provided an apparent philosophical grounding for moral limits to political action. The liberal defence of its revolutionary heritage now demanded just such signs of purity and guarantees of moral restraint.

Tocqueville disagreed on many practical issues with almost all of the figures I have been discussing; nor did he share with them any specific philosophical viewpoint. But he did share a common construction of the tainted legacy of revolutionary liberalism and a similar perception of the urgent need to anchor democratic 'reason' in faith. Tocqueville too recoiled from the Revolution's creation of a political culture in which anything could be countenanced in the name of popular sovereignty or the national will. He struggled throughout his life to understand a bizarre revolutionary dance that, in his view, emboldened those caught up in its rhythms to transgress moral boundaries. The reader of *The Old Regime and the Revolution*, however, can be forgiven for doubting that the moral dilemmas posed by French revolutionary praxis aroused Tocqueville's deepest concern. Indeed, based on that text alone, one might be led to ask whether he thought the French Revolution proper had had any lasting effects at all. Tocqueville's brilliant demonstration of its long incubation in the Old Regime, and of the 'revolutionary' changes in social psychology and social structures that had already occurred by

1780, eclipse the startling particularity of the Revolution itself. But this conclusion would be highly misleading. Although Tocqueville never completed his study of the Revolution and its origins, his fragmentary notes—and many discussions in his other published works—indicate a continuing fascination with revolutionary 'excesses', even if no definitive explanation emerges. 'I can see, I think, the object that I want to portray; but the light illuminating it wavers and does not yet allow me to grasp the image well enough to be able to reproduce it.'[66]

Tocqueville kept his distance from simplistic moral indictments of the crimes of the Revolution, but he was only too struck by the enormity and the contagiousness of the Revolution's 'spirit'. He accepted as fact that this new spirit 'which is still with us' could sweep people away from whatever ethical moorings still anchored their actions (AR, 157). In his notes on the revolutionary decade, one sees him struggling to find the proper way to approach this topic. A preliminary sketch suggests that the Terror could be fully comprehensible only in France. Though a product of general causes, it was pushed beyond all limits by particular facts. It was '[b]orn of our morals, of our character, of our habits, of centralization, of the sudden destruction of all hierarchy'.[67] He carefully notes passages from the memoirs of Mallet du Pin on the dynamic of fear that caused an acceleration of atrocities and a suspension of 'human maxims'. He reminds himself to demonstrate how the dynamic of revolution favours the dominance of minorities. Finally, he signals the need to fathom the 'magical horror' of an atheistic revolutionary ideology that transfixed spectators by its ability to engender religious enthusiasm and even martyrdom.[68]

Tocqueville's instincts, then, were to study revolutionary culture and ideology as the artefacts of human social psychology under particular social and political conditions. But there is no doubt that he believed he was studying a great moral aberration. It was precisely the power of sweeping away traditional moral limits to human action that was of concern. In his view, this macabre phenomenon, a sleeping disorder in French politics, should claim the attention of all who were attempting to create a culture of freedom. Thus, the belief that the Revolution had linked political extremism to moral transgressions haunted Tocqueville's thought no less than that of others of his generation and milieu.

A second way in which Tocqueville was enmeshed in cultural presuppositions that related morality to politics in a quite particular manner was in his understanding of how moral limits functioned in the psyche of the liberal citizen. I have described a general movement to a more spiritualized liberalism, a keen awareness of the alleged failure of eighteenth-century philosophy or republican opinion to lend moral weight to the new order. No longer hostile to religion, this milieu nevertheless yearned for a particular kind of religious sensibility, one that would reinforce a sense of individual responsibility necessary to make self-government work without reviving 'superstition'. This was not in the first instance a concern with the maintenance of external order, but rather a subtle focus on those animating convictions that would allow citizens to act decisively and independently in politics, while preventing them from imagining that they could violate moral rights with impunity. Tocqueville would memorably exploit these motifs of empowerment and restraint in his portrait of religion and politics in America.[69] But his concern was part of a larger question shared by French liberals such as Royer-Collard, Rémusat, and Cousin: how could the human spirit find a reasonable resting-place between incredulity and fanaticism? This awareness of the psychological dimensions of faith was neither obviously secular nor clearly opportunistic. In the case of Tocqueville, explorations of the function of religion in politics would coexist with a romantic religious temperament and with a fitful apprehension of the divine in both nature and history.

Alexis de Tocqueville, then, shared the fear that moral virtues necessary to any civilized existence could be threatened by democratic politics, and that something stronger than reason was required to bolster citizens amid the restlessness of democratic society. Where he parted company with other liberals was in his deliberate refusal to explicate the grounds of such opinions, or to attempt to reconcile reason with faith. Not only did Tocqueville lack the philosophical temperament, but he seemed instinctively to believe that reason was a limited and individualistic power that could not expand to embrace faith, or to sustain collective social purpose. 'Not a man in the world has ever found ... the central point at which all the rays of general truth (which come together only in God) or even all the rays of particular truth meet. Men grasp fragments of truth, but never truth itself.'[70] Though he might in some sense share the moral discomfort of a Rémusat, he would never follow him down the path of attempting to reconcile the worlds of reason and dogma.

Tocqueville would portray the coexistence of faith and reason in America as a fortunate happenstance, comprehensible in light of the history of the Americans and the psychological needs of a democratic people, but nevertheless a happy accident rather than an immanent necessity. Indeed, Tocqueville's moralism appears to be rooted less in reasoned thought of any sort than in a set of moral tastes and fragile epiphanies that he wished to shield from the glare of inquiry. He conveys these moral tastes to the reader less by means of argument than by ironic indirection or aesthetic intimation. This strategy frees him from the demand for consistency in moral argumentation. Fragments of natural law theory, echoes of the romantic law of the heart, traces of Jansenist moral discipline, and deliberate appeals to utilitarianism will jostle one another in his texts; none is fully adequate to capture his moral sensibility. This issue of how he links the morality that lurks in the 'depths of the heart' with the science that emerges from the inspections of reason will form the subject of Chapter 4.

Tocqueville came to maturity in the 1820s under a restored monarchy that was ill-suited to contain either the passions or the interests that divided the French. This regime ended in a new revolution, the occasion of Tocqueville's first oath of allegiance to the new France. He bore troubled witness to another revolution, a republic, and an empire. Like most of his generation, he was convinced that these social and political disturbances reflected a fundamental alteration in the course of French history, and indeed in the history of the West. I have argued, however, that he declined to take up what many of his contemporaries saw as the particular intellectual challenges of their time: an articulation of the independent realm of the social from which to derive the functions of politics; the construction of a theory of history that would make the emergence of the social intelligible within a process of inevitable unfolding; and, finally, a philosophical defence of the moral conditions of liberal freedom. What he has left us instead—a subtle analysis of the mentality that underlies 'democracy itself', an arresting historical portrait of the 'destiny of a people', and a revelation of the inherent difficulties in arguing 'from the depths of the heart'—will occupy us in the next three chapters. In the fifth and final chapter, I will explore the surprising and paradoxical affinities between the passionate concerns of this nineteenth-century displaced French aristocrat and the social and political discontents of the late twentieth century.

Notes

1 For this account of Tocqueville's own statement of his allegiances, see the unpublished fragment entitled 'My Instincts, My Opinions' quoted in Antoine Rédier, *Comme disait M. de Tocqueville* (Paris: Perrin, 1925), 47–8. Among Tocqueville's closest associates were Gustave de Beaumont, his companion in America and in French politics, literary executor, and heir of Mme de Tocqueville; and Louis de Kergolay, childhood friend, invaluable reader of Tocqueville's manuscripts, and intimate correspondent.

2 André Jardin, *Tocqueville: A Biography*, trans. Lydia Davis with Robert Hemenway (London: Peter Halban, 1988), 42.

3 Letter from Tocqueville to Mme Swetchine, 26 Feb. 1857, OC 15:2, 315

4 Jardin, *Tocqueville*, 62.

5 Tocqueville to Henry Reeve, 22 Mar. 1837, OC, B 6:68.

6 From an unpublished note to Mary Mottley, quoted in Jardin, *Tocqueville*, 89.

7 The indispensable guide to Tocqueville's time in America remains George Wilson Pierson, *Tocqueville and Beaumont in America* (Oxford: Oxford University Press, 1938; repr. Baltimore: Johns Hopkins University Press, 1996), which made use of many then unpublished journals and notebooks in the Yale University Archives. Some of this material has since been published in the new OC.

8 Beaumont also wrote a novel about the evils of American slavery, entitled *Marie ou l'esclavage aux États-Unis: Tableau des mœurs américains*, 2 vols. (Paris: Gosselin, 1835); published in English as *Marie, or Slavery in the United States: A Novel of Jacksonian America*, trans. B. Chapman, intro. A. Tinnin (Stanford, Calif.: Stanford University Press, 1958).

9 See *Voyages en Angleterre, Irlande, Suisse et Algérie*, OC 5:2, published in English as *Journeys to England and Ireland*, trans. George Lawrence, ed. J.-P. Mayer (New Haven, Conn.: Yale University Press, 1960). Tocqueville had an important correspondence with John Stuart Mill and with Nassau Senior; see *Correspondance anglaise*, OC 6. On Tocqueville and England, see Seymour Drescher, *Tocqueville and England* (Cambridge, Mass.: Harvard University Press, 1964).

10 Surprisingly little is known about Mary Mottley or her life with Tocqueville. For a judicious assessment, see Jardin, *Tocqueville*, 48–55.

11 Tocqueville's writings on Algeria can be found in *Écrits et discours politiques*, OC 3:1, 130–418, and *Voyages en Angleterre, Irelande, Suisse et Algérie*, OC 5:2, 189–218. For an analysis of Tocqueville's position on Algeria and the colonial problem, see J.-J. Chevalier and A. Jardin, 'Introduction' to OC 3:1; Jardin, *Tocqueville*, 316–42; Michael

Hereth, *Alexis de Tocqueville: Threats to Freedom in Democracy*, trans. George Bogardus (Durham: Duke University Press, 1986), 145–65, and Melvin Richter, 'Tocqueville on Algeria', *Review of Politics*, 25 (1963), 362–98.

12 Keith Baker, 'The Early History of the Term "Social Science"', *Annals of Science*, 20 (1964), 211–26.

13 See Cheryl B. Welch, *Liberty and Utility: The French Idéologues and the Transformation of Liberalism* (New York: Columbia University Press, 1984), 6–14.

14 *État social et politique de la France avant et depuis 1789*, OC 2:1, 33.

15 Welch, *Liberty and Utility*, 23–34.

16 Pierre Cabanis, *Œuvres philosophiques* (Paris: Presses Universitaires de France, 1956), 1:121.

17 Antoine-Louis-Claude Destutt de Tracy, *Élémens d'idéologie*, 4 vols. (Paris: Courcier, 1817), 4:287–8.

18 See François de Corcelles, *Documens pour servir à l'histoire des conspirations des partis et des sectes* (Paris: Paulin, 1831) 8, 19–20, and François-André Isambert, *De la Charbonnerie au Saint-Simonisme: étude sur la jeunesse de Buchez* (Paris: Éditions de Minuit, 1966), 121.

19 See Welch, *Liberty and Utility*, 158–62, 171–8.

20 See Claude Nicolet, *L'idée républicaine en France: essai d'histoire critique* (Paris: Gallimard, 1982), 156, 249–77.

21 I count among the works of social economy the following: J.-P.-A. Villeneuve-Bargemont, *Économie politique chrétienne, ou recherches sur la nature et les causes du paupérisme en France et en Europe*, 3 vols. (Paris: Paulin, 1834); J.-M. DeGérando, *De la bienfaisance publique*, 2 vols. (Brussels: Havman, 1839); H.-A. Frégier, *Des classes dangereuses de la population dans les grandes villes et des moyens de les rendre meilleures* (Paris: J.-B. Baillière, 1840); E. Buret, *De la misère des classes laborieuses en Angleterre et en France* (Paris: Paulin, 1840); L. R. Villermé, *Tableau de l'état physique et moral des ouvriers*, 2 vols. (Paris: Jules Renouvard, 1840); and A.-E. Cherbuliez, *Étude sur les causes de la misère tant morale que physique* (Paris: Guillaumin, 1853). On the social economists, see Giovanna Procacci, *Gouverner la misère: la question sociale en France, 1789–1848* (Paris: Éditions du Seuil, 1993).

22 J. C. L. Sismondi, 'On Landed Property', in *Political Economy and the Philosophy of Government*, trans. from *Études sur les sciences sociales* (London: John Chapman, 1847), 157.

23 Cherbuliez, *Études sur les causes de la misère*, 4.

24 Seymour Drescher, *Dilemmas of Democracy: Tocqueville and Modernization* (Pittsburgh: University of Pittsburgh Press, 1968), 99.

25 The political theory of Benjamin Constant might also be viewed as anomalous against this background, since Constant concerned himself to such a great extent with both political structures and constitutional design. Indeed, the relationship between Constant and Tocqueville—the two French liberals whose reputations have grown in the twentieth century, but who do not seem to have had many points of contact—has intrigued many commentators. Constant, however, was still wedded to an eighteenth-century notion of progress, in which reason, rationalized public opinion, and *doux commerce* would gradually come to enlighten the citizen body and the government. For Constant, the link between society and government was intellectual progress. It is this conception that Tocqueville abandoned in favour of a sociologically more sophisticated view of the interrelations of society and politics. For a systematic comparison, see George Armstrong Kelly, *The Humane Comedy: Constant, Tocqueville, and French Liberalism* (Cambridge: Cambridge University Press, 1992), 38–84. On the political theory of Constant, see Stephen Holmes, *Benjamin Constant and the Making of Modern Liberalism* (New Haven, Conn.: Yale University Press, 1984), and Biancamaria Fontana, *Benjamin Constant and the Post-Revolutionary Mind* (New Haven, Conn.: Yale University Press, 1991).

26 See Drescher, *Dilemmas*, 88–150, and Cheryl B. Welch, 'Liberalism and Social Rights', in C. Welch and M. Milgate (eds.), *Critical Issues in Social Thought* (London: Academic Press, 1989), 173–9.

27 DAI, 60; cf. DAI, 395: 'What is meant by "republic" in the United States is the slow and quiet action of society upon itself.'

28 The image of a second 'journey' comes from George Wilson Pierson, 'Le "second voyage" de Tocqueville en Amérique', in *Alexis de Tocqueville: livre du centenaire 1859–1959* (Paris: Éditions du CNRS, 1960), 71–85, and is elaborated in James Schleifer, *The Making of Tocqueville's Democracy in America* (Chapel Hill: University of North Carolina Press, 1980). Schleifer's work is now an indispensable companion to anyone writing on Tocqueville's *Democracy in America*.

29 *History of the Origin of Representative Government in Europe*, pt. I, lecture 1, in Stanley Mellon (ed.), *François Guizot: Historical Essays and Lectures* (Chicago: University of Chicago Press, 1972), 29.

30 Jardin, *Tocqueville*, 38.

31 On this point, and on Tocqueville's rhetoric in general, see the discussion in Hereth, *Alexis de Tocqueville*, 4–5 and *passim*.

32 Tocqueville regarded the notion of a mixed constitution as a chimera, as did many critics of aristocratic versions of the French constitution: see DAI, 258. He seems always to have deplored the waste of energy expended on dynastic questions in French politics.

33 Jardin, *Tocqueville*, 81; on Tocqueville and Guizot, see also Pierre Rosanvallon, *Le moment Guizot* (Paris: Gallimard, 1985), 84, 195;

Françoise Mélonio, *Tocqueville et les français* (Paris: Aubier, 1993), 16–25, 124–6.

34 Larry Siedentop, *Tocqueville* (Oxford: Oxford University Press, 1994), 40.

35 See e.g., 'Character and Influence of Washington', in Mellon, *François Guizot*, 397–8.

36 Rosanvallon, *Le Moment Guizot* is a stimulating guide to the problematic of the social and political in Guizot.

37 Quoted ibid. 238.

38 *History of the Origin of Representative Government in Europe*, pt. I, lecture 1, in Mellon, *François Guizot*, 28–30.

39 *History of Civilization in France*, pt. I, lecture 1, in Mellon, *François Guizot*, 269.

40 Ibid. 279.

41 Ibid. 195.

42 *History of the Origin of Representative Government in Europe*, pt. I, lecture 23, in Mellon, *François Guizot*, 75. Royer-Collard, anticipating Tocqueville's imagery, perceives that the Revolution has exacerbated this problem, swept away sites of independent resistance to the central government, and left society *en poussière*. See 'On the Liberty of the Press', *Discours*, 2 Jan. 1822, quoted in Siedentop, *Tocqueville*, 26.

43 *History of the Origin of Representative Government in Europe*, pt. I, lecture 23, in Mellon, *François Guizot*, 23.

44 Rosanvallon, *Le moment Guizot*, 171.

45 See Tocqueville's correspondence with Gobineau on this point: *Correspondance d'Alexis de Tocqueville et d'Arthur de Gobineau*, OC 9, 205.

46 George Kelly notes that the second volume of *Democracy*, excluding notes, contains 15 proper names, none of them American. *The Old Regime and the Revolution*, a work of history, turns up only 59. *The Humane Comedy*, 234.

47 From his notes on Barcou de Penhoen's history of India, OC 3:1, 511; quoted in Jardin, 340.

48 See Paul Janet, *Les problèmes du XIXe siècle: la politique, la littérature, la science, la philosophie, la religion* (Paris: Michel Levy fréres, 1872), 59. Janet situated Tocqueville among the great 'observers', including Machiavelli and Montesquieu. Many twentieth-century commentators have nevertheless tried to flesh out a systematic structure they find implicit in Tocqueville. See e.g. Irving Zeitlin, *Liberty, Equality, and Revolution in Alexis de Tocqueville* (Boston: Little, Brown, 1971). More successful, in my view, are those who accept the middle-range nature of Tocqueville's generalizations and the open-ended quality of that work. A particularly stimulating recent example of this approach can be found

in Jon Elster, *Political Psychology* (Cambridge: Cambridge University Press, 1993). For a reading that argues that any attempt to impose consistency on (or even to summarize) Tocqueville's theory of democracy is misguided, and that his essence lies in metaphor and paradox, see F. R. Ankersmit, *Aesthetic Politics: Political Philosophy Beyond Fact and Value* (Stanford, Calif.: Stanford University Press, 1996), 294–341.

49 See e.g. Jack Lively, *The Social and Political Thought of Alexis de Tocqueville* (Oxford: Clarendon Press, 1962), 184–203, and Marvin Zetterbaum, *Tocqueville and the Problem of Democracy* (Stanford, Calif.: Stanford University Press, 1967), 120–1.

50 DAI, 396, 395; Cf. Benjamin Constant's distinction between what revolutionary governments rightfully did and those acts that were 'crimes': *Des effets du régime qu'on nomme révolutionnaire rélativement au salut et à la liberté de la France* (1797), quoted in Stanley Mellon, *The Political Uses of History: A Study of Historians in the French Restoration* (Stanford, Calif.: Stanford University Press, 1958), 22–3.

51 Pierre-Paul Royer-Collard (1763–1845): lecturer in philosophy at the Sorbonne 1811–14; president of the commission on public instruction, 1815–20; member of chamber of deputies almost continuously from 1815 to 1839; leader of the Doctrinaires; Charles de Rémusat (1797–1875): liberal journalist during the restoration, politician and writer associated with the Doctrinaires and then with the liberal opposition under the July Monarchy, Minister of the Interior (1840); exiled to England after the *coup d'état* of Louis Bonaparte; Foreign Minister (1871–3).

52 On the relationship between Royer-Collard and Tocqueville, see Kelly, *The Humane Comedy*, 17–27, and Jean Claude Lamberti, *Tocqueville and the Two Démocracies*, trans. Arthur Goldhammer (Cambridge, Mass.: Harvard University Press, 1989), 130–5.

53 P.-P. Royer-Collard to Tocqueville, 19 Nov. 1836, OC 11:27.

54 Prosper de Barante, *La vie politique de M. Royer-Collard: ses discours et ses écrits*, 2 vols. (Paris: Didier, 1861), 2:18. Quoted in Kelly, *The Humane Comedy*, 18.

55 This judgement was handed down, it is true, after Royer-Collard had left active politics. Royer-Collard to Tocqueville, 21 Nov. 1837, OC 11, 54.

56 Charles de Rémusat, 'Discours sur Royer-Collard', in *Passé et Présent*, 2 vols. (Paris: Didier, 1857), 2:325.

57 See René Taveneaux, *Jansénisme et politique* (Paris: Armand Colin, 1965).

58 Kelly, *Humane Comedy*, 93–114.

59 Charles de Rémusat, 'De l'esprit de réaction: Royer-Collard and Tocqueville', *Revue des Deux Mondes*, 35 (1861), 785.

60 See Charles de Rémusat, *Essais de philosophie*, 2 vols. (Paris: J. Renouard, 1875), 1:17–51.

61 Rémusat was discontented with philosophy because he came to the conclusion that philosophers who escaped scepticism did so through a leap of faith that equalled that of theologians. He ultimately thought that Cousin merely asserted what he had lost the power to demonstrate, but that the Doctrinaires nevertheless deserved credit for trying to reconcile 'le fait avec le droit'. Rémusat, *Mémoires de ma vie*, 5 vols. (Paris: Librairie Plon, 1958), 1:367, 370; see also *Essais de philosophie*, 1:70–86. Rémusat's conviction that it was necessary for liberals to appeal to something beyond the ordinary course of political experience in order to act decisively and to persuade others led him to a series of critical explorations of past attempts to adjust reason to faith, especially in Protestant England. He wrote compulsively on problems of church and state and theology during the Second Empire, remaining most attracted to moderate Jansenism and to Locke's Christian rationalism, though he was also critical of both.

62 Quoted in John Hermann Randall, *The Career of Philosophy*, 2 vols. (New York: Columbia University Press, 1965), 2:448

63 Kelly, *Humane Comedy*, 21.

64 Cousin in George Ripley (ed.), *Specimens of Foreign Standard Literature*, 2 vols. (Boston: Hilliard, Gray, 1838), 2:236, quoted in Kelly, *The Humane Comedy*, 157.

65 On the moral notions of the Eclectics, see Victor Cousin, *Justice et charité* (Paris: Pagnerre, 1848); perhaps more important, see the works of Cousin's followers Adolf Franck and Jules Simon. A good discussion of the latter may be found in John Logue, *From Philosophy to Sociology: The Evolution of French Liberalism 1870–1914* (Dekalb: Northern Illinois University Press, 1983), 17–94.

66 From a letter to Gustave Beaumont, OC 8:3, 522; quoted in Jardin, *Tocqueville*, 515. Tocqueville's notes for the continuation of *The Old Regime* have been carefully edited by André Jardin in OC 2:2, *L'ancien régime et la révolution: fragments et notes inédites sur la révolution*.

67 *Fragments sur la révolution*, OC 2:2, 226.

68 Ibid. 227–8, 239.

69 See e.g. the earliest discussion of religion and politics in the 1835 *Democracy*, DAI, 46–7, which takes the combination of moral certainty and political creativity to be the essence of this new Anglo-American 'type'.

70 Unpublished draft for the 1840 'Preface' to *Democracy in America*, quoted in James T. Schleifer, 'Tocqueville as Historian', in Abraham Eisenstadt (ed.), *Reconsidering Tocqueville's 'Democracy in America'* (New Brunswick, NJ: Rutgers University Press, 1988), 151.

2

American Democracy: The Shape of Democracy Itself

Unlike others who held themselves out as guides to the society that was emerging out of the destruction of the Old Regime, Tocqueville had no clear model on which to base his new 'science'. Neither sensationalist psychology, political economy, biology, mathematics, speculative history, nor idealist philosophy served as a starting-point. Rather, Tocqueville had America. His observations in the United States and the intense intellectual activity involved in writing the two volumes of *Democracy in America* in a literal sense constituted his social and political thought. Yet he discerned 'the shape of democracy itself' in the new world only because he had to some extent perceived its form in the old (DAI, 19). From the beginning, America was less a society deserving of explanation in its own right than a stimulus for meditating on the march of equality and the retreat of liberty in France, twin themes that had preoccupied him for several years.[1] Tocqueville is disingenuous in suggesting on the very first page of *Democracy in America* that only later, when he 'came to consider our own side of the Atlantic', did he detect something analogous to the rapid extension of equality that he had noticed in America. In fact, though he did not carry an extensive baggage of intellectual *systèmes* with him to the United States, he did bring a settled conviction that societies based on permanent inequality of condition were soon to be extinct.

Tocqueville's Point de Départ: Equality and Liberty

Tocqueville wished to understand not the causes of the aristocracy's fall from historical grace, a phenomenon as unalterable as an act of God and as real to him as his own anomalous social identity, but rather its social and political consequences. Nevertheless, his perception of what had been lost deeply marked his analysis of these consequences. From the pen of a middle-class radical, the decline of the European nobility might have been phrased as the 'destruction of privilege' or the 'triumph of freedom over feudal despotism'. Tocqueville, however, never brought into clear focus the exploitative dimensions of aristocracy, either economic or political. Though he recognized injustices connected to a system of hereditary nobility, this recognition did not animate his intellectual work. Rather, his aristocratic background made him sensitive in a particular way to the democracy of everyday life. The end of aristocracy meant for him the disappearance of any existential moral claims based on permanent marks of human distinctiveness, and the disintegration of the social foundations and ethic of the traditional nobility. His attention was correspondingly fixed on the replacement for these claims and belief systems: a demand for recognition on the basis of humanity alone and an attachment to the correlative principle of social equality. Tocqueville did not discover that equality reigned in America. He assumed that any society in which aristocratic status ascribed by birth was absent must substitute equality as a regulating ideal and a motivating passion. His study of America amply confirmed this prescient intuition and made him the first anthropologist of modern equality.[2]

Egalitarian America, like post-aristocratic Europe, and especially post-revolutionary France, presented a particular puzzle. Could a modern society of existential equals organize and perpetuate itself? The ancients, as well as Montesquieu, Rousseau, and several waves of French revolutionaries, had postulated that democratic republics could cohere only on the basis of republican virtue. Revolutionary experience, however, suggested that a quest for virtue under modern conditions was both chimerical and dangerous. It led to terror and dictatorship. Yet equality without virtue seemed to require increasing centralization and reliance on *la police* to maintain order. Tocqueville refused to accept such a grim prognosis. It was not the problem of order, but the question of how to achieve order through the independent efforts and free activity of citizens that drew him to the United States. America's reputation as a *free* republic, vague but widespread in liberal and republican circles in the 1820s, would have been its principal attraction for Tocqueville and Beaumont in 1831.[3] Tocqueville was to struggle for the next ten years with the question: under what conditions could a society of equals also be a free people?

No reader of Tocqueville can miss his devotion to liberty, openly acknowledged as the motivating passion of his life's work, a source of 'sublime pleasure', even an altar at which he is 'disposed to worship' (DAII, 505, 695). Yet he never defined liberty, much less developed a theory of it. When he wrote to John Stuart Mill that he was attached to equality by reason, but to liberty 'par goût', he was being literally truthful.[4] Liberty, like his other moral beliefs, was at bottom an inexplicable attachment that he scarcely knew how to describe for those without the taste for it. Before we turn to a fuller discussion of *Democracy in America*, however, we need such a description, for without an appreciation of what Tocqueville meant by liberty, his obsession with the shape of democracy makes little sense.

Tocqueville believed both in the idea that human beings are in some measure free to determine their own futures and in the idea that civil and political liberties were supremely valuable goods. These are separable notions. One is a metaphysical statement about free will in history, the other valorizes certain social and political practices. Yet these two meanings were linked in Tocqueville's mind through the idea of human choices for which one accepts personal responsibility.[5] Indeed, it was because Christianity affirmed that individuals bore responsibility for their spiritual fate that Tocqueville judged it to be so congruent with the requirements of secular freedom (DAII, 547). The ability to choose and the assumption of responsibility for the future, then, are at the heart of what Tocqueville means by freedom, which alone allows individuals to exercise moral agency. '[Political] freedom is, in truth, a *sacred* thing. There is only one other that deserves the name: that is *virtue*. Yet what is virtue, if not the *free* choice of what is good?'[6] Liberty may be a 'sacred thing', but the issue before Tocqueville was how it could be instantiated in mundane institutions. How can we recognize freedom in-the-world?

Human freedom, Tocqueville tells us, manifests itself in various ways in different times and places. Just as the earth's atmosphere can support many different cultures that would perish in its absence, so freedom can be expressed in different institutions and practices that would lose their human essence without its inspiration.[7] Tocqueville sensed an atmosphere of freedom in the ancient world and under feudalism, among the nomadic tribes of North Africa and the dwindling groups of American Indians, and in 'civilized' forms among the Anglo-Americans, the English, and—more tenuously— the French and other Europeans. What these examples of individuals breathing the air of freedom seem to share is a display of independence and pride, coupled with an intolerance of outside control and a willingness to take responsibility for the fate of oneself and one's group. This ability to act independently and responsibly requires courage, resourcefulness, vigilance, and a certain amount of foresight. It is the opposite of passivity or servility. The feudal notion of being master of oneself and one's realm, responsible for kin and dependents, loyal to one's liege lord, but ultimately accountable only to God and one's peers, constitutes only one manifestation of freedom in history, but this conception is nevertheless close to Tocqueville's core notion of human liberty.

Many of Tocqueville's interpreters have noted that his idea of freedom was largely 'negative'.[8] This judgement is surely right insofar as it captures his revulsion from the claim of any power— monarch or people—to abrogate a minimum area of individual inviolability or to relieve the individual of responsibility for his fate. Security against arbitrary government is a *sine qua non* of freedom, and security ultimately depends on the ability and willingness of individuals to resist. But Isaiah Berlin's famous polar distinction between negative and positive liberty, while nicely calibrated to capture certain differences between Locke and Rousseau or between Constant and Marx, is subtly misleading with regard to Tocqueville.[9]

Implicit in Tocqueville's concept of liberty are two connected ideas that transcend any strict notion of negative liberty as 'the area within which a man can act unobstructed by others': first, service to some collective ideal beyond the self, and second, dignity before one's peers.[10] Tocqueville struggles to express these elements of freedom when he implicitly compares the attitudes of the French in the seventeenth century to those of his own contemporaries. Living under a would-be absolutist monarchy, those earlier French subjects were not truly free, but their *mœurs* retained something of the taste for freedom. Because they still believed in the legitimacy of the monarch, there was something independent, 'firm, delicate, and yet irritable' in their submission to him.[11] In serving the king, they still served their own social ideals. But despite the king's ostensible power, there were many opinions that he was powerless to change and many actions that he could not prevent. The codes of honourable men defined these opinions and actions. In contrast, the French of his own day, who lived under a would-be representative government, seemed to Tocqueville to vacillate between coarse, unrestrained exhibitions of insubordination and an easy submission to centralized power. They had achieved civil and political guarantees, but the atmosphere sustaining their old liberties had evaporated. Freedom, then, is potentially but not automatically available to individuals in democracies.

Tocqueville's idea of liberty always suggests active judgement on matters of collective concern, as well as the right to be let alone. When he speaks more specifically of *democratic* liberty, the participatory and self-governing elements associated with freedom come to the foreground, since obedience to an outside power loses its free character through the disappearance of any compelling claim to legitimacy other than the people itself.[12] Under egalitarian social conditions, in which people stand socially and morally on the same plane, one cannot be free without collective self-rule because obedience to a single figure or a group has become inherently degrading. It is here that Berlin's idea of positive liberty (the desire for collective self-direction, the desire not just to be free of authority but to exercise authority over one's own fate) looks most odd as a foil to Tocqueville's alleged conception of negative liberty. Indeed, wherever it shows itself, Tocquevillian liberty contains some dimension of duty and loyalty to a larger whole; under modern social conditions this element grows into full-blown and active participation in collective self-government, not just as a guarantee of civil rights but as a manifestation of human dignity. Tocqueville's notion of liberty under democratic social conditions, then, suggests a certain kind of self-government even more than the claim to enjoy civil liberties.

Democratic society—a society in which equality of social condition prevails—also offers a grander backdrop for the development of liberty, since one's relevant peers—those others to whom some accountability is due—are not members of a tribe or closed caste, but all citizens. Tocqueville admires the first French revolutionaries, the men of 1789, not because they consolidated the bases of equality in France, but because they exalted the ideal of liberty for all. 'That was once [France's] glory and the most precious part of herself.'[13] Democratic liberty is more just than other forms of liberty precisely because it is distributed to all. 'According to the modern, democratic, and I dare say the just notion of liberty, each man, being presumed to have received from nature the necessary knowledge to rule himself, has an equal and imprescriptable right to live independent of his fellows in everything that relates only to himself, and to direct his own destiny as he sees it.'[14] To direct one's own destiny in democracy, however, proves immensely difficult. The trick of living together under conditions of equality while maintaining individual dignity and independence, as Rousseau had reminded Tocqueville, constituted the moral challenge of modernity.

Alexis de Tocqueville, then, went to America on the alert both for mechanisms of stability that might link existential equals in a new way of life and for sources of freedom that would make that life worth living. His observations, conversations, and close study of American writings became the raw material for a sustained deliberation on these themes. The America and Americans that he saw, or thought he saw, stimulated him to develop a number of abstractions —his *idées mères*—that would henceforth guide his thinking. In his hands these ideas (aristocracy, democracy, equality, individualism, centralization, despotism, revolution) were not static categories, but subtly shifting conceptual tools with which to illuminate his dual focus on the coming of democracy and the potential realization of democratic liberty. Tocqueville's apparent lucidity often evaporates as he shifts his emphases, continually examines phenomena in a new light without revisiting earlier discussions, or occasionally outright contradicts himself. What guides him, however, is not a quest for scientific clarity, but rather the desire to express his ideas in a form that will lead his contemporaries to see their own society with new eyes. As he himself noted many times, Tocqueville wrote from a French perspective and for a largely European audience. In the text of *Democracy in America* he deliberately sculpts his impressions of American life into intellectual shapes intended to provoke and discompose his European contemporaries, to shake them into a self-consciousness about the inevitable effects of their new social order, and to structure the political choices before them. In pursuing this didactic purpose, he arrived by indirection at a provocative use of the comparative method of analysing a culture in 'itself' that has more in common with twentieth-century historians of *mentalité* than with grand narratives of the progress of the West.

American Democracy's Point de Départ

From the time he and Beaumont disembarked at New York, Tocqueville began to keep detailed journals of his impressions and conversations. Because of the careful and imaginative labour of James Schleifer in comparing these notes, journals, and letters of 1830–1 with drafts of *Democracy in America* and the published text, we now know a great deal about the evolution of Tocqueville's ideas. Like other European visitors, he was immediately struck by the prosperity and stability of the American union. In casting about for a way to catalogue the various factors contributing to this success, he sought a schema that would facilitate a comparison with Europe. For this comparison he needed a standard of comparability, some hypothetical collection of causal factors at work in both settings. Eventually he would come to group these common causal factors together under the rubric of the workings of democracy 'itself'.

Drawing initially on his reading of Montesquieu, whose beliefs about the influence of geography and climate were still starting-points for most anthropologically minded voyagers, Tocqueville turns first to particularistic or accidental explanations of American success. His early reflections consider (and then largely dismiss) the effects of geography, isolation from Europe, and especially what he called the national character, or more loosely the race, of the European settlers. The contrast between French and English in America, for example, suggested to him that something inflexible in national character accounted for the persistence of habits and customs over generations.[15] On the other hand, the contrast between Americans and English prompted the opposite thesis, that is, that the effects of national character were much less important than other factors in accounting for the shape of a society. How else could one fathom the vast cultural differences that had emerged in a relatively short time between two peoples of the same national origin? The latter view was to prevail. Like geography, national character would be acknowledged sporadically, but then set to one side as Tocqueville turned to his main task of identifying in America a set of transformative tendencies that also operated in Europe.

Eventually Tocqueville lumped together all those circumstances peculiar to America in the terms *circonstances* or *point de départ*, a notion that included both physical factors (such as the character, size, and location of the land) and historical factors (such as the

English and Puritan character of the first settlers). He takes up these particular circumstances sequentially in the first two chapters of the 1835 *Democracy*. Tocqueville does not claim that this American *point de départ* was uninfluential. On the contrary, he thinks it immensely important. What he claims is that for some purposes it can be identified and set aside. America's exceptional origins facilitated the relatively painless birth of the set of tendencies that he wishes to study, but its origins are separable from those tendencies.

Tocqueville hypothesizes that the English culture of the original settlers disintegrated under the pressure of certain forces and reconstituted itself as American culture under the influence of a new democratic dynamic. Although he sometimes seems to assume that a desideratum of Anglo-Saxon character forms a constant, he argues that in America its aristocratic shell disintegrates, to be replaced by a democratic one that in many ways suits it better.[16] Tocqueville's point is not the continuity of national character, but rather the discontinuity of political culture. Thus, while he never denied the importance of some of the original elements of America's English *point de départ* (in particular its level of civilization, its Puritan religious and legal traditions, its middle-class origins, and its entrenched habits of local government), what he wished to discover was how these given elements had been reassembled, so to speak, in a recognizably *new* set of laws and mores that constituted a society dramatically different from aristocratic England.

Although particular factors involved in America's peculiarly favourable *circonstances* reappear in the rest of the work, and sometimes loom large in Tocqueville's explanation of a particular phenomenon, in general he sets America's *circonstances* to one side in deference to two other classes of phenomena: democratic laws and democratic *mœurs*. By laws, Tocqueville means above all communal and local institutions, constitutional forms, and the organization of the judiciary; by *mœurs* he means nothing less than the whole moral and intellectual state of the people or their 'habits, opinions, usages, and beliefs' (DAI, 287, 308). These laws and *mœurs*, he observes, are quite different from those operating in England and must be the result of the process of democratization itself. Of the three factors that regulate and direct American life (circumstances, laws, and mores), Tocqueville argues that 'the contribution of physical causes is less than that of the laws, and of laws less than mores' (DAI, 308; cf. 307, 309). Explicating democratic *mœurs*, and in particular their great importance in preserving democratic laws, was indeed 'the main object of my work' (DAI, 308).

There are many ambiguities in this attempt to categorize the influences on the state of American society, ambiguities related to Tocqueville's inability to keep his variables conceptually distinct or his terminology consistent.[17] One persistent confusion is worth examining in some detail, for it illustrates the didactic purpose that lies at the heart of the two *Democracies*. Tocqueville never completely decides whether America's particular history (as opposed to its geography) is part of a *point de départ* that can be ignored temporarily for his own heuristic purposes, or whether it is an integral part of democratic *mœurs*. If a nation's *circonstances*—its *point de départ*—includes those habits, beliefs, customs, and ideas that are bequeathed by its particular ethnic or religious past and that persist over many generations, how can these circumstances even be distinguished from existing *mœurs*, let alone considered the least important of the three factors influencing the 'state of a people'? As James Schleifer has pointed out, Tocqueville could maintain the position that the *point de départ* was the least important of his three levels of causes only by conveniently leaving out for the moment its historical elements. When he lists the relative importance of causes, Tocqueville mentions only the physical aspect of *circonstances* (geography). By sleight of hand he slips the idea of historically given beliefs and opinions out of the category of unchangeable circumstances and into the general category of *mœurs*, thus narrowing the compass of *circonstances*. On the other hand, when he wishes to see certain American attitudes (towards art, for example, or towards poetry) as more American than democratic, he widens the notion of *circonstances* to include cultural attitudes and beliefs peculiar to America's origins. This shifting of history into and out of the relevant 'antecedent facts' of American democracy continues throughout the two *Democracies*. Why is Tocqueville so elusive about whether historical circumstances are included in America's *point de départ*?

Tocqueville's difficulties here surely have something to do with his underlying moral belief in the importance of freely willed action. He wishes to set up a polarity between that which is relatively unchangeable (the *circonstances* in which providence has placed us) and that which can be altered (laws and mores), since people will intervene in their own history only if they think they can affect it. Any argument privileging causal factors over which people have no control verges on a 'materialism' that denies the effects of free will. We know from manuscript notes that Tocqueville had originally put circumstances and mores together as the most permanent influences on maintaining a democratic republic, and assigned to laws— the only factor obviously under human control—the least influence. He rejected this preliminary argument, however, because it seemed too deterministic. 'The *idée-mère* of this book is directly the contrary, since I start invincibly from this point: whatever the tendencies of the social condition [*état social*], men can always modify them and avert the bad while adapting to the good.'[18] Because he worried that his account of America would appear to reinforce determinism and fatalism, Tocqueville sometimes reduced the scope of original circumstances to the idea of physical environment, moved history to the category of *mœurs*, and infused the latter with a more voluntaristic element by associating it with laws. If the Americans' *point de départ* is merely geographical and physical, rather than historical, it is plausible to see it as the least important influence on the way they live.[19]

The shifting of history out of circumstances and into the general category of *mœurs*, however, brings its own difficulties: it endangers the comparative enterprise at the heart of *Democracy in America*, which depends on distinguishing historically given American *mœurs* from generically induced democratic ones. Indeed, Tocqueville's desire to create a theoretical space for comparison between America and Europe pushes him in the opposite direction, in the direction of leaving history buried in America's point of departure in order better to isolate and describe a new phenomenon. That phenomenon is the set of laws and *mœurs* (ideas, habits, and customs) that have been profoundly transformed by America's social state and that have taken on a distinct character as 'democratic' because of the very forces which equality unleashes.[20]

Tocqueville's confusions here, and his ability to tolerate them, can be partially explained by the fact that his desire to vindicate a role for voluntarism in history lies at the root of both conceptual schemas. Leaving history out of a society's unchangeable circumstances makes it easier to claim that people can change their fate. But leaving history out of democratic *mœurs* makes it easier to identify the generic democratic *mentalité* that will surely influence that fate, and that people must recognize if they are to act intelligently. Indeed, distinguishing the shape of democracy itself underlies all of

Tocqueville's hopes for appropriating American experience in the cause of France's intervention in her own history.

Tocqueville is struggling here with perhaps the most difficult problem in social and historical explanation: how to set up a useful and meaningful comparison. As he wrote to his friend Ernest de Chabrol from America, 'without comparisons to make, the mind does not know how to proceed'.[21] Because he had abandoned the notion that history itself contained revolutionary laws of development, he was left with the need to create a meaningful comparative framework so that the mind could 'proceed' to understand the limits of and opportunities for human agency. Thus Tocqueville is forever holding one dimension of a problem constant, so as to establish differences along another. He then—with greater or lesser plausibility—hazards an explanation of those differences. A similar problematic would later preoccupy Weber, who achieved a much higher level of self-awareness about the difficulties involved in constructing an explanation of a unique historical phenomenon that would be adequate on the levels both of 'meaning' and of empirical verification.

Tocqueville cared most, of course, about contrasting the effects that democracy has produced in different settings (predominantly France and America).[22] In *Democracy in America*, he argues that certain patterns of social behaviour and belief in America (such as the bent towards civil association or religious belief or stable family life) are inherently *democratic* and hence potentially of great significance for democratic France, rather than merely American and hence of only parochial interest. To make that argument plausible, he must of necessity ignore or downplay unique historical causes of those behaviours. Leaving aside for a moment problems of the definition of democracy 'itself', how does Tocqueville move from a discussion of America's *point de départ*, at once geographical and historical, to a discussion of those newer laws and mores from which the astute analyst may draw out the typical 'shape' of democracy itself?

The crucial mediating argument appears in chapter 3, 'The Social State of the Anglo-Americans'. Tocqueville there hypothesizes that something happens in America to create a 'democratic social state' which *itself* becomes the greatest influence on American laws and mores. 'The social state is commonly the result of circumstances, sometimes of laws, but most often of a combination of the two. But once it has come into being, it may itself be considered as the prime cause of most of the laws, customs, and ideas which control the nation's behavior; it modifies even those things which it does not cause' (DAI, 50; cf. DAII, 417). The particular combination of circumstances and laws that caused the emergence of a democratic social state in America included its favourable *point de départ*, but also new circumstances and laws. First, the American Revolution gave the people a taste for liberty and independence: 'they became a power and wanted to act on their own.' More important, however, the complete democratization of the law of inheritance launched a cycle of changing structures and social expectations ('by acting upon things, it affects persons; by acting on persons, it has its effect on things') that prevented the rise of a new landed elite and favoured an economy based on the rapid circulation of wealth.[23] Together the increased taste for popular assertion occasioned by separation from England and the dynamic of equalization achieved a synergy that launched the creative force of 'democracy' in America. Since the desire of the people to act on their own and the multiplier effects of a democratized law of inheritance are also forces that Tocqueville thinks have accelerated the destruction of aristocracy in France, he has, very early in the *Democracy*, pulled America and France into a common analytical frame. Similar dynamic forces are affecting both societies and pulling them into the same social state—democracy 'itself'—which then independently affects laws, customs, and ideas.

Tocqueville, then, attempts to pour his raw material on America into the following theoretical mould. America's geographical and historical circumstances were on balance highly favourable to liberty and equality of social conditions. For the purpose of using America to learn about French dilemmas, however, we can set aside this *point de départ*. It is of interest mostly because it assured that the birth of democracy would be natural and quiet, rather than unnatural and violent. This favourable environment has produced a usefully instructive specimen of the democratic species. If we hold constant, as it were, its *point de départ*, we can identify and assess the results of democracy 'itself', a social state that continues to transform both the mores and laws of the people and to generate a host of intricate regulating mechanisms that challenge many European assumptions about the meaning of democracy. In this new society it is difficult to unravel the threads of mutually reinforcing behaviours and beliefs, but in general we must recognize that the easiest factor to change—legal arrangements—is probably the least important in maintaining a free and stable form of democracy.

Rather, we must look at the patterns of cultural and social behaviours that shape and are shaped by those laws. A profound study of all the patterns and connections that can be traced to the workings of democracy 'itself', then, must be the starting-point for any responsible plan of action for the circumstances in which European nations find themselves. In the two volumes of his *Democracy*, Tocqueville proceeds to launch that study.

American Tangents

Tocqueville's treatment of those populations that were explicitly excluded both from American democracy and from his analysis of it confirms this construction of the theoretical project at the centre of *Democracy in America*. His relegation of 'The Three Races That Inhabit the United States' to what is functionally a long appendix explicitly marginalizes this subject's relevance to his main concerns. He argues that the situations of African slaves and native populations pose a deep American dilemma, but are unrelated to the conceptual issue of revealing the dynamics of a democratic society. 'These topics are like tangents to my subject, being American, but not democratic, and my main business has been to describe democracy' (DAI, 316).

There are many ironies in this theoretical exclusion of the problems that would pose the deepest moral challenge to American democracy and, one might argue, to any modern democratic society. Some of these ironies were apparent to Tocqueville himself, who did not avert his gaze from the lived contradiction of an 'egalitarian' and 'free' people that practised racial despotism and genocide, but rather gave this contradiction a penetrating look before moving on to his chosen concerns. Whatever his own prejudices, Tocqueville explicitly denies throughout his writings the legitimacy of racist justifications for these exclusionary practices, justifications that would deny the applicability to Africans or Native Americans of the social and psychological tendencies that form a large part of his anatomization of democratic culture. He acknowledges a common humanity, denouncing modern race slavery in the strongest terms and deploring the disappearance of Indian civilizations into a historical void in which their cultural meanings would be forever lost. He particularly scorns the English settlers' treatment of the original inhabitants, contrasting the more 'honest' Spanish version of genocide, which at least left the Indian survivors capable of being assimilated into Spanish culture, with the specious legalism of the Anglo-Americans, which drove whole populations to extinction on a wave of fraudulent contracts and broken promises (DAI, 339). Nevertheless, he does not follow out the implications for subject populations of the democratic psychology he observes among European settlers. Since his primary subject is the irresistible transformative force of democracy itself, the passions it awakens, and the new democratic society it sustains, this lack of interest seems to call for an explanation.

First, and quite simply, Tocqueville ignores the possible effects of the democratic awakening of subject populations in America because he foresees no similar problems of racial subordination in the old world.[24] His real subject was the coming of democracy in Europe, and especially France, not democracy in America. Second, and more troubling, he concludes from his own empirical observations that the forces of democracy will never transcend racial barriers in America in a manner that will allow for the assimilation of currently subordinated groups. Tocqueville's model of equality, based on the breakdown of caste barriers between nobility and third estate in Europe, relies heavily on the homogenizing effects of a common way of life, equal access to wealth and education, and intermarriage. But these are forces that he finds completely lacking in America's racially based caste society.

In the case of native populations, both groups resist assimilation. Indians scorn the European settlers' way of life and agricultural habits. While dependent on European products, they will not condescend to produce such objects themselves. And if they were to try, as did the Cherokees, they could not learn fast enough to compete successfully. Meanwhile the basis of their own social and economic existence is being inexorably destroyed, both by design and through the equally cruel—if sometimes unintentional—consequences of European settlement. For their part, the European settlers make no effort to absorb the Indians. The Anglo-Americans shun intermarriage through a kind of peculiarity of English national character. The French, on the other hand, have no such cultural inhibitions and even exhibit an atavistic affinity for Indian life in the wild. They literally 'go native' rather than absorb the Indians into their own more technically advanced civilization. In any case, the French and others are too few to make a difference. Tocqueville believes that he is watching the rapid and irrevocable disappearance of the Indian races in America, a disappearance that seems to him, as a social scientist might say, overdetermined. His descriptions of the plight of the Indians are haunted by images of extinction. Native pride leads them to 'death'; they have not merely drawn back from the frontier, but have been 'destroyed'; previous tribes have withdrawn and 'died'; the only remaining refuge for existing tribes will be 'the grave' (DAI, 316, 321, 336).

The case of black slaves is different but equally bleak. Tocqueville believes that slavery is an inefficient economic system that will remain profitable only for a dwindling number of crops in the American south. The numbers of blacks, proportionally, will decrease in relation to the rest of the population. But emancipation em;the only just alternative—will inevitably leave these formerly slave populations isolated and victimized precisely because they will be despised and few. Severed from their own lands, languages, and cultures, freed slaves have no choice but to attempt assimilation as an alternative to annihilation. Unlike the Indians, they therefore do seek acceptance by the majority culture. But the experience of freedmen shows that Anglo-Americans will never allow assimilation. Tocqueville drew on his own experience in judging that class prejudice is difficult to overcome even if it is unaccompanied by outward signs of low status. According to Tocqueville, the combination of memories of slavery and its ineradicable badges (among them blackness itself) precludes any meaningful integration. The disastrous effects of modern slavery are hard to overcome because they are 'fatally combined with the physical and permanent fact of difference in race. Memories of slavery disgrace the race, and race perpetuates memories of slavery' (DAI, 341).

Tocqueville does not deny that the human passions and aspirations born of equality will animate freed slaves just as they animated freed serfs, revolutionary crowds, or Anglo-American colonists. In the midst of social equality, ex-slaves will increasingly resent imposed inequalities and struggle against them. But these passions will be stillborn. In the north, where they will remain a small minority, the majority will victimize and isolate them, creating a class of pseudo-citizens. In the south, where they would be a majority if freed, the whites already subject them to a new and terrible species of race tyranny, denying them access to the rudimentary technical and spiritual elements of civilization in order to avoid a bloody insurrection. The Indians achieve a certain dignity in extinction, but even this is denied to the unfortunate victims of race slavery who are humiliated in death as in life. 'When the Negro is no more, his bones are cast aside, and some difference in condition is found even in the equality of death' (DAI, 243). Tocqueville struggled mightily against any deterministic theory based on race, history, or biology; yet he comes close here to accepting—at the same time that he morally condemns it—the extinction of hope for populations subjected on the illusory basis of race. Since whites will always be the majority in America, they will, he thinks, have some inclination to tyrannize over minority populations. Without denying them their humanity, he denies subordinated races a future. Apparently doomed by specific circumstances, they exist outside the dynamic of equality.

If Tocqueville's real subject had been the coming of democracy in America, he might have paused much longer over ideas, customs, and national characteristics that complicated and contradicted the sway of democracy, rather than those that hastened its birth. Among these would certainly have been the institution of slavery and ascriptive theories based on race. He observes in passing, for example, that democratization intensifies rather than lessens race prejudice in America. The personal pride engendered by democratic equality seems to increase the pride of origin that white settlers inherit from the English, raising the possibility of a psychological connection between equality and exclusion.[25] Real integration, on Tocqueville's account, involves intermarriage and the fusion of races, but the English have less than any other people been willing openly to 'mingle their blood' with that of other races. As a consequence, the potential mediating force of a mixed-race group has no strength in itself. Such individuals are simply categorized as non-white. There are many such 'tangential' paradoxes that Tocqueville could have pursued if his subject had been American democracy, or even democracy in America, rather than the puzzle of how to create free institutions in France. His treatment of subject peoples disturbs, however, precisely because his empathetic reconstruction of their plight leads to no corresponding sympathy for their right to a free way of life, and little compunction about dropping them out of the theoretical universe of democracy.[26]

Eventually Tocqueville's single-minded absorption in French affairs will lead him away from America altogether. America itself, like its racial problems, will become a 'tangent' to his growing engagement with France's destiny. In *Democracy in America*, however, he is still struggling to keep the two societies in the same comparative frame. The acknowledgement that America's point of departure might contain unique circumstances that could not be set aside, and that might better account for the shape of its society than 'democracy itself', threatened his comparative enterprise; therefore, he does not acknowledge or pursue those unique circumstances. Similarly, the acknowledgement that France's point of departure might be unique would threaten the structure of *Democracy in America* by putting in question the notion that one democratic template could illuminate both societies. Throughout *Democracy in America* Tocqueville represses the thought that France's circumstances—her experience of state centralization and social revolution—might render her *sui generis*. I will conclude this chapter by considering the return of the repressed, namely Tocqueville's treatment in *Democracy in America* of the effects of the French Revolution. This ambivalence about the significance of the revolutionary legacy will lead him in the end to abandon his focus on America and to turn his attention towards France's unique *point de départ*.

Defining Democracy

Thus far I have argued that Tocqueville's concern to cast his discussion into a form that would shed light on European dilemmas pushed him to slight America's particular history and circumstances in favour of another cause: democracy itself as a transformative force and as a set of cultural tendencies that operated *sui generis* to create a distinctive new society.

I soon realized that the influence of this fact [equality of condition] extends far beyond political mores and laws, exercising dominion over civil society as much as over the government; it creates opinion, gives birth to feelings, suggests customs, and modifies whatever it does not create. (DAI, 1)

Before going on to consider how equality of condition exercises this 'dominion', however, we must confront some difficulties of definition. Tocqueville is an abstract thinker without a technically precise vocabulary, and the bewildering range of meanings he assigns to 'democracy' have caused many commentators to struggle with his various and shifting uses of the terms.[27]

The term 'democracy' had many connotations in France of the 1830s that find echoes in Tocqueville's work: 'democracy' as the rise of a social and political system dominated by the middle classes, as a political system of representative institutions with civil freedoms and wide suffrage, or as a chaotic political system akin to anarchy. Tocqueville's use of the term, however, shifts its meaning away from politics and towards a social and economic state based on equality of condition. As in the passage quoted above, he often uses equality of condition as a virtual synonym for democracy. More typically, however, his usage is a slightly broader one that includes in the term 'democracy' both equality of social condition (the absence of ascriptive classes, with rights, occupations, and social functions open to every citizen) and the psychological tendencies that such equality naturally encourages. The most important of these tendencies are a deep passion for equality itself and a penchant for independent action. This broadened use—equality of condition plus the egalitarian passions and tastes for freedom to which it gives rise—is perhaps Tocqueville's most characteristic meaning for the term 'democracy' (DAI, 12, 19). The inclusion of the passions to which equality gives rise, however, inevitably reintroduces a political dimension, since one of those passions is the desire for independence and self-rule. Thus a certain entailment of rule by the people confounds Tocqueville's attempt to define democracy purely as a social rather than a political concept. Though he often qualifies 'democracy' by 'political' or 'governmental' when he employs it in a more conventional political sense, he sometimes means to include the institutions of self-rule in his unqualified use of the term.

Democracy's Distinctive Spheres: Political Society, Civil Society, and Natural Society

The above quotation from the first page of the 1835 *Democracy* introduces two further notions that play an important part both in Tocqueville's thought and in the structure of his book: the distinction between *political*—rendered indifferently as the 'world of politics', 'political mores and laws', the 'political sphere', or 'political society'—and *civil*—rendered as the 'civil sphere' or 'civil society'. By Tocqueville's time this was a very common distinction, but its significance then as now is not always obvious. Certainly the meanings attached to 'political' and 'civil' society vary greatly depending on the uses to which they are put. With these labels, Tocqueville roughly marks out the territory of social life to be surveyed; he rarely invests them with any metaphysical or transcendent significance. According to his own introduction to the 1840 *Democracy*, his first volume had focused on democracy's transformation of the world of politics, while the second would focus on changes in civil society.[28] Political society includes at least the governmental and administrative framework of the nation—legislative bodies, executives, bureaucracies, and the judiciary (and the relations among these groups)—as well as the jury system and political parties and associations. The political world encompasses both laws (constitutional and ordinary) and particular ideas, habits, and customs that support those laws. For example, hegemonic ideas about political interaction, such as the 'dogma of the sovereignty of the people', an idea that in America 'circulates and bears fruit', fundamentally shape the political world (DAI, 58). Civil society comprises the remaining relationships among citizens and the norms that structure those relationships. It includes such matters as how individuals greet each other in the street; with whom they choose to associate; how they produce, buy, and sell; and how they conceptualize and organize educational, cultural, and spiritual activities.

Tocqueville's distinction between political and civil does not exactly parallel the division between 'law' and 'mœurs'. Both the political and civil spheres are structured by laws as well as by social and moral norms. It is just as clear that 'political' and 'civil' do not correspond in any straightforward way to 'public' and 'private', especially in a culture as saturated with *publicité* as the America that Tocqueville portrays. Moreover, certain aspects of civil society, such as the press and the legal profession, are not squarely in the camp of political or civil life. Freedom of the press in America influences 'not political opinions only, but all the views of men [i.e., civil society]' (DAI, 180). And lawyers, according to Tocqueville, form a living link between civil society and political society (DAI, 262–70). If these quasi-political institutions straddle the two realms, religion and family are areas of human life that exist not between, but beneath—and beyond—civil and political life. Religion, for example, may be considered in relation to politics as well as to the intellectual and material instincts of democracy (the civil sphere), but ultimately it belongs to a 'spiritual sphere' (DAI, 287; DAII, 445). Similarly, Tocqueville believes that marriage, sexual morality, and family life are embedded in a civil and political regime, but are not essentially civil or political matters. Rather, they exist in the realm of 'nature', and as such are linked to some deeper transcendental reality.[29]

Background conditions of civil and political society, religion, and family have effects that need to be analysed 'from the human point of view', but they also must be viewed, presumably, from the divine point of view. Tocqueville sometimes assigns family and marriage to their own sphere, that is, to a 'natural' society outside the civil and political spheres even as it interacts with them. In a characteristic contrast, he proclaims, 'Democracy loosens social ties, but it tightens natural ones. At the same time as it separates citizens, it brings kindred closer together.'[30] I will return at some length to a discussion of these 'natural' aspects of religion and the family; my point here is merely to note that these matters are at once of and not of political and civil society.

There is one more potentially distinct conceptualization of social interactions to consider: economic society. Nassau Senior commented to J. S. Mill that Tocqueville did not really understand economic analysis, and this criticism has since been repeated by many who fault both Tocqueville's command of economics and his understanding of the importance of industrialization. The charge that Tocqueville rejected the theoretical claims of political economy is quite true. I noted in the last chapter that some French liberals had celebrated an economic model of society that identified civil society almost completely with the laws of self-interest, and that devalued the political in favour of an independent realm of human activity governed by economic laws. Tocqueville and Beaumont were certainly aware of this turn in French economic liberalism. We know they spent much of their passage to America dutifully working through J. B. Say's *Cours d'économie politique*.[31] Moreover, Tocqueville's later extensive English contacts, including those with J. S. Mill and Nassau Senior, show that he was not unacquainted with the tendency of the English school to find in the laws of economics the most fundamental and scientific aspects of civil society, if not the whole of social science.[32] Yet this vision failed to attract him either in its utopian French or in its empirical English form. As François Furet has remarked, 'Economics was a dimension of human life that had interested him only for its interaction with social or intellectual life, but never in itself or as a basic mechanism of change.'[33]

Tocqueville rejected the starting-point of political economy: that self-interested behaviour, apart from its social context, produced sufficient behavioural regularity to elevate those hypothetical regularities to the status of laws. He also distrusted what he perceived as a tendency to confound wealth with happiness.[34] Finally, he argued against the central assumption of the French school that interests would harmonize naturally, calling political economy a utopian 'science of words' that reduced complex social phenomena to a huge set of self-interested exchanges.[35] These criticisms reflect common arguments by Catholic social economists as well as moderate liberals in France. Both groups largely rejected the scientific pretensions and alleged materialism of the 'dismal science'. These opinions, however, also expressed Tocqueville's deep conviction that the key to grasping what was most important about democracy lay in unravelling the legacies of particular histories and in deciphering new patterns of social and political psychology. These tasks required an intellectual openness to the ways in which economic behaviour was shaped by other civil interactions and by historical traditions. They pushed Tocqueville away from any independent conceptualization of economics as a science. In *Democracy in America*, his brief discussions of economic topics are often embedded in some larger social or historical point. For example, he links trade crises to the essential temperament of democratic peoples, and refers to rent and wages only in the context of discussing the erosion of social dependence between master and servant (DAII, 582, 554). This is not to say that he rejected all the conclusions of a theorist such as Nassau Senior or that he disdained a free market society. On the contrary, he appreciated many positive affinities between the operations of markets and the independent dynamism necessary to sustain liberty. But he never shared the fundamental outlook of political economists, did not view the social world through a primarily economic lens, and assigned no heuristic value to the laws of 'economic society'.

Tocqueville's deafness to the hegemonic claims of political economy, then, was both culturally induced and the consequence of his intellectual method. The question of his views on the technological and industrial revolutions is more complicated. It has sometimes been thought that Tocqueville was simply ignorant of the causes and effects of industrialization, particularly in America.[36] His perceptive discussions of working-class conditions in Manchester, his interest in the problems of pauperism, and his cryptic warnings of a new manufacturing aristocracy, however, have been hard to reconcile with the view that he was uninformed.[37] Moreover, it is now clear both that Tocqueville knew more about the rapidly changing technological and communications revolutions in the United States than has been generally thought and that he deliberately decided to omit much of what he knew from the published text of *Democracy in America*. 'One can dispute his choices but not his knowledge.'[38] Tocqueville was also quite aware that the industrial developments in England were probably the single most important change in his time.[39] His decision to neglect these matters, then, must be put down to a single-minded focus on his own subject—the social, political, and psychological manifestations of a democratic condition of life—and a lack of interest in the phenomenon of industrialization apart from these consequences. When he attempts to sketch the economic changes that have led to the problem of pauperism, for example, his account owes more to Rousseau's *Discourse on the Origins of Inequality* than to English political economy.

Despite his discussion of the potential threat of an aristocracy of manufactures arising in America, Tocqueville largely ignored problems associated with economic development even as he had pushed the problems of excluded racial groups to the periphery. The reasons for this marginalization of the effects of industrialization, however, differ from his reasons for excluding the effects of racism. He could hardly argue that industrial society was beside the point because it was merely American, rather than generically democratic. Industrialization and its effects—a new dependent class, new forms of wealth, new types of poverty—were intimately tied up with a growing attachment to material well-being, an attachment that he believed to be intrinsic to the coming of democracy in Europe. Democracy, he tells us, 'favors the development of industry by multiplying without limit the number of those engaged in it' (DAII, 555). What he argued, rather, was that industrialization was not likely to generate a new way of life formed by new hierarchical relations that would restructure society as a whole. Though the condition of poverty in some sense trapped the poor, the status of being rich only tenuously ensnared the wealthy. Unable to insulate themselves from market forces long enough to constitute themselves as a new aristocracy, and continuously buffeted by the forces of equality and equalization, the wealthy classes would be able neither to create a new ethic among themselves nor to establish new social relations between themselves and their workers. Since exploitation was not part of Tocqueville's core conception of European aristocracy, he was unlikely to see new forms of economic exploitation as a reincarnation of aristocracy. The reinforcing influence between economic self-interest and the passion for equality, rather than the existence of economic disparities, held his analytical attention.

Tocqueville's conceptualization of social phenomena into roughly delineated spheres—political, civil (including economic), and spiritual or natural—provides a scaffolding that underlies his account of the tendencies of democracy. What interested him were psychological affinities and unexpected fits among the tendencies operating in all these spheres, and much of the excitement of *Democracy in America* for contemporary readers lies in the acuity of these perceptions and their continuing fertility as sources of insight into issues that trouble us. Jon Elster has provided a particularly useful vocabulary for describing the kinds of connections that Tocqueville makes among these spheres. He notes that Tocqueville's insights on how habits and desires are formed and relate to one another in democracy fall into three patterns: the ubiquity of a belief or activity in one sphere may cause the pattern to recur in another sphere (the 'spillover effect'); the lack of a belief or activity in one sphere may cause a person to seek it in another (the 'compensation effect'); and, finally, the dominance of a belief or activity in one sphere may foreclose similar action in another (the 'crowding out effect').[40] Tocqueville uses these patterns of argumentation in many contexts in an effort to show how the underlying passions and behaviours induced by equality of social condition begin to pull societies into a new cultural equilibrium.

Tocqueville's efforts to show how people alter their desires and aspirations to fit new circumstances, and how the psychological spillover, compensation, and crowding out effects combine to establish new cultural patterns, result in a portrait of a distinctively democratic way of life. But his purpose is less to give an adequate historical or structural account of this new cultural universe than to sketch two possible variants of it: one compatible with the absence of political freedom, the other capable of sustaining self-government. Using America explicitly, and France implicitly, as cases that provide the observer with a wealth of data on the social psychology inherent in the democratic social state, Tocqueville draws out for the reader two sets of underlying affinities operating within democratic societies, neither corresponding fully to any existing situation. One set threatens new forms of democratic despotism, the other promises democratic deliverance.[41] Tocqueville's own moral judgements on what he observes shape his presentation profoundly; quite deliberately he both describes a new cultural 'reality' and extracts from that portrait hypothetical cautions and potential models. What follows is a brief reconstruction of Tocqueville's analysis of the 'shape' of democracy, organized around the implicit dichotomy between 'unfree' and 'free' that shapes his own work.

Cautionary Tales

Like Burke and the French reactionaries, Tocqueville conveys an unmistakable sense of fear and trembling before the onslaught of 'democracy'. Unlike those writers, however, he faces obstinately towards the future rather than the past, resolving to unmask the worst in order that it should not come to pass. His fears stem from one 'simple fact'. At some point in the process of democratization the idea of human equality takes hold of people's souls and the desire for it becomes 'ardent, insatiable, eternal, [and] invincible' (DAII, 506). Equality generates a love of equality so strong, and with such close affinities to other democratic proclivities, such as the love of material comfort, that it may become a swirling eddy, pulling all else into its vortex and sweeping the social world towards strange and alien depths. Tocqueville paints several versions of this frightening future. One—stronger in the first *Democracy*—points to the strength of new majorities that smother individual independence and may eventually yield to a Caesaristic tyranny; the other— stronger in the second *Democracy*—evokes a flat Orwellian landscape of servile sameness in which an equal but diminished humanity, ruled by a deceptively benevolent central state, pursues material desires in a spiritual vacuum. Tocqueville's thinking on the subject of despotism clearly evolved in the 1830s towards an ever stronger apprehension of the dangers of administrative centraliza- tion, but he did not abandon his earlier concerns. Rather, one might think of *Democracy in America* as a compendious catalogue of the ways in which the individual spirit might be quenched in democra- cies—by majority opinion, by legislatures, by the executive or a usurper, or by the bureaucratic state itself.[42] What made these despotisms possible were the new links between a society of equals and the forces of political centralization.

Both volumes of *Democracy in America* end with warnings, which are worth quoting at some length:

nowadays, with all classes jumbled together and the individual increasingly disappearing in the crowd, . . . and nowadays, when monarchic honor has almost lost its sway without being replaced by virtue, and there is nothing left which raises a man above himself, who can say where the exigencies of author- ity and the yielding of weakness will stop? . . . For my part when I consider the state already reached by several European nations and that towards which all are tending, I am led to believe that there will soon be no room except for either democratic freedom or the tyranny of the Caesars. (DAI, 313–14)

I am trying to imagine under what novel features despotism may appear in the world. In the first place, I see an innumerable multitude of men, alike and equal, constantly circling around in pursuit of the petty and banal pleasures with which they glut their souls. . . . Over this kind of men stands an immense, protective power who is alone responsible for securing their enjoyment and watching over their fate. That power is absolute, thoughtful of detail, orderly, provident, and gentle. . . . It provides for their security, foresees and supplies their necessities, facilitates their pleasures, manages their principal concerns, directs their industry, makes rules for their testaments, and divides their inheritances. . . . Equality has prepared men for all this, predisposing them to endure it and often even regard it as beneficial. (DAII, 691–2)

These warnings have common elements. Each traces a new social pattern in which the centralizing power expands insidiously into all parts of society, encountering little friction from individuals who cannot resist because they have already succumbed to the centri- petal pull of their own inner lives.

We can begin to unravel the patterns of despotism implicit in Tocqueville's warnings by examining the sources of the new absorption in private life that, in his view, reduces resistance to centralization. Two threads intertwine and reinforce each other in Tocqueville's argument: first, the now universal purchase of material self-interest, and second, the pervasive psychological effects of the passion for equality itself. Under democratic social conditions, according to Tocqueville, these passions feed on one another in ominous ways. He observes that the desire for well-being, present in every human society, takes on a cultural centrality in democratic times that is unprecedented. 'A passion for well-being is . . . the most lively of all the emotions aroused or inflamed by equality and it is a passion shared by all. So this taste for well-being is the most striking and unalterable characteristic of democratic ages' (DAII, 448; cf. 462, 543, 544). How and why is the passion for well-being inflamed by equal social conditions? Since democracy by definition rejects the claim that inherited wealth and status are naturally conjoined, it automatically brings the goods of this world within the compass of everyone's imagination. Under these conditions, everyone develops a desire for material rewards and for the currency with which to obtain them (DAII, 539, 530): 'equality makes not only work itself, but work specifically to gain money, honorable' (DAII, 550). Though work and profit-making are distinct ideas, in democratic society they 'are always visibly united' (DAII, 550). The hope of greater profit by commercial activity gradually leads democratic people away from agriculture and towards trade and industry (DAII, 551).

Once established as the dominant focus of activity, the passion for well-being and absorption in commercial pursuits entrench themselves in civil society. Tocqueville does not grant the economic structure or needs of society causal status here. Rather he declares that the pursuit of material self-interest merges seamlessly with the pursuit of equality; they come to be mutually supportive in many ways and to create an inescapable pattern of motivations and behaviours in democratic civil society. For example, Tocqueville notes that the restless striving characteristic of status-seeking individuals predisposes them to economic activity that is similarly based on chance and risk-taking. The chasing of status in a world open to merit parallels the hazardous pursuit of material rewards from the market.[43] Indeed, insofar as wealth becomes a sign of distinction in a society marked by the competition for status, it becomes part of an ever-receding horizon of desire.

Tocqueville's insights here are Hobbesian and Rousseauian. Once equality becomes thinkable, that is, once the notion that inequalities are eternal and unchangeable is shattered, people begin to seek equality relentlessly and compulsively. Yet equality, always relative, is incapable of earthly fulfilment. An illusory goal, equality generates exquisite resentments and ever-more discriminating sentiments of envy directed against those whose qualities or possessions make them stand out. 'Democratic institutions awaken and flatter the passion for equality without ever being able to satisfy it entirely. This complete equality is always slipping through people's fingers at the moment when they think to grasp it, fleeing, as Pascal says, in an eternal flight; the people grow heated in search of this blessing, all the more precious because it is near enough to be seen but too far off to be tasted.'[44] The pursuit of equality, like the pursuit of material comfort for its own sake, provides no enduring satisfactions.

Although he also recognizes many positive spillover effects from the restless realm of democratic civil society to politics,

Tocqueville's deepest fears are centred on the dangerous affinities between the individualistic pursuit of private interests and quietism in the political sphere. His critique of the profit motive certainly reveals a residual aristocratic disdain for the money-making passion, a passion common not only in the sense that it is shared by all, but in the sense that it is vulgar and unworthy. Yet there is a much subtler analysis at work. Tocqueville objects to the exclusive sway of material self-interest in democratic times primarily because it tends to undermine the conditions of its own existence and subvert its own goals. The universal search for well-being encourages a narrow self-interest that all too easily may exclude consideration of the long-range interests in general prosperity and freedom that all members of democratic society share. A single-minded focus on the achievement of status through wealth simply leaves little time or inclination for deliberating about shared long-term interests; such a focus saps the mental energy necessary for political engagement. 'There is no need to drag their rights away from citizens of this type; they themselves voluntarily let them go. They find it a tiresome inconvenience to exercise political rights which distract them from industry. When required to elect representatives, to support authority by personal service, or to discuss public business together, they find they have no time' (DAII, 540; cf. DAI, 213, 243).[45] The taste for material goods and physical pleasures is so tenacious in democracies that it 'crowds out' everything else. Even worse, this single-minded focus on the goods of this world may dispose people to believe that nothing else but physical matter exists, and thus to adopt philosophical materialism. 'Materialism, in its turn, spurs them on to such delights with mad impetuosity. Such is the vicious circle into which democratic nations are driven' (DAII, 544).

The strong democratic *goût de bien-être*, which fosters a way of life with little room for public affairs, is reinforced by another powerful effect of equality of conditions: withdrawal into the self and attendant social isolation. At the same time as universal participation in the world of work and the continual pursuit of money and status cause democratic men to neglect larger public concerns because their lives are filled up with ceaseless economic activity, they also fall away from political activity of their own accord, since they now lack the feelings of belonging and dependence that make acting in concert with specific others seem natural or desirable.

As social equality spreads there are more and more people who, though neither rich nor powerful enough to have much hold over others, have gained or kept enough wealth and enough understanding to look after their own needs. Such folk owe no man anything and hardly expect anything from anybody. They form the habit of thinking of themselves in isolation and imagine that their whole destiny is in their own hands. (DAII, 508)

Tocqueville terms this democratic permutation of egoism *individualisme*, 'a calm and considered feeling which disposes each citizen to isolate himself from the mass of his fellows and withdraw into the circle of family and friends; with this little society formed to his taste, he gladly leaves the greater society to look after itself' (DAII, 506; cf. 671).

In the second *Democracy*, where he introduces the term, *individualisme* takes on a key role in explaining democracy's potentially devastating effects on civil life.[46] At best, individualism intensifies the materialistic aspects of democratic culture, making it difficult to create bonds of trust and civility among citizens. At worst, it literally drives a person to insanity or suicide, because the drive inward reveals no common truth at the centre of collective life. Human beings, however, cannot tolerate such a psychic vacuum, empty of stabilizing beliefs and opinions. Tocqueville's argument here presages Durkheim on the effects of anomie in modern society and the links between normlessness and suicide.[47] Yet he does not share Durkheim's belief that a new integrating force will arise out of the social interdependence characteristic of modern industry. The difficulty, according to Tocqueville, is that democratic conditions both unsettle current beliefs and make it particularly difficult for individuals to accept any new ones that originate outside themselves; hence, the mental vacuum is likely to be filled by new self-referential authorities. Although these authorities may stave off individual madness or self-destruction, and generally do so, references to the 'will of all' do not necessarily foster the sort of independent yet disciplined psychological characters who can rule themselves.

Tocqueville identifies several dangers to the democratic psyche made vulnerable by individualism: materialism, pantheism, and the pressure to conform to public opinion. On his account, materialism as a way of life and system of thought is literally inhuman. 'If ever the thoughts of the great majority of mankind came to be concentrated solely on the search for material blessings, one can anticipate that there would be a colossal reaction in the souls of men. They would distractedly launch out into the world of spirits for fear of being held too tightly bound by the body's fetters' (DAII, 545). Some Americans already display strange and enthusiastic forms of spirituality. Breaking out of the prison of their relentlessly materialistic culture, they seek to satisfy the soul's needs. But without guidance, 'their minds do not know where to settle down, and they often rush without stopping far beyond the bounds of common sense' (DAII, 535).

Pantheism is dangerous for a different reason. The democratic mind wishes to face reality unmediated by particular forms and unique mysteries and is attracted by single causes and generalizing doctrines. Unity becomes a kind of obsession. Hence pantheistic notions that 'all things material and immaterial, visible and invisible, which the world contains are only to be considered as the several parts of an immense Being who alone remains eternal in the midst of the continual flux and transformation of all that composes Him ... will have secret charms for men living under democracies' (DAII, 452). But pantheistic notions subtly undermine the psychological conditions for human freedom, because they destroy the individual's sense that he governs his own fate. Because it seduces the soul and deceptively satisfies spiritual needs, pantheism is as dangerous in democratic ages as materialism, which starves and denies the spirit.

Finally, democratic individuals may lose their capacity for independent action not in a frenzied compensatory reaction to materialism, or in a soothing philosophic denial of responsibility, but in a blind surrender to the views of all. Democratic individuals, who in any case are likely to have similar beliefs and opinions because they are similarly situated, easily fall under the hegemonic sway of public opinion. Even at the height of his admiration for America's experiment in self-government, Tocqueville thought he glimpsed a tyranny of majority opinion so strong that it crushed all independence of thought. 'I know no country in which, speaking generally, there is less independence of mind and true freedom of discussion than in America' (DAI, 254-5). In a society in which there is no higher appeal than majority opinion, there is a strong desire to abdicate responsibility for contributing to that opinion and simply to conform to its dictates. When the majority 'has irrevocably pronounced, everyone is silent, and friends and enemies alike seem to make for its bandwagon' (DAI, 254). This psychological tendency to defer to some all-powerful 'will of all' was a fault line of democratic, rather than merely American, culture.

Together, the filling-up of social life with the self-interested activities of democratic civil society and the emptying-out of the psychic group life characteristic of aristocracy threaten to produce an egalitarian society that celebrates the abstract individual but ensnares real persons in new webs of intellectual control that undermine the potential for independent judgement. Hence the taste for material well-being and the forces of individualism, both separately and together, make democratic peoples particularly vulnerable to the acceptance of the idea of uniform and ubiquitous state power. I now want to turn more explicitly to a consideration of this democratic vulnerability to political centralization. Why do people in egalitarian times turn so readily to the state?

Among the many connections between democracy and centralization that Tocqueville explores is the central paradox that democratic individuals lack the time for politics, but nevertheless need and crave political stability as an underpinning for their private pursuits. Beyond the order that it provides, a strong central power may be essential to the nurturing of new industries launched by restless democratic maximizers. Even in America Tocqueville was quite aware of the link between the growth of manufactures and the growth of the state apparatus. In Europe he sees the economic role of the state growing steadily, as it draws to itself both the wealth of the rich and the savings of the poor. The sovereign becomes not only master, but steward, banker, and leading industrialist (DAII 683–4). Though in the long run prosperity depends on a vital civil society, in the short run states can deliver powerful advantages. Moreover, precisely because they have no leisure, democratic people are drawn to, even greedy for, general ideas that will save them from wasting time in the painstaking comparisons necessary for political judgement (DAII, 442). This taste for general truths in politics leads to a fatal weakness for the rhetoric of unity and uniformity, a rhetoric that comes naturally to efficient centralizers and administrative rationalizers. Hence democratic individuals are at once pulled away from independent self-governing activities and pushed towards the acceptance of state regulation, even where formal civil and political rights exist. 'Thus men are following two different roads to servitude. The taste for well-being diverts them from taking part in the government, and that love of well-being puts them in ever closer dependence on government' (DAII, 683).

The complex interaction between centralization of state power and growing equality of social conditions emerges as Tocqueville's principal theoretical preoccupation and most powerful image, not only in the later sections of *Democracy in America* but in the rest of his life's work. In the journals kept during his visit to England and Ireland in 1835, he returns obsessively to this subject, querying J. S. Mill about whether the centralizing thrust of the English utilitarian radicals is intrinsic to their democratic ideology, or is merely a temporary expedient to destroy parochial institutions that have become the tools of the aristocracy. He explicitly asks himself, 'why is centralization dear to the habits of democracy (good thing to delve into in *Democracy in America*)?'[48] The urge by those who have power to increase it and use it does not itself arouse his curiosity. The mania to regulate is not French, but is a natural tendency for those in dominant positions.[49] Moreover, he accepts the notion, expounded by Guizot and others, that the drive to increase and consolidate state power is a marked feature of all European history and of civilization itself. Indeed, it is the apparent absence of a centralized state in America, and to some extent in England, that requires explanation.

In thinking through the puzzle of the inevitability of centralization, and of the dangers it posed to freedom, Tocqueville worked out a distinction between 'governmental centralization' (the necessary and inevitable amassing of sovereign power, which defends a nation from its enemies, provides internal order, and is a marked feature of any civilized society) and 'administrative centralization' (the unnecessary expansion of political power into the regulation of ordinary affairs and the details of daily life). Governmental and administrative centralization are related phenomena; indeed, Tocqueville foresaw an ineluctable drift from the former to the latter. 'Now, when one sole authority is already armed with all the attributes of government, it is very difficult for it not to try and penetrate into all the details of administration, and in the long run it hardly ever fails to find occasion to do so' (DAI, 97). When the central power makes its influence felt in the ordinary affairs of civil society, however, it not only becomes more powerful and efficient, but also transforms and destroys existing patterns of social interaction, thereby draining individuals of the capacities of self-government.

One appreciates that centralization of government acquires immense strength when it is combined with administrative centralization. In that way it accustoms men to set aside their own wills constantly and completely, to obey not just once and in one respect but always in everything. Then they are not only tamed by force, but their habits too are trained; they are isolated and then dropped one by one into the common mass. (DAI, 87)

Becoming aware of the accelerating speed of centralization is the sole hope of avoiding an administered future. Unfortunately, 'enlightenment' has tended in the past to increase rather than to diminish the slide from governmental to administrative centralization. With enlightenment and civilization comes a drive towards human rationality in all things, but, paradoxically, a loss of control by individuals over the process of rationalization. 'Eventually that uniformity comes to be loved for itself without reference to its objectives, just as the pious may adore a statue, forgetting the divinity it represents' (DAI, 91).

Power in democratic societies, then, easily extends its reach from the political to the civil spheres, and becomes at once more concentrated, more extensive, and less responsible. The experiences of England and America indicate that the process of administrative centralization may be halted, but these efforts fight against the tide. Centralization of power swells of its own accord, but an atomized society provides little resistance. Indeed, the uniformity in the status of democratic citizens leads them to welcome uniformity in treatment from the central power. Aristocratic bodies that once formed a bulwark against centralizing power have disappeared or been transformed into tools of the state. Democratic society itself erects new barriers only with great difficulty because of its privatizing civil dynamic.

Tocqueville gives differing accounts of where centralizing power is likely to accumulate. When he thinks primarily of America, he fears legislative despotism, albeit with the potential of usurpation by one individual. The dominant tendency is for the majority—*le pouvoir social*—to become all-powerful and to ride roughshod over any particularities standing in its way. Such a power may all too easily invest assemblies with irresistible authority, offer individuals opportunities to usurp the mantle of the majority, or overstep its legal bounds (DAI, 90). This massive social power can be converted into despotism more quickly than the royal authority of a feudal monarch. When he is thinking primarily of France, Tocqueville usually focuses less on majority legislative tyranny than on the possibility of Bonapartism and/or a hegemonic bureaucracy that approaches the ideal type of administrative despotism. In France, justifications in the name of the majority or *le peuple* are still likely to be political ruses masking an individual or group will to power (DAI, 222). In both cases, however, Tocqueville feared that the absence of mediating powers and the withdrawal of citizens into self-interested enclaves could create an entropy leading to a centralized despotism.

The Lessons of America

Tocqueville, then, uses America as well as France to illustrate how the social psychological tendencies operating in democratic societies may lead to an obliteration of liberty by eliminating both the opportunity and desire for independent thought and action. But his portrait of America, filled with examples of how responsible democratic citizens may avoid, reverse, check, or neutralize the insidious tendencies of democracy, is far less cautionary tale than exemplary morality lesson. More important for his European audience and his theoretical project, the example of America shows how democracy can cure itself, how it contains not only the virus of democratic despotism, but also self-generating tendencies that immunize it against that virus. By capitalizing on these tendencies, Americans have achieved a functioning equilibrium in the absence of both social hierarchy and centralized administration. In Tocqueville's account, America emerges as a new species of regime in which the social and political principles of democracy (equal social conditions, social mobility, and majority rule) have been welded together without sacrificing individual freedom.

Despite his cold-eyed judgements about the potential for majority despotism and social conformity, about the lack of grandeur, or about the particular injustices of slavery and racism, Tocqueville admired the Americans' achievement of political freedom—however compromised and exclusive—under the challenge of democratic social conditions. He never recommended, however, slavish imitation of the institutions that made this freedom possible. Rather, he severely edited American experience into lessons suitable for enlightening his European readers. These lessons fall into two characteristic patterns: first, drawing on the initial strengths of their *point de départ*, Americans shore up native barriers and build road-blocks to contain democratic tendencies; second, and more important, they discern stabilizing tendencies within democracy itself, and wisely allow democracy to follow its 'natural' bent in these areas. Both lessons begin from the observation that democracy fosters a desire not only for equality but also for independent action. Self-governing America, in Tocqueville's ideal-ized portrait, has attained a new kind of democratic equilibrium that incorporates this spontaneous desire for freedom. Indeed, if his cau-tionary tales describe an egalitarian *mentalité* that smothers the fragile democratic taste for liberty, his morality lessons draw on an alternative set of interlocking motivations and behaviours in which the spirit of democratic independence—its taste for free-dom—is carefully cultivated rather than allowed to wither or to run wild.

The connection that Tocqueville sees between democracy and lib-erty is often lost amid his warnings about a new despotism. Yet all his hopes for the future depend on a recognition that with equality comes an increase in the desire to be strong, independent, and respected. Democratic peoples have a 'natural taste for liberty' and a 'natural bias towards free institutions' (DAII, 506, 667; cf. DAI, 57). Not merely an inheritance from an aristocratic past, liberty has its own particular democratic form that is itself necessarily bound up with egalitarian passions. Tocqueville stresses that equal social con-ditions beget liberty, and that the human impulse towards freedom will always offer hope for the renewal of a people's political condi-tion. 'Among most modern nations, especially those of Europe, the taste for freedom and the conception of it only began to take shape and grow at the time when social conditions were tending towards equality, and it was a consequence of that very equality' (DAII, 505). Latent in every generation, because inherent in human nature, the taste for freedom intensifies in democratic times and provides the motivations for democratic heroism and selflessness. Tocqueville admired the early French revolutionaries and the American founders precisely because he thought they were motivated by a pure sense of democratic liberty.[50]

Liberty, then, must cast its fate with equality not only because the passion for equality is the dominant trend, but because the only source of liberty in democratic times is equality itself. Liberty finds its vitality in that independent spirit which is an 'effect of political equality' (DAII, 668). The venture is a risky one, however, and Tocqueville presents the Americans above all as lucky winners in a fateful gamble to achieve an egalitarian form of freedom. America represents a 'wonderful harmony between fortune's favours and man's endeavors' (DAI, 132). Europeans may not be able to duplicate the luck of the draw, but they can hope to imitate American skill at beating the odds.

Going against the grain of democracy

One of the arguments about how the Americans have countered the threat of democratic despotism employs images of slowing down or weakening tendencies otherwise natural to democracy. The dangers of extreme political democracy arise above all from the power of majorities to dominate legislatures—and through them governments—and thus to hasten a people into ill-considered or even extra-legal actions that may end in a subversion of their own independence. Also dangerous is the instability and chaos potentially present in the elective process itself. Tocqueville observes these tendencies, so likely to feed into the process of state centralization, everywhere in the American states. Arguments about combating these tendencies can be found throughout the 1835 *Democracy*. They deal primarily with issues of constitutional design, and with American variations on basic institutions inherited from the English, for example the political role of lawyers and juries. Let us consider these two examples—the federal structure of the republic and inherited judicial freedoms—in turn.

The federal constitution, on Tocqueville's account, is admirably designed to balance the dangers of extreme democracy in the states. Bicameralism, indirect election of senators, the organization of the judiciary, and the creation of a relatively independent president (weak by European national standards, but strong in comparison to executives in the states) are all devices to slow down the formation of a national majority, to 'check and direct' or 'correct the aberrations' of democracy (DAI, 287). Tocqueville's principal aim in the chapters that discuss American constitutional law is surely not to recommend the institutions he describes. American political democracy is *sui generis* and may not even represent what is best from some ideal point of view (DAI, 130, 231, 310, 311, 315). What interests Tocqueville, and what he wishes to hold up as exemplary to a French audience, is the skill of the 'lawgiver'. These chapters actually present a primer on how to intervene to shape a nation's political future. He gives the reader only enough information about American institutions to illustrate his thesis that the founding generation purposefully constructed them to address some complex set of problems. To that end he does not fail also to mention the odd lapse in judgement; the American founders emerge as practical guides, not paragons.

The discussion of the presidency is a good case in point. He begins that discussion as 'follows: 'the American lawgivers had a difficult task to fulfill; they wanted to create an executive power dependent on the majority that yet should be sufficiently strong to act freely on its own within its proper spheres' (DAI, 121). His entire discussion of the presidency is organized around how the architects of the constitution designed it to perform this dual role. So as not to bore his audience with extraneous American details—and to reinforce the lesson that creative reform is always a complex mix of circumstances, the art of the possible, and practical understanding—he includes an extended comparison of the American presidency with European constitutional monarchy. The upshot of this comparison is a sharp reminder that American 'solutions' address problems that are theirs alone; adoption of these measures in Europe would be senseless. On the other hand, within the American context the design of the presidency is the result of acute statesmanship because it keeps in view the basic task: how to create authorities that could 'struggle against [the majority's] caprices and refuse to be the tools of its dangerous exigencies' (DAI, 137). Hence, the framers recommended independent election of the president and a legislative veto. According to Tocqueville, their political acumen faltered only when it came to the issue of re-eligibility. In order to maximize experience and wisdom in the executive branch, they allowed re-election, failing to foresee that this would render a president practically dependent on the very majorities from which they had tried to insulate him. In trying to strengthen the presidency they inadvertently weakened it and thereby 'exposed the country to dangers every day' (DAI, 138).

Whatever the merit of this discussion of the American presidency, the focus is ever on the practice of statesmanship and usually on the far-sightedness, courage, and reliable practical judgement of the founding generation. By intervening in their own history at a decisive moment, they slowed the onrush of democracy and gained time for the people to become accustomed to institutions whose wisdom was not immediately apparent. (DAI, 114, 131, 137, 147, 154, 158, 163, 176, 200, 232, 258). In the following description of the founders of the Union, it is difficult not to notice Tocqueville's identification with them, as well as his veiled call for his own political generation to take up the difficult vocation of 'lawgiver'.

They had all grown up at a time of social crisis, when the spirit of liberty had been in constant conflict with a strong and dominating authority. When the struggle was over, and when, as is usual, the passions aroused in the crowd were still directed against dangers which had long ceased to exist, these men called a halt; they looked at their country more calmly and with greater penetration; they were aware that a final revolution had been accomplished and that henceforth the perils threatening the people could only spring from abuses of liberty. What they thought, they had the courage to say; because they felt in the bottom of their hearts a sincere and ardent love for that same liberty, they dared to speak about restraining it, because they were sure they did not want to destroy it. (DAI, 152)

French elites, according to Tocqueville, needed to look at their situation with 'greater penetration' and to attempt a different kind of democratic founding.[51]

A second example of America's success in guiding democracy in a direction 'to which it is not inclined by methods foreign to it' is Tocqueville's analysis of the political role of the legal profession and juries in America (DAI, 266). In his view, the prestige of lawyers and their influence in the government was one of the 'strongest barriers against the faults of democracy' (DAI, 263). Lawyers' conservatism has two causes: first, the habit of order and the taste for formalities that come from the practice of studying law and that turn its practitioners away from revolution or hasty action; and second, the temper of the English common law, which leads attorneys to focus on the past, to cloak innovations in the guise of continuity, and to submerge their own ideas in a bewildering manipulation of precedent. Lawyers, then, have commoners' interests but aristocratic tastes and habits. They serve above all the interests of stability, and only if repulsed by the ruling powers will they put themselves at the head of a revolution. In America these pseudo-aristocratic lawyerly instincts are welcomed into the political system; hence the Americans take advantage of the only 'aristocracy' that can be easily mixed with democracy in order to counterbalance their own worst instincts. 'When the American people let themselves get intoxicated by their passions or carried away by their ideas, the lawyers apply an almost invisible brake which slows them down and halts them' (DAI, 268).

Initially, the institution of juries does not appear to fit into this category of pushing democracy in a direction 'to which it is not inclined'. After all, juries introduce popular judgement into the heart of law itself, and therefore might be seen as the most democratic of institutions. Indeed, Tocqueville calls juries (when he is rhetorically wishing to impress on the reader the irresistibility of the majority in America) 'the majority vested with the right to pronounce judgement' (DAI, 252). The widespread use of juries may seem, in fact, to be a clear case of more democracy curing the ills of democracy. Are not juries analogous to local self-government, a case in which some inefficiencies in execution yield unexpectedly large political dividends because of their unintended consequences? A closer analysis reveals, however, that Tocqueville does not develop a strong argument linking juries to the 'shape of democracy itself'. He notes that while the institution of the jury always has a certain republican aspect, it 'may be an aristocratic or a democratic institution, according to the class from which the jurors are selected' (DAI, 272). Moreover, in America civil juries function less as radicalizing institutions than as conduits for the conservative influence of lawyers and judges to whom juries look for guidance. Most important, Tocqueville believes that juries require individuals deliberately to set aside their own interests in favour of the public interest, rather than to merge their personal interests with the public interest. They are invaluable schools of freedom because they rehearse the difficult practices of equity and teach each person to accept responsibility for decisions (DAI, 274). But precisely because juries so pull against the tide of the gospel of self-interest, they cannot be expected to occur 'naturally' in democratic societies. Rather the jury is an institution that has been carefully husbanded and nurtured by Anglo-American peoples for its freedom-enhancing properties.

So far I have discussed several alleged American successes in slowing down democracy that are facilitated by the peculiar circumstances and the *point de départ* of American society. It is not immediately clear how either the discussion of America's constitution—which Tocqueville calls 'sterile' in other hands and views as the culmination of a particular history of self-government—or her legal traditions—which are the products of common law jurisprudence and a particular English inheritance—further his comparative project of designing a democratic theoretical space in which to take the measure of French democracy. In fact, he means to instruct only indirectly by these examples. Studying a successful example of constitution-making sensitizes the reader to the art of constitutional design and, Tocqueville hopes, presents the tasks facing French politicians in a more dispassionate and analytical light.

The discussion of lawyers and juries also reveals his interest in comparative historical legal studies, an interest fostered by his earlier study of the law and his encounter with Guizot. Throughout the discussion of legal matters, Tocqueville makes a three-way comparison between America, England, and France. He sees

Anglo-American legal traditions as a particular branch of a common
European tree that forked in the distant past, and speculates that it
may at some point be possible to graft certain practices back onto
French stock precisely because of these common roots. (Juries, for
example, had been used in criminal cases in France since 1791 and
Tocqueville wished to see them employed in civil cases as well.)
This discussion, then, is meant to alert the French to effects of foreign legal institutions that 'might recur elsewhere', that is, to effects
that might be possible in France if analogous indigenous institutions
could be revived (DAI, 263). It also draws attention to the historical
role of the French *noblesse de robe*: its independence of sovereign
power, and its roles as arbiter between the individual and the state
and as buffer to state power. Europe, Tocqueville implicitly reminds
us, also had favourable historical circumstances in its *point de
départ* towards democracy (DAII, 683–4).

The general attitudes that underlie Americans' acceptance of constitutional limitations and their respect for inherited legal rights and
practices instruct in yet another sense. These political mores are not
merely the lucky gifts of a unique history, but also the result of
American initiative in attempting to conserve them. The success of
constitutional forms as limits to democracy depends not on mech-
anical obedience to tradition, but on a combination of creative
action and self-restraint. The mystery of rational self-restraint
under conditions in which majorities are all-powerful fascinated
Tocqueville, as well as other continental liberals. His analysis of the
mystery, even when it points to the peculiar success of America in
reinvigorating local traditions of freedom, is not fully focused on
America's fortunate antecedents. Rather he lauds the founders' ability to achieve a rare form of enlightened self-interest and exhorts
his contemporaries to imitate that achievement.

Following the grain of democracy

Of greater theoretical interest than American success in legislating
against the grain of democracy is Tocqueville's belief that American
experience reveals the possibility of turning the very sources of
potential democratic disaster—material self-interest, and the complex psychological dispositions associated with individualism—
into occasions for democratic salvation. His thinking here exactly
mirrors Pope's judgement on learning: a sip of democracy is a
dangerous thing, but a deeper drink sobers rather than intoxicates.

More democracy will eventually subdue democracy. 'Thus in the immense complication of human laws it sometimes comes about that extreme freedom corrects the abuse of freedom and extreme democracy forestalls the dangers of democracy.'[52] The most important lesson Tocqueville draws from America is that new patterns, inherent in the democratic social condition itself, could reinforce rather than destroy freedom. I want to consider here two arguments advocating more democracy as a counter to democracy's own worst instincts: first, Tocqueville's analysis of interest properly understood as the dominant 'principle' of American democracy; and second, his claim that democracy is naturally religious.[53] Together these arguments illustrate something of the range and subtlety of his theorizing, for if both rely on endogenous tendencies of democracy, they present very different configurations of how those tendencies intersect. Moreover, many contemporary readers have paid particular attention to Tocqueville's discussion of these matters. The connection between the art of self-interested association and a healthy democratic civil society, and the link between moral consensus and democratic stability, have preoccupied theorists of democracy in the late twentieth century.

The art of association: virtuous self-interest

America was undoubtedly a republic, and Montesquieu had identified the fundamental principle of republics as virtue. Indeed, during the American Revolution and for decades after, images of Washington and Franklin circulated in France as emblems of a republican simplicity and patriotism analogous if not identical to this ancient republican virtue. And French revolutionaries had conducted their own experiments in reviving pure republican mores. But there was a republican alternative to this emphasis on the need to create self-sacrificing virtuous citizens. Many moderate republicans had relied on a different and less activist, if no less utopian, theory of republican social psychology. Condorcet and his followers, for example, had assumed that once people were educated about their true interests, they would naturally pursue them in a way that produced the public good, both in economics and politics. Like the English utilitarians, they assumed that in an enlightened republic, the general interest would automatically result from individuals seeking their own interests. Citizens of modern commercial republics required not virtue, but enlightened self-interest.

Tocqueville adopts this utilitarian language to describe a crucial self-equilibrating principle of American democracy, rebaptizing it first as *égoisme intelligent* and then as *intérêt bien-entendu*.[54] '[T]he doctrine of self-interest properly understood is not new, but it is among the Americans of our time that it has come to be universally accepted. It has become popular. One finds it at the root of all actions. It is interwoven in all they say' (DAII, 526). In Tocqueville's hands, however, the idea of enlightened self-interest takes on a sociological sophistication and occasionally a detached irony that are quite foreign to the theories of other heirs of the Enlightenment. His fundamental innovation was to view the practical fusion of public and private interest in America as a complex social and psychological artefact, rather than as the automatic result of individual pleasure-seeking. Unlike the utilitarians, who seldom interrogated their most basic premiss about the givenness of individual wants, Tocqueville explores the conditions under which, and the mechanisms by which, individuals come to desire what is in their long-term interest. He then considers, and often obsessively reconsiders, the connections among these precipitating conditions and mechanisms.

If material self-interest and individualism tend to drive democratic individuals away from public concerns, how is it that Americans come to see the public's business as their own? While Tocqueville feared that the all-absorbing game of profit-making had a tendency to crowd out public and patriotic activity, he also acknowledges a positive spillover effect from America's bustling commercial mentality. One can observe in America, he argues, a strong congruence between success in the market-place and success in republican politics, a congruence that can remain hidden in other settings. On the most basic level, people need freedom in order to provide themselves with the goods they crave (DAII, 539). But more important, the qualities of independence and self-reliance needed for success in commerce tend to carry over into political life (DAI, 404, 637). Good business requires order, regular morals, common sense, and practical shrewdness rather than wild speculation. So too does republican politics. Good business practice also demands self-reliance, independent judgement, the ability to calculate risk, and a determination to beat the odds. So too does republican politics. The trick is to effect an identification of these spheres by inducing democratic citizens to attend as passionately and responsibly to public matters as they do to their own affairs, and this in the face of a strong countervailing pull towards privatization. Tocqueville's answer is that such men will act responsibly only if they are in fact responsible for public affairs, only if they pay daily practical attention to them, as they do to their own business affairs (DAII, 442; cf. DAI, 92).

French conservatives, as well as much of the liberal political establishment with whom Tocqueville was allied, distrusted any real participation by *le peuple* in local government, feared the effects of associational freedom, and subjected a 'subversive' press to prosecution in the courts. But in America, Tocqueville argues, associations (including permanent local political associations such as townships, cities, and counties, as well as temporary political and civil groups formed freely by citizens) link self-interest, the only reliable individual motive in democratic societies, to the interest of the whole. Because democratic individuals focus almost exclusively on material pleasures, their desire to gain these pleasures and to prosper are natural spurs to purposeful association, which reinforces the individual's position. Associations make transparent to individuals the link between public purposes and private well-being; they allow for the transference of the habits of responsible action back and forth between civil and political spheres. On Tocqueville's account, successful self-government requires complex patterns of reciprocal action between these spheres. The energy of private life permeates the public sphere and lively political activity in turn reinvigorates civil life. The Americans 'carry a trader's habits into the business of politics' (DAI, 285; cf. 215). At the same time '[t]hat constantly renewed agitation introduced by democratic government into political life passes . . . into civil society' (DAI, 243). Or again 'the Americans almost always carry the habits of public life over into their private lives. With them one finds the ideas of a jury in children's games, and parliamentary formalities even in the organization of a banquet' (DAI, 305). Americans' success in establishing these positive spillovers between civil and political society, in which there is reciprocal positive reinforcement between the two, is a dominant theme of *Democracy in America*.

Vital connections between the civil and political spheres, however, are not automatic. Only participatory democracy—vigorous local self-governing groups—can provide a context in which individuals will be forced to interpret their private interests in a publicly useful manner. The elective principle itself, Tocqueville notes, forces an ambitious man to appeal beyond the confines of his family and friends for votes. Such a man is forced to 'care for his fellows, and, in a sense, he often finds his self-interest in forgetting about himself' (DAII, 510). More important, local affairs provide a constant and accessible focus for attaching individuals to the fate of a larger body. 'It is difficult to force a man out of himself and get him to take an interest in the affairs of the whole state, for he has little understanding of the way in which the fate of the state can influence his own lot. But if it is a question of taking a road past his property, he sees at once that this small public matter has a bearing on his greatest private interests, and there is no need to point out to him the close connection between his private profit and the general interest' (DAII, 511). Decentralization multiplies both the occasions for election and the contexts for cooperation; moreover, it fosters the 'art' of association as the primary technique of governing.

What I most admire in America is not the *administrative* but the *political* effects of decentralization. In the United States the motherland's presence is felt everywhere. It is a subject of concern to the village and to the whole Union. The inhabitants care about each of their country's interests as if it were their own. Each man takes pride in the nation; the successes it gains seem his own work, and he becomes elated; he rejoices in the general prosperity from which he profits. He has much the same feeling for his country as one has for one's family, and a sort of selfishness makes him care for the state. (DAI, 95)

Local political governing bodies, political associations, and civil associations perform similar functions, according to Tocqueville. They are powerful instruments of action formed to facilitate the pursuit of joint goals.

An association simply consists in the public and formal support of specific doctrines by a certain number of individuals who have undertaken to cooperate in a stated way in order to make these doctrines prevail. . . . An association unites the energies of divergent minds and vigorously directs them towards a clearly indicated goal. (DAI, 190)

The purposes of civil associations vary: to plan public festivals, to combat moral evils such as intemperance, or, most important, to carry out some industrial or commercial undertaking. Manufacturing and trading companies, for example, have an invigorating effect on commerce and industry and 'refresh the circulation of feelings and ideas among a great people' (DAII, 516). Associations thus provide a functional equivalent to certain social roles of the nobility. Just as a great territorial magnate might dress very plainly to encourage a contempt for luxury, so the huge temperance societies in America become the grand patrons of sobriety. In politics, Americans associate in endeavours great and small: to clear a blocked road, to attack the tariff laws, to pass new legislation. 'An association may be formed for the purpose of discussion, but everybody's mind is preoccupied by the thought of impending action. An association is an army; talk is needed to count numbers and build up courage, but after that they march against the enemy' (DAI, 193). By pursuing concerns in common, people become habituated to the practice and use it indiscriminately in civil and political life. 'Thus civil associations pave the way for political ones, but on the other hand, the art of political association singularly develops and improves this technique for civil purpose' (DAII, 521).

Local institutions and associations, then, successfully neutralize the potentially pernicious effects of narrow self-interest by altering the context in which individuals pursue their purposes. Tocqueville's main point here is that, in the absence of a state apparatus to organize activities that require more than the efforts of one person, democratic individuals naturally form purposive associations in order to realize their interests. Given a certain level of education, and the natural tendency of people in democracies towards independent action, voluntary association with others presents itself as an obvious and efficacious remedy to the limitations of individual action.[55] The patterns themselves become instinctual and internalized; they eventually form new *mœurs*. 'At first it is of necessity that men attend to the public interest, afterward by choice. What had been calculation becomes instinct. By dint of working for the good of his fellow citizens, he in the end acquires a habit and taste for serving them' (DAII, 512–13). Once established, of course, these patterns of action become a reality to which generations of democratic individuals adapt themselves almost unconsciously.

If the primary function of political and civil associations is to provide a universally accepted means by which weak democratic individuals may attain their various individual aims, this collective purposive activity has the unintended consequence of keeping at bay the moral and spiritual ravages of individualism. Individualism turns people inward, a voyage that may end in a fearful oscillation between doubt and the acceptance of popular forms of authority. Individualism threatens the very capacity for moral and intelligent action because '[f]eelings and ideas are renewed, the heart enlarged, and the understanding developed only by the reciprocal action of men one upon another' (DAII, 515). In aristocracies, the nobility initiates the reciprocal action of men 'one upon the other' by taking up ideas or sentiments and thus 'refreshing the circulation of feelings and ideas' among a people (DAII, 516). In democracies, individuals are too weak to perform this function and governments too strong to do so without tyranny. Hence the progress of civilization itself depends upon associations (DAII, 517). In democratic times, as in any other, the production of ideas arises from voluntary collaboration. Participation in local government and in civil and political associations, then, directly educates individuals to see the ways in which prosperity and all objects of individual action may be increased by cooperating with others. Moreover, the experience of cooperation indirectly renews ideas and feelings, thereby powerfully counteracting individualism's tendency to sap society of its moral and intellectual energies.

So far I have focused on the emboldening aspects of associations, the ways in which they empower weak individuals to coalesce as public or quasi-public agents. But what of the threat that this incessant activity might pose to democratic stability? Tocqueville's European audience would be only too sensitive to the potentially revolutionary effects of political clubs and societies. Tocqueville argues a dual case for the art of association: not only does it foster energetic activity but, if left completely free, also automatically corrects its own excesses. In the latter argument he addresses the issue most salient to his French audience: to what extent should political association be tolerated? Tocqueville makes political association the most fundamental type of free association. It is the more 'natural' type, because association always springs from perceived weakness. In democratic politics people know that they can never look out for themselves without help, while in economic life their initial inclination may be to go it alone. Political association, furthermore, allows for faster social learning. Politics brings into view extensive associations quite rapidly and thus shows people the power of the principle. Finally, the risks to the individual of political association are in some ways less than those of civil cooperation, since no money is directly at stake. 'So one may think of political associations as great free schools to which all citizens come to be taught the general theory of association': how to maintain order among large numbers of individuals, what procedures bring agreement, how to submit one's will to others, how to make one's particular exertions subordinate common action (DAII, 522). Tocqueville concludes that it is a vain hope to wish to reap the benefits of civil or economic group life without tolerating political association as well.

In a full-fledged political democracy, Tocqueville argues, these free schools of political association do not cause excessive disorder because universal suffrage, the rule of the majority, and the circula-tion of public opinion by means of a completely free press change the purpose of political association from violence to persuasion. Polit-ical associations under 'complete' democracy aim at the creation of a new majority, not the overthrow of an existing regime. If they fail, given every chance to succeed, they are marginalized by the force of public opinion itself.[56] Like universal suffrage, a completely free press legitimizes the very idea of majority rule by assuring that pub-lic opinion will be untainted by government censorship. Freedom of political association and a free press, then, are no guarantees against tyranny of majority opinion—other countervailing measures may be necessary for that—but Tocqueville's main concern here is to argue that democratic freedoms do not necessarily lead to chaotic instability. For example, he entertains the objection that the dizzy-ing flow of information and opinion pouring out of an uncensored press may lead to chaos by causing individuals to change their minds with every new idea, and to wreak havoc on public policy by their inconstancies. He denies that such chaos will ensue, however, observing that under conditions of perfect freedom, unexpected and unintended stabilities emerge (DAI, 186). Because people choose their opinions, they become attached to them and hate to abandon them. Furthermore, when everything may be said openly, one becomes fairly sure that everything has been said. If none of the opinions articulated in the public arena is manifestly superior to one's own, one simply holds to current opinion out of habit. Finally, material interests and instincts—so strong in modern democracy—hold individual minds fast within a range of possible opinions.

On Tocqueville's account, then, freedom of association and a free press do not promote anarchy. Indeed, they may even be com-patible with hegemonic forms of public opinion, a new danger that American experience reveals for the first time. In any case, these forms of 'extreme' democracy still guard against some obvious abuses of majority power by providing an arena for the articulation of alternative views and the constitution of new majorities. The complete right to organize for political ends guards against the dan-ger that majorities might impose tyrannical legislation. Whatever the risks of allowing free association, the risks of repressing association are yet greater. Political associations make possible the clarification of ends, give these purposes energy, and ultimately also facilitate the growth of a responsible opposition.

In much the same way as Hobbes envisioned the modern polity as an artificial leviathan made up of the strength of many individuals, Tocqueville saw the democratic polity as a mass of associations, artificial constructs combining the force of their individual members for offensive and defensive actions. If modern Hobbesian sovereignty reconceptualizes the absolutism of kings, Tocqueville's view of political and civil associations similarly transposes the aristocratic conception of a balance between nobility and monarchy into a democratic idiom. Associations both constitute majorities and make it possible to resist current majorities, thus providing an equivalent to the constitutive self-governing activities, as well as the defensive tactics, of powerful nobles (DAII, 513, 516).

Religion in democracy

Like Tocqueville's discussion of enlightened self-interest and associations, his analysis of religion in democracies suggests that the logic of democracy 'itself' naturally promotes religious belief, which contributes to a new democratic equilibrium. This analysis of religion, however, differs from his assessment of the workings of interest properly understood in at least two important ways. First, he relies not only on arguments about congruence and spillover effects among spheres but also on compensations among them. And second, he focuses directly rather than indirectly on the ways in which religion combats the dangerous effects of individualism. Association to achieve human purposes primarily addresses the dangers posed by material self-interest, and only indirectly the dangers of spiritual impoverishment and mental instability. Democracy's affinities with religious dogma and practice meet head on the danger of the spiritual void caused by individualism, though they also moderate the worst excesses of materialism.

Tocqueville's own religious temperament and its importance to his manner of treating moral questions will be taken up in Chapter 4. Here I wish to convey the range and inventiveness of his arguments about religion made 'from a purely human point of view' (DAII, 445). Like Tocqueville's arguments about the benefits of association, his arguments on behalf of religion present no single integrated view of the connection between religious beliefs and a democratic stability, but rather pursue several trains of thought at once. Like his French liberal contemporaries, he defends religious belief as necessary to support traditional moral virtues and to limit the potential excesses of democratic politics. Unlike many of them, however, he neglects philosophical or theological discussions in favour of a functionalist brief that offers several supporting arguments. One line of argument, like his advocacy of associations, relies on the reinforcing spillover effects among spheres of social life that place similar demands on individuals, that is, on the tendency of habits contracted in one sphere to pass over into another. Another train of thought relies on a quite different articulation of the connection between religion and the instincts of democracy. On this second view, religion attracts and holds democratic individuals not because it is familiar, but because it is strange. It offers an arena for the satisfaction of psychological and spiritual yearnings that otherwise go unmet or find dangerous outlets.

Let us consider the congruence arguments first. Tocqueville sees a profound underlying similarity between all forms of Christianity and democracy, because both are based on spiritual equality. Although the Christian religion may be pulled into various shapes by its social and political context—its universalism privileged by the Roman Empire, its elements of particularism and pluralism emphasized in the Middle Ages—Christianity is most easily accommodated in the democratic age, which mirrors its fundamental notion of the equality of all believers. 'Men who are alike and on the same level in this world easily conceive the idea of a single God who imposes the same laws on each man and grants him future happiness at the same price' (DAII, 445; cf. 439). In democracy, Christianity finds its most 'natural' social form.

Beyond this structural similarity, Tocqueville offers several other arguments that religion is natural to democracy 'itself' based on congruence. The most important concerns the psychological parallels between religious discipline and the self-restraint necessary for self-interest to become enlightened. In America the principle of enlightened self-interest pervades the moral sphere as well as all others. Far from chilling religious enthusiasm, this principle quite readily fuses with religious teachings, since the moral habits of self-denial and mutual cooperation preached by Christianity echo existing civil and political practices. Religious and secular psychological dispositions mutually reinforce each other. 'Religions instill a general habit of behaving with the future in view. In this respect they work as much in favor of happiness in this world as of felicity in the next. That is one of their most salient political characteristics' (DAII, 547). Conversely, once enlightened self-interest has been established among citizens in civil and political society, 'they will gradually be led without noticing it themselves towards religious beliefs' (DAII, 549).

American clergy encourage these convergences by forbearing to preach religious ideas that oppose public opinion, or that go against the permanent interests of the people (DAII, 448, 530). 'Far from trying to show that these two worlds [the civil and the religious] are distinct and opposed to each other, they seek to discover the points of connection and alliance' (DAII, 449). Tocqueville is not saying that Americans are religious hypocrites. He is merely pointing to a parallel in structures of thought—American civil and religious doctrines both have consequentialist elements involving rewards—and noting that democratic clergy heed common ground where it exists, and decline to antagonize their members unnecessarily.

A third type of argument based on congruence, introduced in Tocqueville's very first discussion of religion, arises in the context of considering America's specific Protestant heritage and its direct effects on politics. He links Protestantism to individual rights and Catholicism to the authoritarian power of kings. 'Every religion has some political opinion linked to it by affinity. The spirit of man, left to follow its bent, will regulate political society and the City of God in uniform fashion; it will, if I dare put it so, seek to *harmonize* earth with heaven' (DAI, 287). Protestantism, he notes, expresses democracy's impulse towards independent action and judgement whereas 'Catholicism is like an absolute monarchy' (DAI, 288). Just as Protestantism combines freethinking with religious faith and accustoms people to make their own judgements in the religious sphere, so in politics it encourages a kind of independent deliberation and self-reliance that is anchored in settled belief. In a chapter assessing the future of republican institutions in America, Tocqueville states this logic explicitly.

For most people in the United States religion, too, is republican, for the truths of the other world are held subject to private judgement, just as in politics the care for men's temporal interests is left to the good sense of all. Each man is allowed to choose freely the path that will lead him to heaven, just as the law recognizes each citizen's right to choose his own government. (DAI, 397)

The suspicion that Protestantism and republicanism are in some way linked was and is a common one, but Tocqueville does not pursue it very far in the first volume of *Democracy* and ignores it in the second. He clearly wishes to avoid a possible concomitant of this insistence on an affinity between Protestantism and free institutions, namely, the assumption of an attraction between Catholicism and despotism. Catholicism, he acknowledges, is more closely aligned with the passion for equality than with the taste for liberty, but if priests were to be excluded from government, Catholicism itself would not be incompatible with free institutions. 'So while the nature of their beliefs may not give the Catholics of the United States any strong impulsions towards democratic and republican opinions, they at least are not naturally contrary thereto, whereas their social position and small numbers constrain them to adopt them.'[57] An American Catholic, according to this initial line of argument, is a republican *malgré lui.*

Tocqueville then goes on to consider the indirect action of religion on politics. Here he begins to develop a different argument about why democratic peoples may be expected to turn 'naturally' to religion. The dogmas of Christianity that circumscribe human thought and action serve to sustain democratic societies not only because such beliefs are congruent with the discipline required to practice delayed gratification, or because they reinforce responsible private judgement, but also because they answer a psychological need for steadiness that is fulfilled nowhere else. Democratic individuals find a necessary mental anchor in religion and even crave its assurance. '[T]he human spirit never sees an unlimited field before itself; however bold it is, from time to time it feels that it must halt before insurmountable barriers. Before innovating, it is forced to accept certain primary assumptions and to submit its boldest conceptions to certain formalities which retard and check it' (DAI, 292). Tocqueville doubts whether 'deliberate and self-justified conviction' ever inspires the same degree of devotion as do dogmatic beliefs (DAI, 187). Indeed in democratic times, there is a special need for individual minds to compensate for the total lack of structure—the frightening immensity of limitless desires within and unlimited choice without—by gravitating towards some set of beliefs that are transcendentally based and beyond dispute. In this way they find a haven that allows them to function in a heartless world.

When Tocqueville takes up the question of religious *mœurs* in the second *Democracy*, it is this reparative function of religious belief that claims his attention. Neglecting altogether the presumption of a particular affinity between Protestantism and freedom, he instead begins to unravel the close connections between Catholicism, dogma, and equality. He eventually rides this train of thought to a very different conclusion from that of the first *Democracy*: not

Protestantism but Catholicism is specially linked to free institutions in democratic times. The particular mix of faith and personal freedom characteristic of Protestantism appears from this point of view to be inherently unstable. Rather than providing the democratic mind with psychological ballast and thus counteracting the intellectual and spiritual ravages of individualism, Protestantism puts the individual on a slippery slope to nihilism. Only fixed notions about God, the nature of the human soul, and the duties of humanity can prevent humans from descending into 'anarchy and impotence' (DAII, 443). These are the very notions, however, that are impossible for the mind to reach on its own and thus dangerous to leave to the individual conscience. 'General ideas respecting God and human nature are therefore the ideas above all others which ought to be withdrawn from the habitual action of private judgement and in which there is most to gain and least to lose by recognizing an authority' (DAII, 443). Insofar as any form of Christianity has kept a strong hold over the minds of Americans, 'its power is not just that of a philosophy which has been examined and accepted, but that of a religion believed in without discussion' (DAII, 432). Protestantism, however, ultimately performs the task of supplying a minimum of dogma to democratic peoples less efficiently than Catholicism precisely because it encourages unruly independent thought that is difficult to arrest before it dissolves in unbelief or pantheism.[58] Only a very few can 'let their minds float at random between obedience and freedom' (DAII, 451). For most people Protestantism offers only a way station to scepticism and atheism because it does not police adequately the vulnerable borders of faith.

In one of his most famous passages Tocqueville writes, 'For my part, I doubt whether man can support complete religious independence and entire political liberty at the same time. I am led to think that if he has no faith he must obey, and if he is free he must believe' (DAII, 444). Apparently a simplified Catholicism, separated from its medieval excrescences and from the control of the state, can better perform the compensatory functions of religion precisely because of its authoritarian strain. Catholicism is more efficient at producing the necessary minimum of Christian belief. Democratic individuals' attraction to Catholicism's single and uniform authority, moreover, constitutes a hidden instinct that unconsciously urges them towards Rome (DAII, 450). Tocqueville notes an increasing number of conversions to Catholicism in America and even concludes that 'our grandchildren will tend more and more to be divided clearly between those who have completely abandoned Christianity and those who have returned to the Church of Rome' (DAII, 451).

Like the principle of enlightened self-interest, religion also requires a specific institutional context in which to produce the effects that are 'natural' to it in democratic times. Self-interest supplies the energy for reflective patriotism and responsible self-government only when it is activated by the technique of association, when it is embedded in a decentralized political structure and a dense web of group activity that create bridges between civil and political life. These bridges circumvent the need for central coordination. Similarly religion stabilizes democracy only when freed from state sponsorship. Tocqueville's arguments for the strict separation of church and state are rooted in his concern that if religious dogma is fused with secular power, it will lose both its spillover and compensatory effects. He notes that the support of the worldly power always has the potential to harm religion both directly (by corrupting the clergy and dividing their loyalties) and indirectly (by linking its universal claims to ephemeral powers that will vanish sooner or later) (DAI, 298). In crumbling aristocratic monarchies, state support weakens religion by yoking its authority to a doomed and hated ruling class. But in democratic times the political embrace of religion is truly the kiss of death. Religion's strongest attraction in democratic times is its universality; therefore, to ally itself with any particular power is to diminish its appeal. Moreover, to perform its important functions in a democratic world, religious belief must be perceived as untouchable and eternal; however, democratic political authority is by definition responsive to majorities and completely mutable. This variability infects all it touches and compromises religion's ability to demand unquestioned acquiescence to eternal truths (DAI, 298; DAII, 432). Finally, in democratic and enlightened periods the need for dogmatic beliefs is a limited compensatory one; outside its compass people are loath to accept authority. 'This shows that, at such times above all, religions should be most careful to confine themselves to their proper sphere, for if they wish to extend their power beyond spiritual matters they run the risk of not being believed at all.'[59]

Tocqueville anticipates an objection that the French and American situations with respect to religion are completely different. The American government does not need to champion religion because Christianity has no enemies there, whereas faith in France is under attack and needs protection. But he argues that this objection entirely misses his point. Religion flourishes in America only because the state leaves it alone. Individuals are therefore free to follow their limited but real spiritual interests, and those few who do not believe are constrained by opinion to keep quiet. Although religion does have ardent adversaries in France, Catholicism loses power over souls not because enemies attack it but rather because fanatical friends, who fail to discern the true religious affinities of democracy, defend it with clumsy political weapons. In France, the 'close union of politics and religion' prevents those affinities from becoming apparent; all sides regard religion as a political battleground and hence politics as religious war (DAI, 300).

The position that only more democracy could cure the ills of democracy attracted Tocqueville because it reinforced the existential choice he had himself made: only a complete commitment to the new democratic France, rather than accommodations to the remnants of aristocracy, could create liberty in the 'new regime'. And he felt a certain urgency to convey these lessons about the equilibrating instincts of democracy because they were counter-intuitive to his audiences. Among the self-corrective tendencies that he thought he had discovered in democratic America were precisely those measures dreaded most by many French liberals and conservatives: complete freedom of association, extension of political rights, and disestablishment of the Church. Ultimately, however, only such measures offered leaders the chance of creating a democratic form of liberty. Tocqueville had come to the conclusion that only by drinking deeply of the waters of democracy could the French arrive at democratic sobriety.

Tocqueville's Method of Explanation

Tocqueville had little interest in questions of methodology. Indeed, his elegant rhetoric often masks or even distorts the structure of his arguments. All discussions of the Tocquevillian 'method', then, are more reconstructions than critical engagements with a theorist self-conscious about the tools of his trade. Yet he was passionately interested in explaining the causes of social and political beliefs and behaviours. How does he structure such explanations in *Democracy in America*?

Perhaps every sociologist or theorist who has written about

Tocqueville has noted that Tocqueville practiced 'ideal-typical' analysis before Weber invented a name for it.[60] *Democracy in America* teems with types: 'democracy', 'aristocracy', and the 'revolutionary spirit', but also the 'Puritan mind' or the Indian 'mentality'. These abstractions accentuate certain features of reality, rendering them internally more logical for the purposes of clarity in analysis. Tocqueville was quite aware of having constructed such notions. He described the practice as seeking the 'shape' or 'image' or 'model' of a phenomenon: 'Beginning from the facts furnished by American and French societies, I wished to paint the general traits of democratic societies of which no complete model yet exists.'[61] Ideal-typical analysis, practiced with a greater or lesser level of self-awareness, was inseparable from Tocqueville's use of the comparative method; he devised models and 'typical' trains of thought in order to compare and contrast, in order to divine that which was significant enough to be noticed, in order to identify the differences to be explained.[62] Many have also noted that Tocqueville's types— especially democracy and aristocracy—sometimes seduced him, that he spun out deductions from his *idées mères*, and confused these deductions with the reality he wanted to illuminate.[63] But in moments of clarity he realized that creating a type is not explaining a social phenomenon, but merely facilitating such an explanation. Tocqueville used 'types' to build two kinds of explanation in *Democracy in America*: first, an account of the emergence of democracy (which he 'typified' as democracy itself) in history, and second, an account of the causes of behaviours and beliefs characteristic of democracy when it had established itself as a functioning system. In the second case, Tocqueville implicitly argued that interlocking patterns of *mœurs* caused beliefs and behaviours to perpetuate themselves in democracy.

The first type of explanation plays a limited role in *Democracy in America*. Tocqueville's early chapters sketch the emergence of democracy 'itself' in America with a few broad strokes that outline —rather than detail—the role of favourable geographical circumstances, political and religious institutions and practices inherited from England, and multiplier effects produced by the impact of separation from England and by changing inheritance laws. Similarly, in the famous introduction to the first *Democracy*, with its rhetorical conclusion that equality is fated and irreversible, Tocqueville runs rapidly through the pages of French history in order to suggest a number of causes that have intersected to produce democracy in

France (DAI, 1–20). Later, in *The Old Regime*, Tocqueville will turn his attention more fully to the emergence of democracy out of aristocracy in France. But what strikes the reader, even in the brief sketches of historical transformation in the two *Democracies*, is Tocqueville's focus on the complexity and multidimensionality of historical change. As a political actor deliberately attempting to shift the weight of history's legacies, he leaves himself open to the view that social phenomena have multiple causes, causes that are entangled in complicated and sometimes indeterminate ways.

Tocqueville's attribution of so many consequences to the protean concept of democracy, an aspect of his work that J. S. Mill criticized in his review of the second *Democracy*, may seem to contradict this awareness of complex causation.[64] But the causal historical 'force' implicit in such overarching concepts as 'democracy' or 'centralization' is usually either rhetorical or representative of a host of smaller analyses and judgements. It is these judgements, and his recognition of the simultaneous effects of many factors, that form the core of his analysis. Despite his rhetoric about the fatedness of democracy, then, Tocqueville believed that theorizing the contingency of historical transformations was of more use to the political actor than generalizing about the sweep of history. In *The Old Regime and the Revolution*, he took up the difficult task of deciphering the effects of France's general and particular *circonstances* on the structure of possibilities that confronted his own generation. I will turn to those efforts in the next chapter.

The second type of explanation, an extended analysis of how the interlocking grid of democratic mores shapes attitudes and behaviour in a society that has reached democratic equilibrium, lies at the heart of *Democracy in America*. Among the 'general' causes that explain behaviour, a people's *mœurs* are the most important. Tocqueville was powerfully attracted to this Montesquieuian notion of the 'spirit' of a people, in this case the complex of basic attitudes that exist within a new democratic cultural formation. As Tocqueville tells us in the introduction, he sought to capture democracy's 'inclinations, character, prejudices, and passions' (DAI, 19). This search for the shape of a culture has much in common with the practices of other historians of *mentalités*.[65] Tocqueville was concerned with how people adjust their aspirations to their environment, and how they are in turn shaped by the mental patterns that come to seem natural in that environment. In his discussion of the affinities between the passion for equality and the passion for profit, of the bridges between civil and political society constructed by the psychological bent towards association, of the mental affinities between a new kind of atomized individual and pantheism or philosophical materialism or Catholic dogma, he takes as his special subject neither disembodied ideas nor the socio-economic foundations of societies, but rather a conceptual space somewhere between the two. This rather amorphously defined theoretical world between the history of ideas and social history resembles the territory explored in the *Annales* histories of Lucien Fébvre and Marc Bloch, or the idiosyncratic narratives of Philippe Ariès, Norbert Elias, or Michel Foucault. Like these twentieth-century cultural historians, Tocqueville considers collective more than individual attitudes, the thoughts of typical people rather than elites, unspoken general assumptions rather than elaborated philosophical theories, and the general structure of beliefs rather than their specific content.[66] Tocqueville's Americans—their passions, interests, tastes, and desires—are shaped by the possibilities inherent in a particular mental organization of culture that he terms democracy 'itself'. He approaches the study of this society by imaginatively reconstructing what Montesquieu would have called a distinctive *manière de penser* or what recent scholars might call *l'imaginaire social.*[67]

Like the practitioners of the history of *mentalités*, Tocqueville does not always avoid certain pitfalls of the method, such as overestimating the amount of consensus in a given culture or treating the belief system (democracy itself) as autonomous and self-replicating. Moreover, he shared the tendency to dichotomize collective representations. Early *Annales* historians, for example, fell into a pattern of contrasting premodern with modern thought, and of using the former (allegedly more spontaneous and direct) implicitly to criticize the latter (more disciplined, desiccated, and abstract). Tocqueville's division of belief systems into aristocratic and democratic and his nostalgic appreciation for the former sometimes betray a similar form of covert romantic critique. '[T]he sight of such universal uniformity saddens and chills me, and I am tempted to regret that state of society which has ceased to be' (DAII, 704). But perhaps the most striking reason to place Tocqueville in the tradition loosely termed the study of *mentalités* is a certain ironic construction of the map of cultural history. Throughout *Democracy in America*, he explores the paradox that the democratic patterns of living and thinking that have come to structure American and French societies represent at once a complex process of collective human innovation and a constraint on the human capacity to innovate in the future. Democracy 'itself' imposes new psychosocial forms of discipline and uniformity, and hence an increased threat of despotism. Thus historical change produces paradoxical outcomes and troubling antinomies.[68] Tocqueville, then, escapes the narrative of progress that generally characterizes both idealistic and materialistic historical theories of civilization. His view of the emergence and prevalence of the democratic 'mentality' in some ways has more in common with Foucault than with Guizot.

If the broad outlines of Tocqueville's method prompt comparison with the tradition of mentalities, we ought not to push the analogy too far. The implicitly critical perspectives of certain historians of mentalities—their concerns about social conformity and psychological repressions associated with the modern self—are secondary to their more explicit goals of reconstructing a particular cultural formation. Their methodological and historical objectives take centre stage, and they often pursue these goals with sophisticated quantitative techniques or systematic and detailed historical research. But Tocqueville's 'presentist' concerns are not at all oblique, and he treats the ambitious methodological project of unearthing and analysing the *mœurs* of aristocracy and democracy as a mere preamble to the real tasks of the public intellectual. His normative goals are quite explicit: a moral and civic regeneration of the French polity that will institutionalize democratic 'freedom', protect civic spaces, and foster practices of self-government in the potentially hostile world of democracy. These purposes quite deliberately influence his articulation of the social psychology that shapes democracy 'itself'. In his discussion of how to recognize and exploit the equilibrating psycho-social mechanisms associated with creating interest well-understood or religious belief within a democratic social state, for example, he takes deliberate rhetorical aim at a particular set of French understandings. He calibrates his discussion in such a way as to convince French readers that certain reforms have a chance of success because they correspond to the deepest instincts of the new society. Tocqueville's analyses, then, rather openly serve his own ends. Yet what grips the contemporary reader are not these specific ends, but rather his subtle exploration of the psychology underlying democratic *mœurs*, an exploration rich enough to be appropriated by those with other assumptions and very different ends.

A Return to Democracy's Point de Départ

At the beginning of this chapter I suggested that Tocqueville saw America's particular and irreproducible circumstances as both crucial and beside the point. They were essential in setting the stage for the emergence of a relatively transparent form of democracy from which an observer could construct a useful type of democracy 'itself'. But the cumulative and self-reinforcing tendencies of the democratic social state, rather than its precipitating geographical and historical conditions, were most responsible for the character of the new society. Because he assumed that a similar set of dynamic forces was transforming Europe, and especially France, Tocqueville was able to create a novel theoretical space from which he could diagnose the problems of his own society. But were those democratic types in fact the same?

Throughout the two *Democracies* (and increasingly in the second) Tocqueville struggles to maintain this heuristic fiction that America and France were two instantiations of a common type. Though he urges Europeans not to take America as a model in any conventional sense, he does claim a theoretical relevance for America that would evaporate if the same democratic tendencies were not operating in both settings. Tocqueville never confronted this possibility directly in *Democracy in America*, but many of his comparisons between the Old World and the New did suggest that the manner in which democracy appeared in France was of more importance than democracy 'itself'. France's political culture seemed to be shaped at least as much by revolution as by democracy.

Complicating the Tocquevillian schema by which all democratic societies contain two hypothetical futures—one unfree, one free— is a third possibility. A society may fall victim to the special ills of the *esprit révolutionnaire*, which has effects that are powerful enough to rival the causal dynamic of the *esprit d'égalité* itself. 'In Europe it is hard for us to judge the true character and permanent instincts of democracy, for in Europe two contrary principles are contending, and one cannot precisely know what is due to the principles themselves and what to the passions engendered by the fight' (DAI, 196). To conclude that the debilitating and disorienting passions 'engendered by the fight' fatally compromised Europe's political future would be painful indeed. Tocqueville does not reach this conclusion in *Democracy in America* (though he approached it by the end of his life). Underlying his project in the *Democracy* is in part the desire to conquer these recurrent fears of a permanently disfiguring revolutionary spirit by normalizing the French Revolution and its legacy, that is, by making them intelligible within a larger comparative picture.

Like every central concept in Tocqueville's theoretical arsenal, 'revolution' may have different meanings depending on the context and his immediate purpose. One meaning is simply that of a discrete political event, or series of events, that precipitately adjusts political society to the social state of a people.[69] More often, however, he refers to revolution as the historical transition from an aristocratic to a democratic social state, as in his famous sketch of the 'great democratic revolution' in the introduction to *Democracy in America* (DAI, 1). The first meaning—largely political—refers to a discrete series of historical events; the second refers to a long historical process with both social and political ramifications. The French Revolution was revolutionary in both senses. It was a particular political event, but its real significance lies in its complex relationship to the protracted revolutionary transformation of France from an aristocracy to a democracy. In contrast, according to Tocqueville, the American Revolution was a revolution in neither sense. The Americans were both equal and free before their separation from England, hence their 'revolution' marked a fundamental continuity with their past.[70] Singularly absent in America was the revolutionary spirit, the passions inspired by 'the heat of the struggle' (DAI, 16).

When Tocqueville was composing *Democracy in America*, he believed the French Revolution to be over, the impulse towards political revolution to be largely exhausted, and the democratization of France in its final stages. His conviction that the greatest danger for France during the first decade of the July Monarchy was not rebellion but stagnation, as well as his belief that what distinguished mature democracy was its lack of the revolutionary spirit, underlay one of the most famous chapters in the second *Democracy*, 'Why Great Revolutions Will Become Rare' (DAII, 634–45). Tocqueville's rhetorical adversaries in that chapter were the nervous liberals of the *juste milieu* in France who feared that extending democratic rights would endanger social stability. His arguments have long been viewed as a *tour de force* in which he turns Burke on his head and reveals the unexpectedly conservative tendencies of modern democracy. Great revolutions will become rare because widespread property ownership attaches citizens to the status quo, because commercial characters fear the turbulence of revolution, and because revolutionary ideas and opinions lack appeal in a country truly under the sway of majority opinion. Revolutions come from unequal social conditions, not equal ones.[71] Even if democracy stabilizes itself over the long run, however, its revolutionary origins may still be profoundly important. Indeed it is the admixture of revolution that muddies French democratic experience, rendering it, in contrast to the allegedly transparent America, less capable of clearly revealing democracy 'itself'. This mutant form, democracy disfigured by revolution, haunts the pages of both the 1835 and the 1840 *Democracies*.

In the first *Democracy* Tocqueville argues that revolution temporarily perverts democracy because its lingering effects prevent a society based on equal social conditions from achieving its natural shape, and make more likely a fall into despotism. In France class warfare and political extremism left a legacy of divisive rancour and distrust that interfere with the stabilizing mechanisms of democracy and immensely complicate the task of creating self-governing institutions. Tocqueville notes that democracy arrived and continues to exist 'amid the disorders and agitations of conflict. In the heat of the struggle each partisan is driven beyond the natural limits of his own views by the views and the excesses of his adversaries, loses sight of the very aim he was pursuing, and uses language which ill corresponds to his real feelings and to his secret instincts' (DAI, 16). Moreover, the revolutionary spirit innovates recklessly, scorns formalities and legal limits, and rides roughshod over vested rights. These attitudes render the task of creating a stable constitutional structure infinitely more difficult. Whereas the Americans have a deceptively chaotic politics due to the instability of their secondary laws, the French have real chaos because of the lack of agreement about 'the very basis of the Constitution'. This latter kind of instability 'attacks the creative principles on which the laws are founded' (DAI, 398).

In the second *Democracy*, Tocqueville develops these two initial observations about the revolutionary spirit—its tendencies to intensify mutual distrust and to ignore all limits—as temporary exacerbations of democratic *individualisme*. 'There is a tendency in democracy not to draw men together, but democratic revolutions make them run away from each other and perpetuate, in the midst of equality, hatreds originating in inequality' (DAII, 509). In a society infected with revolutionary forms of individualism 'envy, hatred, and distrust of his neighbor, together with pride and exaggerated confidence in himself, invade the human heart and for some time hold dominion there' (DAII, 432). Natural to democracy, the passion for equality assumes a virulent form in revolutionary democracy. 'At such times men pounce on equality as their booty and cling to it as a precious treasure they fear to have snatched away' (DAII, 505).

Revolution, moreover, increases the central aspect of individualism itself, the tendency to look inward for human meaning and to withdraw from intellectual *commerce*. 'Every revolution must shake ancient beliefs, sap authority and cloud shared ideas. So any revolution, to a greater or lesser extent, throws men back on themselves and opens to each man's view an almost limitless empty space' (DAII, 432). Because of pervasive distrust of others, this space can be filled only by ideas that are peculiar to the individual. Intellectual liberty thus becomes a sterile rather than a fertile freedom. 'No longer do ideas, but interests only, form the links between men, and it would seem that human opinions were no more than a sort of mental dust open to the wind on every side and unable to come together and take shape' (DAII, 433). Mental dust cannot sustain any ordinary social consensus on rules of behaviour, a consensus that normally functions as a brake on reckless innovation. 'As ordinary ideas of equity and morality are no longer enough to explain and justify all the innovations daily introduced by revolution, men fall back on the principle of social utility, political necessity is turned into a dogma, and men lose all scruples about freely sacrificing particular interests and trampling private rights beneath their feet in order more quickly to attain the public aim envisaged' (DAII, 700). Thus the revolutionary spirit prevents the formation of new intellectual and moral ties even as it undermines basic notions of decency and restraint, leaving humanity with no moral ballast at all.

If revolutions corrode the shared ideas essential to civilized life, they at the same time increase aspirations and unleash boundless human ambitions. Tocqueville espies a kind of limitless longing in post-revolutionary France that has no exact analogue in America. He attributes it to historical memory, to an unconscious reaching towards the splendour of the vanquished aristocracy combined with the memory of revolution itself. That memory conjures up the fantasy of unlimited desires and the power to satisfy them, of a place where everything is possible and all judgements contestable, of a time when men and women performed unimaginable deeds. 'Men do not in one day forget the memory of extraordinary events which they have witnessed; and the passions roused by revolution by no means vanish at its close. A sense of instability is perpetuated amid order. The hope of easy success lives on after the strange turns of fortune which gave it birth' (DAII, 628).

In his analysis of democratic societies, Tocqueville had identified psychological patterns potentially hostile to freedom: the increasing sway of material self-interest, which both feeds and is fed by the privatizing stream of individualism. The spirit of revolution, on his account, intensifies the separate effects of self-interest and individualism, and accelerates the processes by which they reinforce each other. An atmosphere of envy and distrust in which citizens experiment wildly in disregard of all limits effectively stifles the more benign self-equilibrating tendencies of democratic culture. The centralizing tendencies of the state, however, are ominously freed to do their worst.

among democratic nations the only form of government which comes naturally to mind is a sole and central power. This applies particularly to those democratic nations which have seen the principle of equality triumph with the help of a violent revolution. The classes that managed local affairs were suddenly swept away in that storm. . . . Centralization becomes a fact, and in a sense a necessity. (DAII, 675)

The final section of the 1840 *Democracy*, 'On the Influence of Democratic Ideas and Feelings on Political Society,' consists of five short chapters that sum up Tocqueville's thinking about the fatal attractions between revolutionary democracy and centralization. The underlying theme of these chapters is that all participants and all phases of the revolution in France combine, as if in some secret conspiracy, to increase the prerogatives of the state. Power seems to rush 'spontaneously' to the centre, leaving the already weakened democratic individual defenseless and isolated (DAII, 674).

Tocqueville's method of integrating the effects of a revolutionary legacy, then, is to portray them as weakening democracy's inherent immunities to despotism. The resulting afflictions are 'confusing', 'miserable', 'wretched', and 'abnormal', but will disappear in time as enlightened citizens learn to profit from the countervailing tendencies of democracy (DAI, 236; DAII, 578, 606, 625).

At times, however, the discrete legacies of revolution seem to merge together and to offer to the reader a powerful new historical type: *la société révolutionnaire*. Though it might be only a 'moment of hesitation' between aristocracy and democracy, revolutionary society possesses distinct and internally connected mores that sharply define that moment. The distrust between master and servant, for example, mirrors the 'intestinal war between permanently suspicious rival powers' characteristic of the world of politics (DAII, 578). Manners are unsettled, and notions of honour appeal to no common rule (DAII, 606, 625). As long as this moral netherworld could be envisioned as a painful but temporary period of adjustment, Tocqueville could accommodate it within the structure of his thought by assigning it transitional status. If the finitude of revolution were to come into question, however, this model of a revolutionary society might present a theoretical puzzle in its own right. Rather than an unfortunate collection of 'secondary and accidental causes', revolutionary society might need to be considered as a unique political culture with its own historical logic and mentality. The possibility that revolution carried its own pervasive *mentalité* disrupted Tocqueville's uneasy settlement of the theoretical problem of a nation's *point de départ* and suggested that his method of extracting an ideal democratic type that could serve as the principal tool for insight into both French and American society might have to be reconsidered. To study revolutionary society on its own terms would be to study modern France, its history and its destiny. Indeed, bringing history into the foreground in this way might also suggest that America's own history had affected her destiny in more complicated ways than he had acknowledged. Perhaps America's *point de départ*, as so many subsequent theorists have concluded, made it exceptional rather than typical of any generic concept of modernity. Or perhaps a meditation on the dark side of America's freedom—its racist exclusions, its bizarre forms of spirituality, its restless adventurism—might suggest a variant of democracy as distinctive as France's own.

Tocqueville never reopened the question of national identity and its historical roots in the context of America. But he did begin to seek France's modern identity by interrogating her past with increasing intensity. In the wake of the Revolution of 1848, Tocqueville became preoccupied with France's singular political fate, and in particular with the origins and effects of revolutionary democracy, a concept that was now released from the particular comparative integument within which it had been contained in *Democracy in America*.[72] In *Souvenirs* and in *L'Ancien Régime et la Révolution*, Tocqueville would struggle continually to understand the significance of France's *point de départ*, to comprehend how the destiny of modern France had been forged by the interaction of inherited circumstances, the forces of democracy, and the shock of revolution.

Notes

1 See Tocqueville to Louis de Kergolay, Jan. 1835, OC 13:1, 374: 'For almost ten years I have been thinking about some of the things [the themes of the 1835 *Democracy*] I have just expressed to you.'

2 As Tocqueville developed a picture of democracy, he also created a contrasting portrait of aristocracy. Some commentators, especially those focusing on his status as a founder of sociology, have considered aristocracy separately, as a contrasting ideal type. See e.g. Gianfranco Poggi, *Images of Society: Essays on the Sociological Theories of Tocqueville, Marx, and Durkheim* (Stanford, Calif.: Stanford University Press, 1972), 3–28. The contrast between aristocracy and democracy is foundational to almost everything Tocqueville wrote, but I will treat aristocracy (as he did) as a foil to democracy, rather than attempting to reconstruct it.

3 The reasons that Tocqueville and Beaumont chose to go to America certainly include considerations of career as well as larger intellectual concerns. See A. Jardin, *Tocqueville* (1805–1859): A Biography, trans. Lydia Davis with Robert Hemenway (London: Peter Halban, 1988), 90–5; See also François Furet, 'Naissance d'un paradigme: Tocqueville et le voyage en Amérique (1825–1831)' *Annales*, 39/2 (Mar.–Apr. 1984), 225–7.

4 Tocqueville to J. S. Mill, June 1835, OC 6:1, 293.

5 Jack Lively gives a particularly clear exposition of this conjunction. See *Social and Political Thought of Alexis Tocqueville* (Oxford: Clarendon Press, 1965), 8–10.

6 *Voyages en Angleterre*, OC 5:2, 91

7 Ibid. 92.

8 Lively, *Social and Political Thought*, 10; J.-C. Lamberti, *Tocqueville and the Two Democracies*, trans. Arthur Goldhammer (Cambridge, Mass.: Harvard University Press, 1988), 53–63.

9 For Berlin's discussion, see Isaiah Berlin, 'Two Concepts of Liberty', in *Four Essays on Liberty* (London: Oxford University Press, 1969), 118–72. Tocqueville scholars are always forced to qualify this judgement, by 'adding' elements, or by referring to Tocqueville's liberty as negative liberty on a moral basis. See e.g. Lamberti, *Two Democracies*, 62.

10 The phrase is from Berlin, 'Two Concepts', 122.

11 *État social et politique*, OC 2:1, 60. In a late letter to Mme Swetchine, Tocqueville complains of the privatizing quality of contemporary

French life. To throw this isolating individualism into relief, he quotes the advice of his grandmother to her son about living a free and honourable life under the French Old Regime. 'And then, my child, never forget that a man above all owes himself to his homeland; that there is no sacrifice that he must not be ready to make for it; that he cannot remain indifferent to its fate, and that God demands of him that he always be ready to consecrate, in case of need, his time, his fortune, and even his life to the service of the state and the king.' 10 Sept. 1856, OC 15:2, 293.

12 *État social et politique*, OC 2:1, 62.

13 Speech in Chamber of Deputies, Jan. 27, 1848, in DAII, 752.

14 *État social et politique*, OC 2:1, 62.

15 See J. T. Schleifer, *The Making of Tocqueville's 'Democracy in America'* (Chapel Hill: University of North Carolina Press, 1980) 64, quoting from George Wilson Pierson, *Tocqueville and Beaumont in America* (New York: Oxford University Press, 1938), 270–5; cf. his comments on Germans in Pennsylvania, OC 5:1, 189–90, and French in Canada, OC 5:1, 189.

16 François Furet argues that Tocqueville believes that this transformation is in some ways the true emergence of the English character, purged of its aristocratic overlay: 'Naissance d'un paradigme', 235. Thus America offers Tocqueville a crucial way to pursue the classic English/French comparison. Yet not only does Tocqueville argue that democracy has altered the American character, but also that aristocracy—rather than Englishness—explains much of the allegedly English national character. He speculates that 'the English character might well be nothing but the aristocratic character'. See Dec. 1831, Pocket notebook 3, quoted in Schleifer, *Making*, 66.

17 Melvin Richter has a useful discussion of how Tocqueville adopts and changes Montesquieu's notion of a 'level of causes', and of some of the difficulties that ensue. See 'The Uses of Theory; Tocqueville's Adaptation of Montesquieu', in M. Richter (ed.), *Essays in Theory and History* (Cambridge, Mass.: Harvard University Press, 1970), 74–104.

18 From undated drafts, quoted in Schleifer, *Making*, 68. On Tocqueville's shifting assignment of priorities to circumstances, laws, and mores, see ibid. 58–61.

19 Tocqueville indeed contradicts himself at DAI, 279 and calls its *point de départ* the most important influence on American prosperity. But in this case he is clearly thinking of the *point de départ* as containing the legacy of national character and religion, not just 'physical circumstances'.

20 Lamberti argues that the causal force of the Americans' English heritage vs. the causal force of democracy itself is the real criterion on which the distinction between Part II ('The Influence of Democracy on the Sentiments of the Americans') and Part III ('The Influence of Democracy on

Mores Properly So Called') of the second *Democracy* is based. Lamberti notes that attempts to distinguish between Tocqueville's definitions of 'sentiments' and 'mores' are therefore misleading; the real difference is in Tocqueville's attempt to maintain the space of comparison between America and France. See Lamberti, *Two Democracies*, 191–3.

21 Tocqueville to Chabrol, 7 Oct. 1831, in *Selected Letters on Politics and Society*, trans. J. Toupin and R. Boesche, ed. R. Boesche (Berkeley, Calif.: University of California Press, 1985), 59.

22 There is of course a third comparative dimension here, i.e. the trajectory of democracy in England. In the second volume of the *Democracy*, England is an increasing presence, an example of an alternative evolution of aristocracy under the pressures of democracy. When Tocqueville turns to writing the *Old Regime*, the counter-examples of England and Germany, rather than America, emerge as central. See below pp. 128–9 On the place of England in Tocqueville's thought, see Seymour Drescher, *Tocqueville and England* (Cambridge, Mass.: Harvard University Press, 1964).

23 DAI, 51. Tocqueville always was struck by the importance of changes in the law of inheritance, which he believed to be a crucial factor in the destruction of any landed aristocracy. See DAII, 456–7, 66, and *Voyages en Angleterre*, OC 5:2, 41. Many commentators have noted that the connection between inheritance laws and social equality was an *idée fixe* of Tocqueville's, though he was not consistent in his attribution of a causal connection (i.e. he said both that the abolition of the law of entail causes equality and that equality causes the abolition of the law of entail). See Schleifer, *Making*, 37; Pierson, *Tocqueville and Beaumont*, 126–8. Lively, *Social and Political Thought*, 46–7.

24 Tocqueville and Beaumont were very active in the study of slavery in the French colonies. See below, pp. 172–4.

25 The issue of whether democracy and exclusion are 'logically' linked in America, and how Tocqueville might bear on that issue, is explored in Rogers Smith, 'Beyond Tocqueville, Myrdal, and Hart: The Multiple Traditions in America', *American Political Science Review*, 87(3) (1993), 549–66. For a contrasting view, see Michael Rogin, *Fathers and Children: Andrew Jackson and the Subjugation of the American Indian* (New York: Vintage Books, 1975).

26 Compare Tocqueville's treatment of the Algerian question, which similarly envisions without undue anguish the destruction of aspirations of the native peoples in Algeria. OC 3:1, 130–418 and OC 5:2, 189–218. For particularly good discussions of the contradictions involved in Tocqueville's position here, see Melvin Richter, 'Tocqueville on Algeria', *Review of Politics*, 25 (1963), 362–98, and Michael Hereth, *Alexis de Tocqueville*, trans. George Bogardus (Durham, NC: Duke University Press, 1986), 145–65.

27 On the shifting and ambiguous meanings of democracy in Tocqueville
    see Lively, *Social and Political Thought*, 49–50; Seymour Drescher,
    Dilemmas of Democracy: Tocqueville and Modernization (Pittsburgh:
    University of Pittsburgh Press, 1968), 30–1; François Furet, 'Le système
    conceptuel de la 'Démocratie en Amérique', preface to Tocqueville, *De
    la démocratie en Amérique* (Paris: Flammarion, 1981); Lamberti, *Two
    Democracies*, 15–17; and esp. Schleifer, *Making*, 263–74.

28 Schleifer, ibid. 7, notes that the division between political and civil
    society parallels the distinction between Parts I and II of the 1835 *Dem-
    ocracy*. Yet Tocqueville hardly kept in any consistent way to this plan.
    Schleifer, ibid. 20, also notes that in a letter to Molé, Tocqueville indi-
    cated that the 1835 *Democracy* had treated democracy's influence on
    laws and political institutions, while the '*dernier développement*' (the
    1840 *Democracy*) would deal with civil society. For Tocqueville's
    statement of this division between the first and second *Democracy*, see
    DAII, 417.

29 Elster argues that Tocqueville anatomizes social life into four distinct
    spheres: family life, economic life, political life, and religious life: *Polit-
    ical Psychology* (Cambridge: Cambridge University Press, 1993), 123–4.
    I do not believe, however, that Tocqueville thought of economic life
    consistently as a separate sphere. The real tendency of his thought was
    to erode the distinction between purely economic relationships and the
    larger civil context. Religion is certainly separate, but the nature of its
    'apartness' is qualitatively different.

30 DAII, 589. He sometimes also uses the term 'natural' in this sense to
    describe those apparently spontaneous human groupings—tribes, ham-
    lets, or communes—that form the basis of all known cultures and
    spring, as it were, from the hand of God. See below, p. 171.

31 Pierson, *Tocqueville and Beaumont*, 22; Jardin, *Tocqueville*, 97.

32 See *Correspondance anglaise: Correspondance et conversations
    d'Alexis de Tocqueville et Nassau William Senior*, OC 6:2. For
    Tocqueville's views on economics, see Drescher, 'Introduction' to
    Tocqueville and Beaumont on Social Reform, ed. S. Drescher (New
    York: Harper & Row, 1968), pp. ix–xx, and Drescher, *Dilemmas*, 51–88.

33 François Furet, *Interpreting the French Revolution*, trans. E. Forster
    (Cambridge: Cambridge University Press, (1981), 151; cf. Drescher,
    'Tocqueville never felt it necessary to do more with economic institu-
    tions than to draw from them circumstantial evidence for psycho-
    logical portraits, and only insofar as they impinged on social or political
    behavior': *Dilemmas*, 66.

34 Tocqueville to Nassau Senior, 21 Feb. 1835, OC 6:2, 70.

35 *Le Commerce*, 6 Jan. 1845, quoted in Roger Boesche, 'Tocqueville
    and *Le Commerce*: A Newspaper Expressing His Unusual Liberalism',
    Journal of the History of Ideas, 44 (1983), 286.

36 See e.g. René Rémond, *Les États-Unis devant l'opinion française,
    1815–52,* 2 vols. (Paris: Armand Colin, 1962), 1:384–5, and Pierson,
    Tocqueville and Beaumont, 762–3.

37 *Memoir on Pauperism,* in Drescher, *Tocqueville and Beaumont on
    Social Reform,* 1–27.

38 Schleifer, *Making,* 83.

39 Drescher, *Dilemmas,* 54.

40 Elster, *Political Psychology,* 180–91.

41 In the following account, I shall neglect the issue of changes of emphasis
    between the two volumes of *Democracy in America,* originally brought
    into focus by Seymour Drescher in 'Tocqueville's Two Democracies',
    Journal of the History of Ideas 25(2) (1964), 201–16, and restated in
    'More than America: Comparison and Synthesis in *Democracy in
    America*' in Abraham Eisenstadt (ed.), *Reconsidering Democracy,*
    77–93. Drescher argued for a sharp disjuncture between the works
    related to empirical referents (1835, America; 1840, France) and political
    concerns at the time of composition. Beyond the different foci (political
    society in the first, civil society in the second), there are certainly differ-
    ences in level of abstraction (more concrete and tied to America in the
    first, more abstract and reflective of France in the second) as well as
    differences in the evolution and elaborations of key concepts. These
    differences in the elaboration of concepts (particularly his deepening
    variations on the themes of *individualisme* and *despotism,* and his
    fluctuating comments on the revolutionary spirit) are clearly tied to
    Tocqueville's differing political concerns at the times of composition.
    These are important matters, especially for understanding the impact of
    Tocqueville's participation in French politics on his writing. However,
    the notion of a radical break (an early and late Tocqueville) is less per-
    suasive if one stresses, as I do, the French focus of both volumes. The ideas
    in the 1840 *Democracy* almost always expand on earlier formulations.
    On the essential 'harmony of the whole', see Schleifer, *Making,* 285–6,
    and Furet, 'Naissance d'un paradigme'. In 'harmonizing' the materials
    from the two *Democracies,* of course, I run the risk of obscuring many
    differences of emphasis between the works. At certain points, I have
    called attention to these differences, but more often I set them aside.

42 There is a large secondary literature on the subject of democratic des-
    potism in Tocqueville. See esp. a series of articles by Melvin Richter,
    who has shown that, whatever Tocqueville's changes of emphasis, he
    did not abandon a central preoccupation with Bonapartism. See esp.
    'Tocqueville, Napoleon, and Bonapartism', in Eisenstadt, *Reconsidering
    Tocqueville's Democracy,* 110–45; 'Toward a Concept of Political
    Illegitimacy', *Political Theory,* 10 (1982), 185–214; and 'Tocqueville and
    French Nineteenth-Century Conceptualizations of the Two Bonapartes
    and their Empires', paper delivered at the International Meeting of the

Conference for the Study of Political Thought (Hunter College, New York, Apr. 1999).

43 Tocqueville also notes an opposing tendency. The uncertainties of life in the market lead to a need for compensatory stability: in political life, in religion, and in family life. See pp. 98–9, 197–8.

44 DAI, 198; cf. DAII, 536–8, a passage recalling Hobbes's famous depiction of life as a race ceasing only in death, or DAII, 531: 'They are therefore continually engaged in pursuing or striving to retain these precious, incomplete, and fugitive delights.' On this aspect of Tocqueville's argument, see Joshua Mitchell, *The Fragility of Freedom: Tocqueville on Religion, Democracy, and the American Future* (Chicago: University of Chicago Press, 1995), 40–101.

45 DAII, 540; cf. DAI, 213, 243, and DAII, 671: 'in our time a secret force constantly fosters [such narrowing inclinations] in the human heart, and if they are simply left unchecked, they will fill it all.'

46 The individualism of the second *Democracy* is an evolution of the notion of democratic egoism in the first. On the relationship between these two concepts, see Schleifer, *Making*, 232–59.

47 Tocqueville notes that Americans are more likely to go mad; the French to commit suicide. Americans are kept from suicide by the influence of Christianity, but even so, 'forms of religious madness are very common there' (DAII, 534).

48 *Voyages en Angleterre*, OC 5:2, 77.

49 Ibid. 83.

50 See e.g. DAI, 258, where he praises the 'virile candor and manly independence of thought' of American leaders of an earlier generation.

51 Tocqueville's focus on the difficulties of incorporating executive power within an effective system of checks and balances has continued to find contemporary readers. See e.g. Lilia Shevtsova on the difficulty of institutionalizing executive authority in 'third-wave' democracies, a discussion that takes its bearings from Tocqueville's analysis of the American presidency: 'The Problem of Executive Power in Russia', *Journal of Democracy*, 11(1) (2000), 32–9.

52 DAI, 195; Cf. DAII, 668: 'I admire the way [equality] insinuates deep into the heart and mind of every man some vague notion and some instinctive inclination towards political freedom, thereby preparing the antidote for the ill which it has produced.'

53 Other arguments that take the form of more democracy curing the ills of democracy are his position on women and the democratic family and his arguments about widespread property rights. See below, Chap. 4, pp. 187–207.

54 Lamberti, *Two Democracies*, 179, comments: 'Tocqueville was thus led to rediscover one of the key ideas of the Idéologues, inherited from

Condorcet himself.' For a comparison between Montesquieu's idea of the 'principle' of a republic and Tocqueville's notion of interest rightly understood, see Melvin Richter, 'The Uses of Theory': Tocqueville's Adaption of Montesquieu' in Richter (ed.), *Essays in Theory and History: An Approach to the Social Sciences* (Cambridge, Mass.: Harvard University Press, 1970), 93–7.

55 Tocqueville also notes that Americans form associations so readily because of their English inheritance. However, they have taken this technique far beyond its roots because it is consonant with democratic instincts: DAI, 514. On associations in England, see *Voyages en Angleterre*, OC 5:2, 59–60.

56 DAI, 193–4. Tocqueville compares the internal organization of political sects in Europe, which mimic military hierarchy, with the internal organization of associations and parties in America, which mimic republican government.

57 DAII, 289. Tocqueville does not consider Madisonian arguments about Protestantism being less dangerous to democracy because multiple sects tend to cancel each other out and to lessen the threat of establishment. He also does not extensively consider the affinity between congregational forms of self-government in Protestantism and in politics, except briefly in the case of Puritanism. Conversely, Tocqueville's notes from his *Journeys to England and Ireland* are filled with speculations about Catholicism's affinity with notions of popular independence in Ireland, and discussions of the elements of democracy within the Irish church. He emphasizes the opposition of the Irish clergy to close ties between church and state, the simplicity of their forms of worship, their endorsement of popular education and freedom of the press, and their closeness to the common people: OC 5:2, 112, 122–3, 135, 143, 149–50.

58 Joshua Mitchell has an interesting discussion of Tocqueville's use of Christianity to elucidate the paradox of 'rightful obedience': *The Fragility of Freedom: Tocqueville on Religion, Democracy, and the American Future* (Chicago: University of Chicago Press, 1995), 194. He also notes that the need for stable limits that religion satisfies may be answered less well by Protestantism, which exacerbates the contrary tendency towards universality (217). In Tocqueville's very first references to religion in the first volume of *Democracy in America*, he illustrates what I have called the compensatory argument for religion in the context of Puritanism. Because of the influence of Puritanism, two 'tendencies' show their 'traces': 'In the moral world everything is classified, coordinated, foreseen, and decided in advance. In the world of politics everything is in turmoil, contested, and uncertain. In the one case obedience is passive, though voluntary; in the other there is independence, contempt of experience, and jealousy of all authority' (DAI, 47). But this favourable inherited 'moral capital' is being extinguished as Protestantism fuses with modern democratic tendencies.

59 DAII, 445. One of the reasons Tocqueville thought Islam incompatible with democracy and enlightenment was its inability, in his view, to separate the religious from the political and civil spheres. See his notes on the Koran, OC 3:1, 154–63. But his travels in Canada and in Ireland during the gestation period of *Democracy in America* reveal an obsession with the liberation of an active pastoral (and patriotic) role for priests, once they are completely disassociated from any official role in a polity. *Voyage en Angleterre*, OC 5:2, 109, 149–50. He also focuses, especially in Ireland, on the unusual spectacle of priests encouraging 'enlightenment' and on the false association between ignorance and mass religiosity. OC 5:2, 143.

60 See e.g. Raymond Aron, *Main Currents in Sociological Thought*, 2 vols., trans. Richard Howard and Helen Weaver (New York: Doubleday Anchor, 1968), 1, 279; Poggi, *Images*, 4; Pierre Birnbaum, *Sociologie de Tocqueville* (Paris: Presses Universitaires de France, 1970), 29–39; Robert Nisbet, 'Tocqueville's Ideal Types', in Eisenstadt, *Reconsidering*, 186–91; Melvin Richter, 'Comparative Political Analysis in Montesquieu and Tocqueville', *Comparative Politics*, 1(2) (1969), 153–7; Schleifer, *Making*, 271–2; Larry Siedentop, *Tocqueville* (Oxford: Oxford University Press, 1994), 142–3; Irving M. Zeitlin, *Liberty, Equality and Revolution in Alexis de Tocqueville* (Boston: Little, Brown, 1971), 14.

61 Tocqueville to J. S. Mill, 18 Dec. 1840, OC 6:1, 330.

62 On Tocqueville's use of the comparative method, see Richter, 'Comparative Political Analysis'.

63 Birnbaum, *Sociologie de Tocqueville*, 38–39.

64 'De Tocqueville on Democracy in America [II] 1840', in *Collected Works*, xviii: *Essays on Politics and Society* (Toronto: University of Toronto Press, 1977), 191–200.

65 James Schleifer notes that a comparison of Tocqueville and the modern French *Annales* school 'presents another fascinating set of parallels and dichotomies': 'Tocqueville as Historian', in Eisenstadt, *Reconsidering*, 164. He gives a very brief comparison that differs in some respects from the one presented here.

66 See the useful characterization of the distinctive features of the history of mentalities in Peter Burke, 'Strengths and Weaknesses of the History of Mentalities', in *Varieties of Cultural History* (Ithaca, NY, Cornell University Press, 1997), 162. See also Roger Chartier, 'Intellectual History and the History of *Mentalités*', in *Cultural History*, trans. Lydia B. Cochrane (Ithaca, NY: Cornell University Press, 1988), 19–52.

67 See ibid. 19–52.

68 For a discussion of this ironical construction as the common ground linking diverse theorists of *mentalités*, see Patrick H. Hutton, 'The History of Mentalities: The New Map of Cultural History', *History and Theory*, 20(3) (1981), 237–59.

69 *État social et politique*, OC 2:1, 65.

70 The real analogue—though very weak and hardly amounting to a revolutionary spirit—of France's Revolution in America was the brief period in which political majorities were flexing their muscles and the changes in inheritance laws were rapidly eradicating the vestigial remains of aristocratic English influence and transforming Americans into a 'thoroughly' democratic state. The Jacksonian 'revolution' was a sort of political consolidation of equality that already existed. But it was hardly a great revolution in the European sense, for there was so little to overcome. On the idea of revolution in Tocqueville, see Melvin Richter, 'Tocqueville's Contributions to the Study of Revolution', in *NOMOS VIII: Revolution* (New York: Atherton Press, 1966), 75–121; Lamberti, *Two Democracies*, 191–208; Zeitlin, *Liberty, Equality, and Revolution*, 95–162.

71 Hence his observation that any revolution in America will be linked to the situation of blacks. For the rhetorical purposes of this chapter contra Guizot, see Lamberti, *Two Democracies*, 197–203.

72 This change of opinion can be followed in his letters. See e.g. Tocqueville to Corcelle, 26 Sept. 1840, OC 15:1, 147–52, and Tocqueville to Eugene Stoffels, 28 Apr. 1850, OC, B5, 460–2. See also Edward Gargan, *Alexis de Tocqueville: The Critical Years, 1848–1851* (Washington, DC: Catholic University of America Press, 1955), 181, 188.

3

French Democracy:
The Natural Destiny
of a People

Two decades separate the publication of *The Old Regime and the Revolution* (1856) from the first volume of the *Democracy* (1835). In those years the puzzle of democratic America retreated in Tocqueville's consciousness—though it never entirely disappeared— to be replaced by an intense practical engagement with the political fate of France.[1] Only when the Second Empire abruptly ended his political career did Tocqueville again take up the threads of his scholarly work. As early as 1841, however, he seemed to have had in mind a new project that would focus directly on the coming of democracy in France and on the true significance of its Revolution.[2] And when he turned to this task in earnest he began at precisely the point at which he had concluded the second *Democracy*, i.e. with the question of why democratic France—unlike America—had developed a profound attachment to centralization, and why a violent but sterile revolutionary spirit had come to plague every attempt to break this attachment, thus apparently dooming France to a permanent oscillation between administrative domination and political chaos.

French Democracy's Point de Départ

In *Democracy in America* Tocqueville had first attempted to establish the Anglo-Americans' distinctive *point de départ* (geography, national character, inherited institutions, and religion) in order better to isolate the tendencies of democracy itself. He argued both that a particular democratic *mentalité* had come to dominate the United States, and that this collective mentality had transnational significance. To sort out the effects of democracy 'itself' from those causes peculiar to America was precisely the theoretical point of his American project. When he turned directly to a study of the making of democratic France, he similarly began from France's distinctive *point de départ*. Unlike America—or indeed France's European neighbours—the French struggled with the legacies of intense administrative centralization and a unique revolutionary tradition. Yet Tocqueville's theoretical intentions with regard to these circumstances were now different. Far from setting aside France's peculiarities in order to reveal democracy in general, he put these particular historical circumstances at the centre of his inquiry. Not democracy 'itself' but France was his subject. Her unique confrontation with democracy oriented his research, guided his comparative method, and ultimately structured his explanation. How had France's most important national characteristics—a powerful administrative machine and a singular defiance of its constraints—shaped and been shaped by the forces of democracy to create the political culture of contemporary France? Tocqueville's France had inherited both centralization and revolution. He explicitly took on the task of revealing the intricate elective affinities of these variables with democracy and with each other, of tracing their twining into a distinctive pattern of norms and structures that constricted the ways in which the French could shape their destiny.

Napoleon and the Destiny of France

Tocqueville's first impulse—later abandoned—was to write a book on the key historical period in which centralization, revolution, and democracy had consorted openly in French history for the first time: the Consulate and Empire of Napoleon Bonaparte.[3] His 1842 address to the Académie Française sketching the history of the First Empire already focused on his belief that centralization had come to dominate post-revolutionary France precisely because that society was more thoroughly democratic, and democratic societies offered less resistance to centralizing governments than did aristocratic ones. Napoleon, Tocqueville believed, stood at a fateful crossroads on this journey towards an administered society. His regime decisively resolved the unstable political equilibrium that had plagued the last years of the monarchy and the revolutionary decade. The new Napoleonic equilibrium, however, was not republican democracy, but rather 'the despotism of one man constructed on a democratic foundation'.[4] Tocqueville in fact produced two chapters on this period, entitled 'How the Republic Was Ready to Receive a Master' and 'How the Nation in Ceasing to Be Republican Remained Revolutionary' before shelving the project in favour of a more careful study of the prelude to the Revolution. But he still intended to conclude his work on the significance of the Revolution with a volume on the Empire, for it was during this period that the French had fully enacted a new and sinister drama in modern French political culture for the first time.

Tocqueville was originally drawn to a study of Napoleon not only because he believed that a focus on the Empire would allow him to dramatize the profound mutual attractions that existed among democracy, centralization, and revolution in France, but also because the effects of Napoleon's leadership fascinated and repelled him. Identifying opportunities for human intervention and choice that would move France towards a free democracy was the very point of his life and scholarship. Although Napoleon had ushered in a despotic form of democratic equilibrium, Tocqueville refused to believe that this was an inevitable development, even in France. He speculated that the period of the Directory could have paralleled the period of leadership and consolidation in America subsequently known as the founding, a crucial era in which—so Tocqueville believed—American leaders had acted decisively to mould political *mœurs* in order to promote liberty under the new democratic republic. Hence Napoleon's emergence from the 'anarchic' phase of the Revolution was an event of great significance. Unlike his nephew fifty years later, Napoleon had both the historical opportunity and the personal genius to attempt a republican founding. Though the French were weary and demoralized under the Directory, their very vulnerability and disarray left them open to inspired leadership. The charismatic Napoleon might have broken, or at least begun to dismantle, the patterns of administrative centralization that had come to structure French political society and he could thus have altered its destiny.[5] That Napoleon pursued exactly the opposite course was a national tragedy. Though Tocqueville praised his 'personal grandeur' and judged him 'the most extraordinary being ... who has appeared in the world for many centuries', this grandeur was a species of evil genius.[6]

Napoleon's diabolical accomplishment was to perceive the deep compatibility between the dogma of popular sovereignty and despotism, and to act decisively on this intuition. He took over and perfected the machinery of the central state and made a sham of representative government while accommodating the democratic passion for civil equality that was the lasting legacy of the Revolution. 'His powerful intelligence saw that his contemporaries were closer to subjection than they themselves realized, and that it was hardly folly to aspire to a new throne and a new dynasty.'[7] Upon the tabula rasa of a traumatized society, Napoleon was able to build his despotism far more rationally and skillfully than anyone had dared to do before him. 'After having uniformly promulgated all the laws regulating the relations of citizens among themselves and with the state, he was able at the same time to create all the powers charged with executing those laws and to assemble the whole into a vast but simple machine of government. He alone was its motor.'[8]

Not only did the emperor directly eviscerate liberal institutions, but he indirectly fostered an assault on the norms of citizenship by enshrining the worst individualistic and privatistic tendencies of the bourgeoisie in the Civil Code. In this complaint Tocqueville echoes the social economists, who believed that the laws of property and labour in the new Civil Code established a barren individualism that destroyed old methods of public cooperation without putting anything new in their place. On Tocqueville's account, one of the greatest potential weaknesses of democratic societies was the economic self-interest that drew citizens away from public life. Perfectly aware of this vice and its consequences, Napoleon deliberately manipulated the legal consolidation of the Revolution in a privatistic direction.

Tocqueville, then, initially thought to begin his work on modern French history by investigating the link between centralization and democracy as it had emerged from the revolutionary period and had been forged anew in the Empire. A preliminary sketch of administrative centralization under France's kings would be little more than a long introduction to a work on this theme. Yet sometime in 1853 or

1854 this introductory sketch took on a life of its own. We do not know exactly why Tocqueville changed his mind. But it had something to do with his growing sense—stronger the more he delved into the archives of eighteenth-century France—that he could explore the fateful connection between centralization and democracy with more originality and power by concentrating on France's *point de départ* than on her subsequent ports of call.[9] Indeed, his reading of administrative records suggested that the most salient characteristic of French politics in the nineteenth century— its oscillation between despotism and defiance—was born before the Revolution. Moreover, focusing on this earlier period, like his original notion of beginning with the Revolution's dénouement in Napoleon, still allowed him to put off the difficult task of integrating into his account the particular course and development of the French Revolution itself. His first plan had been to highlight the marriage of centralization and democracy and their unfortunate progeny, rather than to consider the officiating presence of the Revolution itself. His second, which he carried out in *The Old Regime and the Revolution*, was to investigate the courtship of centralization and democracy under the monarchy. In *The Old Regime*, he in fact stops short of considering the Revolution itself, bringing his readers to the brink of conflict without leading them into the abyss. I do not believe this avoidance was accidental, for Tocqueville found the Revolution a country peopled by strangers whose mentality was in some ways more foreign than that of the Americans.

Themes of The Old Regime and the Revolution

The virtues that impressed its original reviewers—freshness, originality, and the ability to express 'many thoughts in few words' — continue to strike the contemporary reader of the *L'Ancien Régime et la Révolution*.[10] It is not a work of narrative history, but rather a philosophical and sociological essay that throws into relief both a vision of the political psychology of Tocqueville's time and the roots of this psychology in pre-revolutionary France. Tocqueville's first innovation was the concept of the *ancien régime* itself. Unlike most of his contemporaries, he did not use the term to refer to an undifferentiated pre-revolutionary constitution or to a nostalgically idealized time before the 'troubles'. Rather, he used it to describe a drastic transformation of feudal France that had occurred during the final 150 years of the French monarchy, a transformation in which the prejudices, habits, and passions that dominated his own time were born. A seminal period of deep disturbance and transition, Tocqueville's Old Regime was of interest not because it represented a lost past, but because it contained within it all that was most important to his own time. The theme of *The Old Regime*—announced immediately in the forward and sketched in Part I—is deceptively simple. Tocqueville argues that the apparent disruption of the revolutionary period masks a profound continuity in French history; the changes effected during the period of royal absolutism—changes unintended and largely unrecognized at the time—were to emerge after the Revolution as the defining characteristics of the 'new France'.

According to Tocqueville, when the men of '89 had overthrown the ancient political edifice, they revealed the foundations of an even more powerful state structure, a foundation that 'had been laid immutably in the minds of all Frenchmen, even its destroyers' during the Old Regime itself (AR, 72). Habits and customs that had provided the life of the feudal monarchy were in fact defunct long before the Revolution. What had displaced them was a new and at first unrecognized set of *mœurs*: egalitarian and highly susceptible to despotism. Like a river, this new French *mentalité*—'the ways men thought and felt, their habits and their prejudices'—went underground in the early years of the Revolution, when there was a mania to destroy everything. But the river re-emerged afterwards, 'ready to carry all before it' (AR, 20). During the Old Regime, in Tocqueville's account, France had already become a democratic society fuelled by egalitarian passions, but these passions were still embedded in an anachronistic set of inegalitarian civil and political forms. To paraphrase Marx, it was inevitable that this inegalitarian integument would be burst asunder. The meaning of the revolutionary movement, then, even as it continued into Tocqueville's own time, was to excise from the body politic 'a host of ideas, sentiments, manners, and customs which, so to speak, adhered to [the old feudal institutions]' and were inconsistent with the new democratic spirit (AR, 20).

Insofar as there was an identifiable agent of change in France's transformation into a democratic nation, it was the monarchy of the Bourbons. Kings pursued a relentless—if incomplete—process of centralizing their power and thereby effected a secret metamorphosis in

French *mœurs*. They undermined the social hierarchy even as they left its outward trappings intact. The very people most responsible for destroying the patterns of social cooperation characteristic of feudal aristocracy temporarily avoided the consequences of this policy by regulating everything themselves. Royal ministers progressively administered alongside, above, and beneath older aristocratic institutions in order to hold together the separate elements of a France that was more and more fragmented in social condition. Administrative centralization during the Old Regime, in this account, lay at the heart of France's modern predicament. As the French became more equal, they developed habits of dependence and servility that would doom the Revolution's attempts to create liberty.

For Tocqueville, equality and indifference to the public business had a potentially fatal mutual attraction. In democratic times, Tocqueville argued in *Democracy in America* and reiterated in the introduction to *The Old Regime,* 'people are far too much disposed to think exclusively of their own interests, to become self-seekers practicing a narrow individualism and caring nothing for the public good' (AR, p. xiii). The policies of generations of kings ensured that this potential connection between equality and apathy would become a reality in France, for monarchs and their ministers actively deprived the people of the only possible antidote to democratic individualism: self-government. Tocqueville announces from the beginning, then, the tragic implications of *The Old Regime and the Revolution*. The most important casualty of France's unique path towards democracy was liberty. Tocqueville's penetrating examination of that singular path, with its dual focus on an increasingly administered society and a secret equality that dared not speak its name, remains a model for those who reflect on the problems of constructing a democratic politics in the face of a hostile history.

An Administered Society

Tocqueville begins Part II of *The Old Regime* with a snapshot of the peculiar status of feudalism in eighteenth-century France: politically defunct, morally bankrupt, yet socially entrenched within an administered society. But it should be said at the outset that the historical origins of European feudalism's decline, and the ultimate cause of the rise both of kings and of social equality, remain obscure to Tocqueville and to the reader. He does not seriously try to pinpoint the beginning of this process, since it is not part of his plan 'to trace the gradual decline of this ancient constitution of Europe' (AR, 16). Indeed, for much of the work he simply takes the progressive evisceration of feudalism as a given. Tocqueville's intention was not to question fate, but to trace the *particular* trajectory of this providential process in France: first, the rapid and accelerating growth of royal power; and second, the unusually quick disintegration of the institutions, norms, and customs associated with a functioning aristocracy. These developments together cause the levelling and isolation of classes, and eventually, a revolutionary crisis. To bring out this unique process of development, Tocqueville instinctively reaches for a comparative case: a country that is similar to France, in that it is also subject to the general cause of feudal dissolution, but sufficiently distinct to allow him to pinpoint key differences.

The important comparative case for clarifying America's *point de départ* was England, since Tocqueville wished to hold constant America's Englishness in order to isolate its allegedly new democratic character. Tocqueville knew more about England and its history than about any European society other than France; moreover, he had for years thought comparatively about English and French social and political development. Indeed, England's historical development plays an important role in *The Old Regime*; it points out to the reader the 'road not taken', and functions—much as America did in *Democracy*—as a source of morality lessons for French readers.

Tocqueville soon decided, however, that the example of England could not clarify France's *point de départ*. He needed a country that was subject to the same general cause (the dissolution of feudalism and a transition to a democratic social state) but was relatively free of France's unique circumstances. England did not meet the first test: she was not subject in the same way as France either to the 'normal' European experience of feudalism or to its decline. On the contrary, England was exceptional by virtue of the Norman conquest, the fusion of Norman feudalism and Saxon institutions, and, most important, the evolution of a caste nobility into a functioning aristocracy. England's nobility, in a choice of inestimable significance, had declined to decline. Creating common cause with elements of the middle classes against the crown, the English nobility, in Tocqueville's view, had salvaged key elements of feudal traditions of liberty and self-rule. Hence, even though England had experienced the centralizing push of its monarchy, the rise of the middle classes, and the spread of social wealth, it had escaped a pattern of aristocratic decline more common on the Continent.[11] England's relative political decentralization and its lack of a revolutionary tradition were closely tied to this exceptional development. Tocqueville's view of English history thus echoed the themes of English Whig historiography, without unduly sentimentalizing England's providential escape from continental corruption.[12]

If England was too different to serve as a useful foil in illuminating the unique historical interplay among democracy, centralization, and revolution that formed the core of Tocqueville's study of France, Germany provided a better comparative case. Similar in both feudal traditions and their decline, Germany nevertheless lacked an indigenous revolutionary tradition. Thus it might serve to throw into relief the factors that had set France on its particular democratic course. Whereas during the writing of *Democracy* Tocqueville went to aristocratic England to check his perceptions about the birth of democracy in the Anglo-American colonies, in his work on the Old Regime he visited Germany to improve his comparative understanding of the death throes of feudalism. What especially interested him were the interaction in Germany between a fading feudal inheritance and a new administrative bureaucracy, the lack of an indigenous revolutionary tradition, and the reaction to French political developments.[13] Tocqueville's relatively imperfect mastery of German and the briefness of his stay (cut short by his wife's ill health) limited the usefulness of this visit, but he nevertheless frequently employed German examples to clarify and set apart France's social and political distinctiveness in the final years of the monarchy.

The decaying feudal order that Tocqueville describes is filled with complex conflicts of interest. From the dissolution of feudal ties emerge squabbling subjects nursing secret grievances, haughtily guarding caste privileges, or jealously policing petty distinctions. Set against this picture of distrust and division, however, is a series of contrasting images of unity: the glittering dominance of one capital city, a powerfully unified chain of bureaucratic command (from *conseil du roi*, to *controller-général*, to *intendant*) and an efficient exceptional court system that usurped the faltering functions of older local courts. Indeed, the tentacles of an increasingly centralized and powerful monarchy reach everywhere; the French monarchy 'had taken to playing the part of an indefatigable mentor and keeping the nation in quasi-paternal tutelage' (AR, 41). At the heart of *The Old Regime* is the spectre of an administration inexorably arrogating authority and power to itself, a process that is by Tocqueville's definition the very obverse of freedom.

How can this centralization be explained? On the one hand, Tocqueville assumes that kings wish to increase their power and influence by the very nature of things. There is an 'instinctive desire of every government to gather all the reins of power into its own hands' (AR, 58). On the other hand, this natural penchant towards expansion does not explain why European monarchies managed (with varying degrees of success) to subvert older constitutional forms at roughly the same time in early modern Europe, and explains even less the unusually rapid success of centralization in France. After all there is also a 'natural' wish on the part of the people to retain independence. 'Left to itself, the people would probably prefer an assembly or elected magistrate, rather than a king.'[14] Tocqueville dismisses the idea that a series of accidental causes in each European country could have simultaneously caused the rise of kings. Such a general phenomenon must have a 'general' cause. At times he speculates that the revival of Roman law might be such a cause. The law of a highly civilized but 'enslaved' Roman Empire was available to centralizing monarchs everywhere, and they invariably made use of it.[15] Tocqueville eventually decides, however, that it is the success of kings that explains the triumph of Roman law, rather than the spread of Roman law that accounts for the victory of kings (AR, 222–3).

In the last analysis, Tocqueville offers no satisfactory historical account of the rise of royal absolutism. He merely derives a 'general' explanation from the 'general' premiss of his work, namely the historical shift from aristocracy to democracy. The success of European kings, Tocqueville tells us in a formulation reminiscent of Guizot, was simply a by-product of the coming of democracy, a temporary artefact in the steady, but uneven development of equal social conditions. The underlying cause of absolutism was simply

the transition from one social state to another, from feudal inequality to democratic equality. The nobility was prostrate; the people had not yet risen up; the one was too low, the other not high enough to embarrass the movements of the supreme power. For a period of 150 years kings enjoyed a golden age. They were all-powerful, and their thrones were stable, advantages usually inconsistent with each other. They were as sacred as the hereditary chiefs of a feudal monarchy, and as absolute as the masters of a democracy.[16]

As in the *Democracy*, the coming of equality and the death of his own class exist as providential forces, of which monarchs are both the witting and unwitting agents. France, then, was not alone in having a monarchy that successfully consolidated its authority. European social equality brought absolutism in its wake. Unique, however, was the rapidity of the French monarchy's rise and fall. In *The Old Regime and the Revolution*, Tocqueville analyses the factors associated with this meteoric trajectory: the acceleration and institutionalization of the royal bureaucracy, the lack of resistance on the part of French civil society, the cumulative and unintended consequences of such events for French political culture, and, finally, the monarchy's radical misapprehension of the bases of its own power and its spectacular revolutionary demise. These factors provide the logical structure of Tocqueville's book; they structure this chapter as well.

Noble Failures and Bourgeois Weakness

The adroitness and patience of a long line of monarchs and royal ministers, who moved gradually but steadily to centralize both authority and power in their own hands, were crowned with unimaginable success. Yet they did not set out deliberately to deprive France of liberty or to destroy the bases of aristocracy. Each individual encroachment had particular short-term goals, almost always the desire to raise money. Nevertheless, the cumulative effect was greater than anyone could have predicted. A series of claims by the monarchy to exercise alone what had previously been jointly shared responsibilities with local estates, and a simultaneous string of surrenders by nobles and commoners to those usurpations, sealed the fate of France. In a statement reminiscent of Rousseau's rhetorical claim that the first person to erect a fence around his land had subverted human freedom, Tocqueville exclaims,

It was on the day when the French people, weary of the chaos into which the kingdom had been plunged for so many years by the captivity of King John and the madness of Charles VI, permitted the King to impose a tax without their consent and the nobles showed so little public spirit as to connive at this, provided their own immunity was guaranteed—it was on that fateful day that the seeds were sown of almost all the vices and abuses which led to the violent downfall of the Old Regime. (AR, 99)

131

That 'fateful' day brought together the monarchy's willingness to subvert the ancient constitution for financial expedience, the nobility's withdrawal into sterile caste privilege, and the weary middle class's preference for prosperity and order over freedom: a conjunction of tendencies that colluded in the creation of a society that was administered rather than governed.

At the heart of Tocqueville's portrait of the ancient feudal nobility was a romanticized vision of independence, honour, and responsibility, the qualities that most inform Tocqueville's understanding of the 'free man'. Perhaps for this reason he judges the French nobility especially harshly for their historical submission to kings and their withdrawal into caste privilege. He does not blame them for the underlying erosion of their economic and social base. The rise of equality (and its obverse, the fall of legalized inequality) were beyond their control and not peculiar to France. In all parts of the Continent where the feudal system was in the process of dying out without being replaced by a new form of aristocracy, the nobility found themselves progressively impoverished. In German territory, along the Rhine, 'the decadence of the indigenous nobility was particularly marked and attracted much attention' (AR, 80). Tocqueville reports that a man of gentle birth, writing in 1755, laments: 'Despite its privileges, the nobility is being starved out, and all its wealth passing into the hands of the Third Estate' (AR, 78). Tocqueville charges the nobility not with the decline of feudalism, which no one could prevent, but with the short-sighted indulgence of feelings of caste honour and a willingness to trade practical influence in the countryside—over their peasants and over the bourgeois of the towns—for a ceremonial role in the monarchy. Worn out by private wars, the nobles let down their guard against the encroaching prerogative of kings and let their liberties slip away without ever taking an intelligent stand against the centralizing power.

The middle classes, according to Tocqueville, made a similar Faustian bargain for which future generations of French citizens would pay dearly. At one time they had cooperated with the nobility to rule the countryside, exercising real power in the cities, on the manor, and in the general assemblies. But the middle classes eventually gave up their aspirations for self-rule. At the end of the seventeenth century kings began the practice of selling 'to certain members of the community the right of governing in perpetuity their fellow citizens' (AR, 42). These expedients for raising money displayed 'well-nigh diabolical ingenuity' (AR, 100). Tocqueville, we should recall, believed that freedom and equality have a certain affinity. Thus, as the French became more equal in social condition, they also developed an increasing taste for independence and self-rule. The desire for independence, moreover, would have been further stimulated by spillover effects from the bustle and energy of commerce. Inclinations towards freedom, however, are not proof against systematic countermeasures. The monarchy manipulated the desire of the towns for independence by revoking the charters guaranteeing them local autonomy in order to sell back these very charters, sometimes revoking them again at a later time in order to resell them yet again. Eventually, of course, a town ceased to desire independence, gave up its claims, and permitted itself to be ruled by royal bureaucrats. Indeed, individual members of the bourgeoisie made alternate careers in the central bureaucracy and rapidly developed an insatiable appetite for such offices. The monarchy created new offices specifically for sale to these ambitious bourgeois, thereby assuring a steadier flow of cash. In the end, the struggle against the central powers exhausted and strangled the impulse to freedom associated with growing equality, and the middle classes succumbed to being administered.

If the nobility and bourgeoisie did not realize what these habits of dependence would mean for the future, neither did kings foresee the unintended consequences of their efforts to weaken or destroy provincial freedoms. In their short-term successes, the king's ministers were actually digging the grave of the monarchy itself, since they were destroying the allies they would later need to save it. In a long appendix on the exceptional case of Languedoc, which retained a version of local self-rule, Tocqueville works out a domestic counterexample that he believes might have served as a model for constitutionalizing the French monarchy and adapting local assemblies to a modern version of limited government and democratic freedoms. But '[u]nhappily our Kings' one desire was to keep power in their own hands at all costs and they turned a blind eye to the needs of modern civilization' (AR, 221). By accustoming people to constant changes in the personnel and organization of the bodies that ruled them, and by inuring them to governmental bad faith and arbitrariness, the monarchy assured both its own demise and its replacement by something worse. The result of short-term royal success in eviscerating local government was a system of degenerate petty oligarchies dependent on government initiative. In the long term, however, these apparently successful royal subversions contributed to those petty oligarchies' willingness to support a lawless revolution. Taught by kings, the French were ready to accept the arbitrary and lawless actions of revolutionary assemblies without any sense of outrage, and eventually to acquiesce in the even worse despotism of Napoleon.

The assumption of day-to-day administrative power over local affairs also had unexpected effects on the monarchy itself, increasing its taste for despotism and its inability to effect real reform. Surveillance—a new and ominous term—became compulsive and almost second nature, even when its use was self-defeating. Tocqueville notes that the monarchy did not necessarily always use its power unwisely or malevolently; indeed, it was sometimes efficient and often well-intentioned. But the compulsion to oversee everything prevented monarchs and their ministers from recognizing the need to undertake long-term reform. They did not understand until it was too late that they required intelligent cooperation from key members of civil society to save the monarchy. The shared notion of caste honour by which they had conciliated the nobility eventually proved a fatal stumbling-block to any reasonable scheme of cooperative reform. Irrationally based in notions of blood purity, such feelings proved impervious to rational argument. Thus the monarchy had inadvertently helped to kill off the personal influences and political contacts that alone could support joint action. 'And, preposterously enough, it often showed surprise on discovering that those very people whom it had, itself, deprived of life were dead' (AR, 132). Ironically, the loyalty of the nobility to the crown—however foolishly based in illusory caste honour—would survive a revolutionary reversal of the king's fortunes. But Tocqueville argues that the middle class's long-standing alliance with royalty proved to be highly conditional and tied to the main chance. When the monarchy failed to deliver financial and administrative reform, the middle class deserted it without compunction.

Tocqueville marvels that the legitimacy of the monarchy, which in retrospect seems to him so fragile, could have been treated so recklessly. Both autocratic and lax, at once antagonistic to their subjects and tolerant of a disrespect for authority that their pride refused to take seriously, French kings had a blind confidence in their authority. Like Lear, they did not feel the need to consult the opinion of their children and could not even imagine rebellion against patriarchy. Royal indifference to the effects of a regime that mixed arbitrary severity with fitful indulgence would be fatal.

Civil Society in the Old Regime

If the monarchy's drive to centralize its power, and the lack of resistance on the part of nobles and bourgeois, dissolved the glue that had held aristocratic France together, how did the now separate social elements of the Old Regime interact? Tocqueville describes a complicated society that was ultimately unstable because 'ill-adjusted'. Yet his description of the irregular set of social and political attitudes and behaviours that characterized France in the last century of the monarchy has its own compelling logic. It is a story of growing divisions among classes, and of the gradual and unnoticed formation of a new and equal individual within those classes. Unbeknownst to its inhabitants, Old Regime civil society was being encoded with patterns of distrust and exclusion that would outlive the Old Regime itself.

A Pariah Class

The peasantry or the 'people' has a special place in this analysis, literally outside or beneath Old Regime civil society. By the 1830s and 1840s most French writers on social and political affairs were using the term 'people' to mean workers, artisans, and peasants, as distinct from the middle and upper classes. In *The Old Regime* Tocqueville generally follows this usage, distinguishing clearly between the common people living in the rural countryside and those 'who ranked above the common herd' (AR, 81).[17] It is the latter who experienced a growing equality and similarity of social condition. The 'common herd', on the other hand, underwent a peculiar debasement. This degradation was the ironic fruit of increased independence, for the French peasantry was freer than its counterparts elsewhere on the Continent in that it could technically own the land that it worked. In his 1836 sketch of French history Tocqueville had already argued that, because of the breakup of feudal estates, many French peasants had become landowners before the Revolution. A multitude of domains of feudal origin had gone out of the hands of the nobility by 1789, and much other land had also been subdivided. Hence, the number of those with a middling fortune was increasing in a great number of provinces. The phenomenon of the division of land into small properties always remained crucial to Tocqueville's definition of democracy. Such division promoted equality and broke up the ideas and special habits associated with aristocracy, which depended on the influence and power of concentrated wealth rooted in a specific locale. The Revolution generalized this trend of land subdivision and the dissipation of aristocratic influence to all areas of France, Tocqueville argued, but it did not initiate it.[18]

In *The Old Regime* Tocqueville expands on this argument about the subdivision of feudal lands by analysing its effects on the peasantry. Long emancipated from literal serfdom, the peasants in the last 150 years of the monarchy were also freed from the control and influence of the lord, even as they struggled to secure their small holdings. By the end of the eighteenth century, the nobility had no say in parish councils and exercised feudal rights only to raise money, not to rule their people. Indeed, the people no longer 'belonged' to the nobility, but did not yet belong to themselves. They existed in a vulnerable netherworld, with no power to evade the financial and military demands of the other classes or of the state, but also with no way of making common cause with others. Paradoxically, the French peasant's emancipation from day-to-day control by the lord caused the levies, taxes, and duties of forced labour and conscription weighing upon him to rankle more keenly than did similar burdens on peasants in other European countries. In France these onerous duties were counterbalanced by no perceived benefits, such as the keeping of order, the administration of justice or charity, or intercession with the central government. Indeed, French peasants were more exploited and shunned than their counterparts elsewhere on the Continent. Both the nobility and the middle classes had fled the countryside.

For different reasons, nobles and bourgeois were repelled by rural life and attracted to what was on offer by a powerful centralizing monarchy. Tocqueville argues that by the eighteenth century the substance of feudalism—loyal service in exchange for protection— had everywhere disappeared. Yet if aristocracy was dead, one particular aspect of the civil relations of feudalism—reliance on legal status as a basis from which to press material advantages and evade financial obligations—persisted and insinuated itself into labour relations, incomes, and the calculation of every person's material self-interest. These anachronistic feudal dues fostered increasing resentment among the peasantry. Ignored by the other classes and the church, treated arbitrarily and insensitively by the central government, peasants bore the brunt of a dysfunctional system that progressively effaced their very humanity. In Old Regime France anyone with resources sought to distance himself from rural life, and the nobility and middle classes callously abandoned the people to a pariah existence in the rural countryside.

Marx has left us a vivid rhetorical picture of the proletariat as objectified labour, demeaned and dehumanized by the brutal forces of capitalism. Tocqueville offers an even colder-eyed view of a breakdown in social relations in a pre-capitalist society. Not only did the material exploitation of the peasantry form the basis of the economy, but in Tocqueville's account the higher classes isolated the peasants geographically and socially in a particularly cruel way. The French peasantry existed in a state of 'spiritual estrangement' whose unforeseen consequences provided much of the energy for the French Revolution (AR, 121). Though treated as subhuman, peasants were of course neither deaf, dumb, nor incapable of acting on their perceived interests. Deceptively cheerful, they brooded on their grievances and slowly developed a mentality that was prepared to absorb and act on any promise of deliverance.

An Equality that Dared not Speak its Name

If the peasantry was developing a mentality centred on the land and compounded of a dangerous mix of humiliation and hope, those above them in the social ladder, according to Tocqueville, were fleeing the land to inhabit cities where they lived parallel but unconnecting lives. He describes the typical eighteenth-century noble and bourgeois as individuals who had similar interests, activities, and even grievances, but who nevertheless did not have these interests, activities, and grievances in common. Indeed, given the social and political structure of the Old Regime, their similarities drove them apart rather than brought them together. As the material circumstances of their lives converged, relations between the classes broke down and hostilities increased (AR, 96).

The nobility eventually paid in blood for turning its back on the peasants of the countryside. According to Tocqueville, however, what truly consigned the French aristocracy to historical oblivion was its failure to renew its dwindling economic and social capital by co-opting and conciliating wealthy members of the Third Estate. Recall that Tocqueville is always attuned both to the tensions between commerce and liberty and to the affinities between them. In his analysis of the fall of the French nobility, it is the affinities

that are uppermost in his mind. The loss of political liberty accelerated the material impoverishment experienced by the nobility with
the advance of commerce. 'And yet, in proportion as both the
instinct and the practice of leadership declined among them, their
wealth passed out of their hands' (AR, 79). Only a few families, tied
to the court, kept their wealth. Lack of political freedom meant a
decline in the practice of foresight, in delayed gratification, and in
cooperation for larger ends. These virtues, however, were precisely
the qualities necessary for material success in the new commercial
economy. As in *Democracy*, Tocqueville evokes the spillover effects
that can occur between political and economic behaviours. He contrasts the different strategic choice made by the nobility in England,
who sold their lands not for money but to engage in commerce. One
of the most famous sections of *The Old Regime* uses the etymology
of the English word 'gentleman' to track the collapse of the English
nobility into an amorphous aristocracy of education and wealth,
an upper class in which blood nobility and commoners 'joined forces
in business enterprises, entered the same professions, and—what
is still more significant—intermarried' (AR, 82–3). In France, where
no counterpart to 'gentleman' existed, the original antithesis
between *gentilhomme* and *roturier* (plebeian) retained its force
until the Revolution, when both words dropped out of common use
altogether.

The barriers between the privileged sections of the Third Estate
and the nobility were especially problematical. In contrast to England, there was no grey area to cushion class hostility through
ambiguous and open-ended interactions at the margins of caste. The
no-crossing signs were too clearly posted. Paradoxically, however,
the clarity of the line between noble and commoner did not mean
that boundaries could not be traversed in practice. The need for infusions of money was too great for the nobility to scorn alliances with
new wealth, and the monarchy always had offices on offer. It did
mean, however, that border-crossing increased, rather than miti-
gated, resentment and envy of the *arrivistes* among all concerned.
Moreover, the nobility's disdain for the middle classes intensified as
the ways of life between these groups became more similar. If the
only thing that marked a noble as different from a privileged bourgeois was birth, that noble would cling all the more strongly to his
prerogatives and to small differences in manners. To ask a noble to
fill the position of *intendant*, for example, would have been
unthinkable, since only commoners filled those roles. And since

nobles no longer had to interact with commoners in local affairs—
and thus to bring down their self-regard to a level that others could
tolerate—they could afford to cultivate feelings of superiority. But
Tocqueville notes that pretending to have feelings of regard for
others often engenders authentic fellow-feeling. The lack of need for
such pretence—since nobles had no need to conciliate or propitiate
others—deprived them of the opportunity to establish patterns of
cooperation and influence. Finally, if nobles on occasion resented
their loss of power to a bureaucracy staffed by middle-class officials,
they consoled themselves by scorning such common offices, taking
solace in their exclusive personal and military service to the king.

Despite its myopia, the French nobility does not appear in *The
Old Regime* as either despicable or corrupt. Indeed, insofar as it
remained true to its own admittedly perverse sense of honour—
service to the king and protection of its own caste purity—
Tocqueville portrays it with a certain sympathy.[19] But the French
nobility exhibited weaknesses of character and intellect that loom
very large in Tocqueville's explanation of the failures of the Old
Regime. He believed that a functioning aristocracy by virtue of its
very existence formed a dyke against the rising encroachments of
the central power (AR, 60). As this structural barrier weakened with
the rise of 'democracy', great skill was necessary to prevent the natural consolidation of central power. It was this skill and statesmanship that the English nobility displayed and the French nobility
lacked. In driving away its only possible allies, the nobility ensured
that middle-class insecurity and passion for place would develop
outside its tutelage and would doom aristocracy as a social system.
Generations of privilege without responsibility further incapaci-
tated the French nobility for leadership and left them morally and
mentally crippled (AR, 30). Like children, members of the nobility
had become self-absorbed and thoughtless. Like children they could
also be high-spirited and daring, but these qualities were exercised
spontaneously and utterly without judgement. Indeed, it was the
impulsive actions of the aristocracy that would precipitate France's
revolutionary crisis and destroy them as a class.

If the noble in Tocqueville's *Old Regime* brings to mind a careless
child, the bourgeois resembles a greedy and calculating one. If the
nobility missed out on the disciplinary and invigorating effects of
commerce, the middle classes gave in to its debilitating and privatizing effects. The bourgeois, after all, switched masters easily, and
gave up his self-governing role in the countryside to enrich himself

in commerce and to staff the growing central bureaucracy. 'For he had now, to all intents and purposes, only one ambition: that of securing an official post of some kind in the place where his lot was cast' (AR, 91). He abandoned the countryside above all to escape the *taille*, a tax to which, unlike the nobles, he would have been subject if he had continued to live in rural France. Eventually the bourgeois became separated from the peasantry not only by conflicts of interest but by way of life and place of residence. 'When we turn from the nobility to the middle class we find a very similar state of affairs; the bourgeois was almost as aloof from the 'common people' as the noble from the bourgeois' (AR, 89). Moreover, unlike the old nobility, who were insulated by caste, the bourgeois feared identification with those from whom he had sprung. Hence he did everything possible to distance himself from the ignorant peasant and to shore up any claim that would differentiate him from the common herd.

Within the middle classes this psychological dread of 'commonness' led to great internal differentiation and a host of associations in civil society. A dynamic of exclusion drove wigmakers, winemakers, and bankers to articulate narrow group interests. The power to keep others out—subconsciously modelled on the practice of the French nobility—signified social worth. 'Each group was differentiated from the rest by its right to petty privileges of one kind or another, even the least of which was regarded as a token of its exalted status' (AR, 94). Personal vanity caused disputes among these proliferating groups, but, more important, the structure of expectations and the exclusionary norms that governed civil society ensured an atmosphere of distrust and envy (AR, 95). This method of marking social differences was especially pernicious because reminders of distinctions cropped up at every turn, successfully preventing the positive social effects of commerce from emerging. Cooperation, even for long-term economic gain, appeared to be more trouble than it was worth. Moreover, the entrenched petty passions involved in policing barriers between groups doomed schemes of tax reform, as did the monarchy's indulgence of these passions by collecting even supposedly uniform taxes in different ways to avoid trampling the jealous sensibilities of groups.

Tocqueville's portrait of civil society under the French Old Regime is less a faithful historical reproduction than a theoretical ideal type that forms an arresting counter-image to his portrayal of associational life in America. In his Old Regime, both exemption from public duties and the inclination to exclude others from one's group in order to demonstrate standing became normative in social relations. Noble, bourgeois, and peasant alike associated status with exemption from public demands. Paying taxes, the pre-eminent public duty, had become anathema (AR, 86). A perverted sense of honour rather than merely material self-interest fuelled this avoidance of public duty. Tocqueville quotes from a letter from a noble petitioner who objects to paying a special direct tax imposed by Louis XV: 'Surely your natural good feeling will prevent you from taxing for the full vingtième a man of my position with a family to support, as you would tax a member of the lower class in such a case' (AR, 71). In an exact inversion of Tocqueville's America, the French fused self-interest with harm to the public; they practised 'self-interest ill-understood'. In a similarly dysfunctional association of ideas, the consciousness of inhabiting a respected social rank was defined completely—rather than partially—by the power to exclude others from one's group. This passion for exclusion led to a host of petty distinctions. Only the ability to expel others as different, to police social boundaries no matter how irrational, assured one of social recognition. Groups minded their 'own' business, not the public's business or even the interest of their class as a whole. Indeed, in this civil society there were a host of associations, but no facilitating political culture or structure that could function as a medium in which human attachments that developed in groups could 'spill over' into more extensive public sentiments. Tocqueville calls this situation 'group individualism', a phenomenon less analogous to the vibrant associational civil society that he discerned in Jacksonian America than to the incipient democratic individualism that he deplored there.

Old Regime society, then, was held together by a shared set of values of sorts, but these values were ultimately incapable of producing long-term stability. They were premissed on a denial of the new realities of equality, for beneath the barriers of caste and the artificial distinctions erected by middle-class groups to distinguish themselves, a new and similar type of individual was emerging. Living in the same places, educated in the same institutions, consuming the same goods, these new Frenchmen in fact thought and acted alike.

had anyone with a gift for psychology delved into their inmost feelings, he would have found that these very men regarded the flimsy barriers dividing people so much alike as contrary both to the public interest and to common sense and that already, theoretically anyhow, these ancestors of ours were all for unity. Each set store on his status as member of a particular group because he saw others asserting their personalities in this way; yet all were quite ready to sink their differences and to be integrated into a homogeneous whole, provided no one was given a privileged position and rose above the common level. (AR, 96)

The privileged classes of France, then, were isolated from one another by the norms and social structures of the Old Regime, '[b]ut basically all who ranked above the common herd were of a muchness; they had the same ideas, the same habits, the same tastes, the same kinds of amusements; read the same books and spoke in the same way. They differed only in their rights' (AR, 81). For a time, however, legal and cultural signifiers of status masked these similarities; these signifiers entered into the warp and woof of material interests and ideological needs. Only when the whole tissue of rights and privileges unravelled would the sameness of social conditions be revealed, and the characteristic psychological profile of the new French citizen—unfortunately deformed by his singular historical encounter with absolutism—become obvious. Tocqueville believed such a man to be '[a] familiar type . . . we have all met him!' (AR, 92).

The Endgame

Tocqueville's Old Regime was a complex society highly dependent on central initiatives, but still subject—with increasing strain—to a set of pervasive status norms derived from feudalism. Ultimately unstable because of the growing tensions between the passions of a democratic people and inherited inegalitarian forms that frustrated and irritated those passions, Old Regime society was for a time stabilized by the monarch's willingness—indeed eagerness—to administer it. Yet kings and their ministers proved neither far-sighted enough to create a self-governing society in which they could themselves participate nor ruthless enough to resolve social contradictions by imposing a new democratic despotism. As a consequence, the monarchy's days were numbered. Tocqueville, however, still had to explain how its time ran out. In this task, he faced two formidable challenges: first, to account for the emergence of the ideology that came to dominate the Revolution, and second, to explain how a nation so dependent on central direction could summon the initiative to launch a revolution. How did the French break through the confining fetters of self-interest ill-understood and the norms of social exclusion to embrace an ideology of public utility and the rights of man and citizen? And how did a people emasculated by 'quasi-paternal tutelage' defy its government with such world-shattering spirit?

Let me turn first to the question of the formation and appeal of revolutionary ideology, that is, to the ways in which an explicitly democratic self-understanding replaced Old Regime norms. Tocqueville describes the emergence of democratic ideology as a process of increasingly feverish collective 'dreaming', a process that eventually overtakes reality and for a short time completely replaces it. Because of the absence of a political class in France, this alteration of collective perceptions was accomplished largely through literature, a phenomenon that, according to Tocqueville, was to have lasting effects on French politics. Again he contrasts England, where literary figures existed only on the margins of practical politics in the eighteenth century, or Germany, where most writers retreated to an ivory tower and did not engage directly in social criticism. Only in France did the literati participate actively in the creation of a democratic social identity, and only in France was that identity shaped by the lability of a literary imagination unanchored to experience. In France intellectuals created a 'republic of letters' where notions of natural law and universal rights prevailed. This alternative vision of civil society eventually succeeded in estranging the French completely from the day-to-day psychological realities of life in the Old Regime. Seductive because they provided a space to indulge real feelings and passions that as yet had no outlet in the real world, the egalitarian theories of the philosophes were both increasingly widespread and unconnected to the day to day administrative practice of the regime.[20]

On the surface Tocqueville's preoccupation with the unreality of French natural rights ideology echoes Burke's diatribe against the dangers of universalistic abstractions in politics. Like Burke, Tocqueville argues that writers had usurped the traditional role of the political aristocracy in guiding public opinion and had in this way ushered in a new sort of revolution. Tocqueville alleges that there were no statesmen in the entire country. His definition of statecraft—'a clear perception of the way society is evolving, an awareness of the trends of mass opinion and an ability to forecast the future'—also recalls Burke (AR, 144). France lacked these judicious qualities because 'it is only in an atmosphere of freedom that the qualities of mind indispensable to true statesmanship can mature and fructify' (AR, 144). Indeed the French nobility was politically naive and imprudent enough to toy with dangerous abstract models of politics as a mere diversion. Instead of articulating a rationale for their own privilege based on public interest (a rationale that Tocqueville thinks could at least have been attempted), French nobles inadvertently courted their own destruction. He notes that the relations between the literati (mostly commoners) and this nobility were complex. Rather than elevating writers into their own ranks and thus co-opting their pens, nobles themselves temporarily joined the ranks of writers. They fraternized in an imaginary republic, a shadowy democracy where each person was reduced to his or her natural advantages.[21] Those who should have been most wary about the possible effects of utopian theorizing rushed to create even more radical schemes of regeneration. Tocqueville describes a naive devotion to abstractions in politics. The French believed that the complex of traditional custom governing the social order could be replaced by simple, elementary rules deriving from the exercise of human reason and natural law.

Burke had viewed the propensity to theorize in this way as a delirium both false and dangerous. Such theories were condemned to failure because simplistic arithmetic could never capture the complexities and contradictions of politics. Insofar as the delirium took on religious intensity, he found it blasphemous. But Tocqueville makes a different and subtler point. The abstractions of natural right were potentially dangerous, but they were neither completely false, doomed to fail, nor inherently sacrilegious. In fact, the philosophy of the natural rights of man and citizen expressed a deep psychological truth about the democratic psyche, as it had already emerged in the Old Regime, a truth that represented the politics of the future, or at least one aspect of that politics. Moreover, Tocqueville explores the religious aspects of the rights 'delirium' with objectivity and distance. Like Christianity, natural rights ideology was universalistic, abstract, and aimed at the regeneration of the species. Indeed, his point was not to excoriate this new 'religion' but to explain why it was able to make so many converts in France. Tocqueville's answer—like most of his answers to questions about the affinities among ideas, interests, and passions—has several layers. Not only had a conjunction of circumstances undermined Catholicism's grip on the minds of the French and destroyed it as a living faith, but French civil society, as it had been transformed in the Old Regime, provided the perfect medium for an egalitarian creed.

The French church, in Tocqueville's view, had lost the allegiance of the people for many reasons. The inherent gulf between reason and faith, while real, was the least important of these reasons. Of course Catholicism could not acknowledge rationality as the highest authority, thus setting up a certain tension with the Enlightenment project, but this unavoidable tension was not necessarily fatal in practice. More devastating were the church's assumption of the role of apologist for secular authority and its identification with a hated but ineffective censorship. According to Tocqueville, these failures of the Catholic Church played a crucial though still 'accidental' role in the coming of the French Revolution. Indeed, he is careful to link loss of faith in Christianity to particularistic French developments rather than to generic democratic ones. His study of democracy in America had argued that democracy 'itself' was far from incompatible with a religious sensibility. The Americans used religion both to reinforce democratic mores and to compensate for democratic ills.

Tocqueville argues that the French church's interpretation of Catholicism, in direct contrast to Americans' use of both Protestantism and Catholicism, quite unnecessarily ran head on into democratic mores. Moreover, the French church foolishly enmeshed itself in the confused and transitional patterns of civil society in the Old Regime. The absence of religion's natural defenders (political statesmen with judgement) and the clerical hierarchy's own short-sightedness combined to ensure that the existing church would be swept away with the Old Regime. Tocqueville thus dismisses the prevalent idea that enlightenment and scepticism necessitate a transcendence of the age of religion. For him such a notion was a dangerous red herring. Though the French Revolution attacked established religion, irreligion is not a necessary corollary of democracy.[22]

French Catholicism's failures, then, precipitate a revulsion from established religion. The consequent lack of spiritual ballast partially explains why the French were so vulnerable to the powerful currents of new ideas. They were peculiarly prepared to receive 'a host of new loyalties and secular ideals that not only filled the void but (to begin with) fired the popular imagination' (AR, 156). Secular ideologies of natural rights ignited the imagination, however, not only because the fires of Catholicism burned low, but because the new ideas themselves had an explosive affinity with attitudes fostered by equality of social condition. Ideas of universal rights appealed because they were already implicit in the 'living conditions, customs, and mores' of the French people, who were steadily drifting towards a mooring in existential equality, though this destination was hidden from them by the confused fog of daily life in the Old Regime. Theories of natural law and rights had the force of revelation because they lifted the tattered veil of the Old Regime's 'ill-regulated' norms and allowed people to face the truth about themselves. Such recognition was at first a heady and intoxicating business, and it occasioned a period of exhilaration and real fervour. Tocqueville in fact argues that people who have become equal can tolerate spiritual representations that deny that equality only at the cost of their souls. The widespread participation in the *rêve de Jean-Jacques* was ultimately disastrous for France, but it had 'grandeur' because it was at first both authentic and sincere.

According to Tocqueville, then, the French had succumbed to a religiously infused philosophy of the rights of man because it reflected the equality latent in Old Regime civil society. But to move from ideas to action required at least two more intervening steps: a generalized optimism about reform—people more often act out of hope than despair—and the courage to make a leap of faith. The first step was accomplished during the last twenty years of the Old Regime, which experienced prosperity and demographic growth despite the inefficiencies of its social structure. 'In 1780 there could no longer be any talk of France's being on the downgrade; on the contrary it seemed that no limit could be set to her advance. And it was now that theories of the perfectibility of man and continuous progress came into fashion. Twenty years earlier there had been no hope for the future; in 1780 no anxiety was felt about it' (AR, 177).

Accounting for the second step—i.e. how the French mustered the will to attempt to implement the dream of equal rights—posed a greater theoretical and stylistic problem for Tocqueville. The earlier parts of *L'Ancien Régime* create such a vivid picture of a dysfunctional civil society, dependent on royal initiative and lacking in public spirit, that one is hard put to understand how such a people could launch a world historical revolution. The peasantry, of course, waits in the wings: an immense and unsuspected source of energy ready to be tapped. Yet they do not launch the Revolution. In Tocqueville's view, the lower classes react rather than act. Neither peasants nor workers make revolutions; they are caught up in them, duped by them, or temporarily put at the helm by them. Once the enthusiasm of the elites touched off peasant rancour, the alienated and resentful peasantry would deepen and radicalize the Revolution. 'Now that his grievances were ventilated, now that the men responsible for them were pointed out to him and he realized how small was their number, he was emboldened to take arms against them, while in his heart were kindled the primitive emotions of envy, malice, and cupidity.'[23] But the more difficult question was how the privileged classes—noble and commoner alike—summoned the energy to break normative patterns that might have been increasingly fragile but still retained the persuasiveness of everyday life and that more or less served their immediate interests.

Tocqueville's analysis of the elements that would carry the French over the brink into revolution contains both general observations about the evolution of public opinion and particular comments on the changing psychology of the middle classes and the nobility. Central to his discussion of public opinion is his identification of what subsequent theorists of revolution have called the 'revolution of rising expectations'. We have already seen that France's long period of prosperity and population increase induced a hopeful attitude towards the future in general. Tocqueville argues that royal policies intensified these hopes, even as they failed to enlist the support of public opinion for the monarchy's programmes. Louis XVI's attempts at reform, for example, created heightened expectations that were frustrated when the reforms inevitably fell short. Failed royal policies had other unintended consequences as well. Most important, they prepared the population for wholesale social change by disrupting settled *mœurs* and even modelling revolutionary action. Attempts to overhaul the judicial system and other changes in the system of administration unsettled habitual forms of action, set classes against each other, and changed the relative positions of individuals. Attempts to bring individuals together to address entrenched inequalities in fact brought to a head the crisis that had long been brewing in the Old Regime: classes could not cooperate to reform the system of taxation precisely because of the divisive effects of that system. The problem was in fact 'insoluble' (AR, 198). Tocqueville notes the underlying irony that the only king who attempted seriously to remedy the inequities in the Old Regime mounted the scaffold.

People turned against royal reforms, then, not for substantive reasons—many of the reforms in fact served their interests—but because the affinity between the proposed new laws and the egalitarian *mœurs* that had come to life beneath the surface of the Old Regime was not yet evident. Moreover, the way the authorities went about reform helped to doom their efforts. By committing civil and criminal irregularities, the government further undermined respect for law, already compromised by a long period of irresponsible centralization, and edged its critics towards open rebellion. 'The Old Regime provided the Revolution with many of its methods; all the Revolution added to these was a savagery peculiar to itself' (AR, 192). What ensued was a crisis of immobility, or suspended animation; 'thus the nation as a whole was now in a state of unstable equilibrium, at the mercy of that final stroke of destiny which was to have such tremendous effects and to produce the most formidable social cataclysm the world had ever seen' (AR, 203).

Into this eerie calm burst the clamour for change expressed in the form of demands for equal rights and republican self-rule, ideas that had been seeping into the consciousness of French elites throughout the latter years of the Old Regime. To account adequately for how the middle classes and the nobility could become the vehicles of 'that final stroke of destiny', Tocqueville must explain how a population whose deepest patterns of interaction were oriented towards being ruled could demand self-rule. He has already prepared the way by reminding his readers that centralization under the Bourbons was never as thoroughgoing as it was to become under its successors. Precisely because despotism was inefficient, memories and reflexes associated with freedom could survive in the interstices of Old Regime society. These reflexes may have produced a 'curiously ill-adjusted intermittent freedom' but nevertheless they prevented the population from becoming totally subservient and servile (AR, 119). Beyond this general observation, Tocqueville notes important changes in the mentality of the middle classes and the nobility.

Although the middle class was generally conservative and politically risk-averse because revolution is bad for business, its tolerance for governmental incompetence nevertheless had its limits. By the end of the Old Regime, the monarchy's financial bankruptcy and its antagonism of its bourgeois creditors, as well as its failure to find a viable mechanism of reform, went a long way towards removing the innate psychological resistance to reform among the bourgeoisie. 'Rentiers, merchants, manufacturers, businessmen, and financiers—the section of the community usually most averse to violent political changes, warm supporters of the existing government, whatever it may be, and essentially law-abiding even when they despise or dislike the laws—now proved to be the most strenuous and determined advocates of reform' (AR, 179). What the middle classes most wanted, however, was not political liberty, but egalitarian reform. It is the nobility which initially demanded freedom and lit the spark that resulted in a brief burst of creative collaboration, an evanescent period of 'self-rule'.

Unaware that it existed with extreme fragility 'like a foreign body in the State', like officers with no troops, the French nobility was crucial in launching the revolution of 1789. Drawing on its traditional fearlessness and willingness to confront kings when its prerogatives were questioned, the nobility, in Tocqueville's account, provided the energy and patriotism to carry out the 'virile' phase of revolution. They occupied the point of maximum resistance and presented the strongest demands for safeguards against abuse of power.[24] Only in jealously guarding its honourary privileges did the nobility 'turn its back on the prevailing spirit of reform' (AR, 267). Paradoxically, it was in this anxious clinging to privilege that they showed themselves most like commoners, and—so Tocqueville implies—least worthy of their heritage. 'When the Revolution broke out, the nobility, destined as they were to be swept away with the throne, still maintained in their dealings with the King an attitude vastly more arrogant and a freedom of speech far greater than those of the Third Estate, who were soon to overthrow the monarchy' (AR, 110). Tocqueville thought it a national tragedy that the nobility, instead of being disciplined and forced to obey the rule of law, was ejected from the French body politic. Yet he accepted that ejection as final. Though 'restored' after the Revolution, the nobility had irrevocably lost its ability to lead the nation. In retrospect its actions in 1788 and 1789 were analogous to the final rush of strength and lucidity that sometimes accompanies death: reflexive, spirited, and doomed.

Tocqueville as Historian

The Old Regime and the Revolution concludes with a judgement summing up Tocqueville's understanding of his own vocation as an historian: 'To those who study it as an isolated phenomenon the

French Revolution can but seem a dark and sinister enigma; only when we view it in the light of the events preceding it can we grasp its true significance' (AR, 210). He wished to present a philosophical account and analysis of historical events that would reveal their meaning for the contemporary reader. That this account remains compelling to many readers, while the 'philosophic' histories of Tocqueville's contemporaries interest only scholars of the history of histories, calls for some explanation. What is it about Tocqueville's interpretation of the Revolution that makes this account still significant in our time?

Tocqueville's brand of cultural history stood apart from much historical writing of his day because it lacked the sense of moral progress or necessary 'unfolding' of a larger plan that suffused the narratives of writers from Guizot to Marx. Owing more to Montesquieu than to his own contemporaries, he modelled *The Old Regime* on *Considérations sur les causes de la grandeur des romains et de leur décadence*. But he remained uneasy that he would still be charged with the cardinal sin of democratic historical writing: an abstract determinism. In the 1840 *Democracy* Tocqueville famously pronounces on the characteristic vices of aristocratic versus democratic historians. Historians in aristocratic times attribute all to individuals; they particularize, chronicle, and fail utterly to perceive a generalizing trend. In democratic times, on the other hand, historians generalize, pursue abstractions, and obliterate human singularity and agency by privileging only impersonal historical forces. It was the latter vice with which Tocqueville charged contemporaries like Michelet and Hegel. Yet according to this categorization Tocqueville himself—as well as his model, Montesquieu—were more in the democratic than the aristocratic camp. In *Democracy* and *The Old Regime* there are remarkably few proper names. Tocqueville, however, was anxious to be seen as a democratic historian of a new type: one whose account did not paralyse decisive action, but rather freed political actors to make the most of their circumstances. Therefore, he remained uneasy that his pronouncements about the fated arrival of democracy would be misunderstood as another species of historical determinism.[25]

Tocqueville's vulnerability to the charge that he elevates abstract historical forces over human agency may be examined by a brief comparison with Hegel. In both the Tocquevillean and Hegelian narratives of modern European history, the 'depression' of the nobility and the concurrent consolidation of royal absolutism mark the emergence of 'the modern time'.[26] But the texture of their specific accounts of feudal decline, and the consequent effects of these accounts on the reader, are quite different. What follows, then, is not a general evaluation of Tocqueville and Hegel, but rather a more targeted attempt to elicit these distinct effects.

There are many passages in Hegel, especially in his early political writings, that describe the decline of feudalism and the rise of the modern state in terms that Tocqueville might have used. His portrait of the 'old German freedom', for example, expresses a view of aristocratic liberty that is close to Tocqueville's:

in that period the individual refused to be restricted by the whole; his limitations he imposed on himself without doubt or fear. But what lay within his sphere was so much, so entirely, himself that we could not even call it his property; on the contrary, for what belonged in his eyes to his sphere ... he risked life and limb, soul and salvation. Out of this arbitrary activity, which alone was called freedom, spheres of power over others were built by chance and character, without regard to a universal and with little control by what is called the public authority, since this authority scarcely existed at all in opposition to individuals.[27]

Like Tocqueville, Hegel believed that France's particular misfortune lay in the complete disintegration of the representative functions of this spirited aristocratic class, who had been willing to risk 'life and limb, soul and salvation' for things within their sphere. They had lost any public function and settled for an intensification of their merely personal privileges.[28] Moreover, in the context of post-Napoleonic Germany, Hegel employs a rhetorical strategy similar to Tocqueville's: he condemns what he thought were sterile attempts to restore institutions rooted in these feudal notions of liberty, once they had been bypassed by history. If Tocqueville portrayed the Old Regime as a period in which the blood had rapidly drained out of France's aristocratic institutions leaving 'corpses' that would soon be swept away by the Revolution, Hegel frequently warned his fellow Germans that '[t]he dead ... cannot be revived' or that 'an actual positive right a hundred years old rightly perishes if the basis conditioning its existence disappears'.[29]

In contrast to holding futile séances aimed at raising the dead, both Hegel and Tocqueville wished to have a real role in renewing public culture, that is, in creating a public *mœurs* consistent with modern liberty. And neither theorist believed this could happen apart from the concrete practices of self-rule. In Hegel's view, 'a political consciousness is principally acquired ... in habitual preoccupation with public affairs. By this means not only is the infinite intrinsic worth of the general [weal] felt and recognized, but experience is gained of the resistance, hostility, and dishonesty of private interest, and the battle with it. . . . '.[30] For both Hegel and Tocqueville, then, again in Hegel's words, 'the right way to pursue improvement is not by the moral route of using ideas, admonitions, associations of isolated individuals, in order to counteract the system of corruption and avoid being indebted to it, but by the alteration of institutions'.[31] Indeed, one might argue that Tocqueville indulged more frequently than did the politically shrewd Hegel in moral platitudes and vain regrets—a weakness that both condemned in theory.

In the midst of these shared perspectives, the differences in the impact of their narratives emerge more starkly. For example, though both emphasize the spontaneous way in which the European noble took responsibility for everything in his orbit and the quality of his attachment to his own dignity, Hegel quickly moves on to condemn the limitations of an aristocrat's sense of freedom, and its historical inadequacy to become the spirit of a larger social entity based on the rule of law. Tocqueville, on the other hand, while he notes that aristocracy is undoubtedly less 'just' than democracy (because its conception of freedom is limited to its own caste), focuses on the psychological qualities of mind and heart that aristocrats displayed and that appear to him to be necessary for any human liberty. He is drawn to empirical speculation about the various social mediums that could conceivably sustain such an empirical fusion between the self and a larger social entity, to the question of the connection between *mœurs* and the conditions of freedom. Tocqueville's fascination with America comes from his belief that early nineteenth-century America was one such medium.

Beyond these differing interests in the psychological and social conditions of freedom, Hegel and Tocqueville describe the processes that 'determine' the disappearance of feudal liberty in quite different ways. For Hegel this disappearance is part of a larger purpose that is 'inherently right and rational'.[32] He subsumes the decline of European aristocracy under a larger development that had long been going on in the continental states: the scientific remodelling of law and the rise of princes who took an active interest in the whole. These monarchs adopted a sense of absolute justice 'with a view to making way for these principles and giving them reality in the face of merely positive privileges, traditional private interest, and the stupidity of the masses'.[33] A larger scheme of calibrated liberty, in Hegel's view, properly preserves but transcends feudal liberties. 'But a necessity higher than that lying in the positive bond of a promise lies in the nature of the concepts which have risen to become a universal conviction and which attach to monarchy, as essential characteristics, the formation of a representative constitution, the rule of law, and popular influence on legislation.'[34] Hegel, then, scorns the Württemburg assembly, which had foolishly dismissed the 'rational' constitution the king offered. He is similarly impatient with claims for England's vaunted free constitution, in his view an 'Augean stable' of inconsistent private law and public corruption that survives due to the skilful machinations of a political class.[35] Indeed, Hegel eschews the pursuit in any detail of the processes by which the aristocracy declined or the monarchy rose. This decline takes its place in his narrative only as a necessary step in the evolution of the concept of liberty; the nobility needed to be subject to kings in order to purge the notion of right of personal connotations and to facilitate a recognition of the Universal as against positive personal rights.[36] It is the fate of particularity to be subsumed under universality.

Tocqueville, however, struggles to convey to the reader a complex social and psychological story: not the decline of nobility as one instance in the emergence of rational freedom, but the human drama of a class's collusion in its own extinction. Tocqueville attends to the interactions between circumstances and human action at a much more detailed and less abstract level than does Hegel. Indeed, Tocqueville's account of the fall of the nobility, the rise of kings, and the triumph of the commons persuades us not so much because it illustrates the historical inevitability of the change from aristocracy to democracy as because it enlarges our understanding of how such historical transformations in *mentalité* can happen. As we have seen, he entered deeply into the psychology of the Old Regime nobility to speculate on a number of psychological mechanisms that distanced the nobility from the middle classes, and made all future cooperation unlikely: the narcissism of small differences, the notion that psychological pretence often turns into the real thing, and the phenomenon of sour grapes. Similarly, his account of the rise of bourgeois consciousness just before the outbreak of the Revolution depends entirely on the interplay between long-term trends (his 'general causes') and the immediate events and changed psychological perceptions that lead to decisions to act ('secondary causes').

Bad harvests and economic crises precipitate political disturbances because they alter characteristic psychological responses and motivations. It is the subtle texture of this alteration—the transformation of the bourgeoisie from an anxious supporter of the status quo to an intense constituency for reform—with which Tocqueville is most concerned.

Perhaps the best example of Tocqueville's examination of the ways in which collective *mentalités* emerge in history is his account of the transformation of rural France, i.e. his analysis of the emergence of a technically independent but virtually powerless French peasantry, a class living 'in a state of isolation and abjection, as inaccessible to outside influences as a prisoner in jail' (AR, 134). Tocqueville simultaneously pursues two strategies of explanation. First, he uses empirical evidence of various sorts to place certain facts and historical trends in the foreground. By setting this evidence in a comparative context, he emphasizes the distinctiveness of the French situation and sets up the argument that the French peasantry's unique situation helps to explain why the Revolution occurred in France and not elsewhere. Second, he enters into the minds and hearts of 'typical' actors, empathetically recreating their motivations and the plausibility and significance of their actions. Finally, he sets these actors in motion so that the reader may watch the drama unfold.

According to Tocqueville, the rapidity of the devolution of land ownership and the swiftness of feudal decline were trends unique to France. He quotes confidential reports made to an *intendant* on the ways in which inheritances were being subdivided 'to an alarming degree' and also quotes contemporary observers (both obscure and famous) on the Frenchman's inveterate craving for land and the growing numbers of peasant owners (AR, 24). He himself makes a survey of land distribution based on parish reports required by a tax law of 1790, which had requested a listing of all privately owned land within parish borders. He concludes that the number of landowners in 1790 had already reached half or even two-thirds of the number in his own time.[37] He also studies records of revolutionary sales of the lands of the nobility and the clergy to support his contention that most lands were purchased by people who already were landowners. As far as he is able, he contrasts this situation to England (where the once considerable number of peasant proprietors had dwindled and been absorbed into urban areas) and to Germany (where independent peasant ownership had never been very prevalent). In the case of Germany, he adds that in those exceptional regions where a landed peasantry similar to the French existed, the people tended to welcome revolutionary ideas, thus strengthening his case about the indirect effects of land ownership on the psychological predispositions to support a social revolution (AR, 232).

Tocqueville also uses empirical evidence of various sorts to support his account of the deterioration of social relations in the countryside. He quotes letters of *intendants* on the arbitrary and inequitable ways in which taxes were collected from the peasantry and describes the strategies for tax evasion that were taken for granted by all concerned. In short, he attempts to establish a vivid prima facie case for his thesis that peasants had become a unique sort of proprieter: 'higher' in social condition than anywhere else in Europe, but exceptionally ignorant, exploited, and harassed, and with no natural allies to protect them from social oppression and financial extortion (AR, 131).

In these efforts to establish a pattern of differences, Tocqueville does not scorn statistical evidence; indeed, he is one of the first to see the significance of large-scale studies of land sales to an understanding of the Revolution. Like original documents and memoirs, however, such evidence takes on meaning only as it is shaped by its interpreter into a plausible narrative. For this shaping one must draw on imaginative insight into the motivation of the dramatis personae.[38] At the same time as he is establishing an empirical case for the devolution of land ownership, Tocqueville enters into the sentiments of the people placed in such a position, imagining their responses to their changing circumstances. 'I would ask you', Tocqueville says, 'to picture to yourself the French peasant as he was in the eighteenth century . . . . [See] how he appears in the records from which I have been quoting.' Tocqueville evokes the feelings and intentions of such a typical peasant proprietor, arguing that his passionate devotion to the soil would have given birth to a sense of pride and independence. He asks us to share this peasant's feelings towards faceless absentee neighbours who trample his seedlings in the hunt, exact tolls at the river, force him to use their mills and ovens, and drag him away from his land to 'work elsewhere without payment'. He then recreates this hypothetical peasant's attitude towards the official 'men in black' who proceed to take the rest of his harvest (AR, 31).

In these ways Tocqueville historically contextualizes the allegedly 'natural' secretiveness and craftiness of the French peasant. Like the persecuted Jews of the Middle Ages, peasants would naturally try to hide any wealth or good fortune to avoid being despoiled by powerful neighbours from whom they have no protection. Similarly, he offers a social psychological explanation of changing peasant attitudes towards military service. The same peasants who would in a few years proudly swell the citizen armies of the Republic and the Empire fear and despise conscription in the Old Regime. It is not the economic and physical hardships of conscription that particularly repel the peasant—these will remain in later times and will always account for a certain level of avoidance and desertion—but rather the painful psychological fact that inability to avoid the draft in the ill-adjusted democratic *mentalité* of Old Regime France signifies worthlessness. Like taxation, conscription constituted a virtual denial of status. Underneath the common peasant's traditional meekness in the face of adversity, then, was a hunger for social recognition based on incipient economic independence. The continued denial of such recognition would ultimately affect the peasant's disposition to rebel. Born of the discrepancy between the hopes and passions engendered by (limited) land ownership and the frustrations of having those hopes and passions blocked at every turn, the peasant's resentments constituted a revolutionary time-bomb. French peasants were all too ready to welcome the ideas of the democratic age, and the ways in which those ideas took shape in the 'cramped, obscure retreats of their minds' would contribute to the peculiar ferocity of the French Revolution (AR, 134).

Tocqueville notes that with effort he—and we—can enter this peasant's mentality. Yet these psychological insights were difficult for eighteenth-century men and women, for 'whenever the poor and the rich come to have hardly any common interests, common activities, and common grievances, the barriers between their respective mentalities become insuperable, they are sealed books to each other even if they spend all their lives side by side' (AR, 235). The increasing likelihood that peasants would lash out against their perceived oppressors, then, remained a secret buried in the complex new peasant *mentalité*; as a class the peasantry was sealed off as if by the barriers of caste untouchability. Tocqueville's efforts to recreate the sense of grievance and yearning experienced in the past induces a sensitivity to the possibilities of empathetic reconstruction in the present, and an awareness of the preconditions of any collective action. Unlike accounts of the past (such as those of Hegel) that bring narrative closure and a sense that an idea or purpose will be realized in the fullness of time, Tocqueville's historical writing evokes a sense of the possibilities of disruption and unintended consequences that lie just beneath the surface of everyday life.

Neither drowning in facts nor losing himself in abstractions, Tocqueville wished to work in 'that half-light that allows one to glimpse the country and ask the inhabitants to point out one's road'.[39] His success in achieving this controlled illumination, in creating an explanation without robbing the past of its individuality or the present of its possibilities is what gives *The Old Regime and the Revolution* its 'classic' quality. Even in assigning a retrospective meaning to events, thus terming them 'general' or 'fated' or 'overdetermined', Tocqueville engages the reader on a ground of contingency, plurality, and choice. In unravelling a pattern of multiple causation, he always provokes the question 'what if?' and implicitly invites his reader to answer it. It is not surprising that contemporary French intellectuals emerging from the hegemony of Hegel discover new affinities with Tocqueville.[40] We can exonerate him, then, from the charge he most feared. The effect of his narrative is not to paralyse either thought or action, but rather to stimulate them both.

The Revolution and its Spirit

At the end of *The Old Regime and the Revolution* Tocqueville concludes that the antecedent circumstances that he has discussed were more than enough to have led to revolution anywhere. Nevertheless, he admits that he has not accounted for the 'drastic' character of the French Revolution, which he proceeds to attribute to the innate character of the French. They are so full of contrasts and extremes, so emotional, so loath to be guided by fixed principles that their revolution necessarily embodies these characteristics. 'France alone could have given birth to revolution so sudden, so frantic, and so thoroughgoing, yet so full of unexpected changes of direction, of anomalies and inconsistencies' (AR, 211). Here we see Tocqueville invoking the sort of explanation to which he turns in moments of frustration, but with which he is seldom satisfied. Perhaps because of their deterministic overtones, arguments based on innate national character seem to represent a failure of the comparative method rather than its exercise. The Revolution itself, then, remains opaque to Tocqueville.

In describing the explanatory method of *The Old Regime*, Tocqueville had used the metaphor of 'half-light'. He in fact combined an impulse to understand the intentions of actors and the significance of actions in historical contexts different from his own—the impulse of empathetic reconstruction—with an appreciation of historical structures and patterns that were slowly developing, unperceived by the actors themselves, and which could be revealed only by patient empirical investigation. He tries to find his way in this half-light in which subjective recreation and empirical generalization come together to create neither subjective description nor universal laws, but rather a contextually grounded account with explanatory power.

If Tocqueville had lived long enough to fulfil his ambition of explaining the significance of the Napoleonic period, he might have achieved such an analytically and empathetically informed account of the end of the Directory and the emergence of the Consulate and Empire, because he had a certain confidence that he could recognize and understand—even when he did not admire—the characters who lived in those times. His unfinished chapter on the Directory fascinates because of its evocation of the decay of the revolutionary impulse. The weariness and ennui of the populace, the corruption of the government, the state of hopeless paralysis, the sensation of waiting in a web for the sting of the spider—these characterizations arise to some extent out of Tocqueville's own experiences in 1849–50. They provide him with an imaginative bridge by which to enter the world of the First Empire. Such an account of the coming of Napoleon, were he to have completed it, might or might not have revealed Napoleon's 'true' significance, but it would undoubtedly have constituted yet another nuanced elaboration of one of Tocqueville's deepest preoccupations. We may doubt, however, if he would have struck gold in mining the revolutionary record. Indeed, in his private letters during this period—to Freslon, to Beaumont, to Kergolay—he reveals his struggle to find a coherent thread that would lead him through the details of revolutionary history. He returns to the 'light' metaphor only to express his frustration.

I must interweave ideas and events, I must say enough about the events to make the ideas comprehensible and make the reader feel how interesting or important they are, and yet I must not write a history properly speaking . . . . I can see, I think, the object that I want to portray; but the light illuminating it wavers and does not yet allow me to grasp the image well enough to be able to reproduce it.[41]

The object that he is referring to in this passage from a letter to Beaumont is the period of the Revolution, the years from 1789 to 1795. In the first chapter of *The Old Regime*, he states that no one at the time of the French Revolution—friend or foe, French or foreign—recognized the real significance of this Revolution. It seemed then 'a grim terrific force of nature, a newfangled monster, red of tooth and claw' (AR, 3). Even in his own time the Revolution was more likely to be attributed either to satanic forces or to God's beneficent providence, depending on one's politics, than to human causes. Tocqueville uses this arresting image of an inexplicable act of God to set up his own contrary thesis, namely that the Revolution was the inevitable yet unforeseen outcome of a preceding democratic revolution in civil society that had been silently eating away at the aristocratic foundations of the Old Regime for generations. Yet Tocqueville neither satisfactorily theorized the Revolution itself nor the aspirations, distrusts, and patterns of interaction that it seemed to have engendered in French political culture. Writing to his friend Louis de Kergolay near the end of his life he admits to being unable to penetrate this mystery.

there is moreover in this malady of the French Revolution something peculiar that I sense without being able to describe it well or analyze its causes. It is a virus of a new and unknown kind. There have been violent revolutions in the world, but the character of these Revolutionaries is so immoderate, violent, radical, desperate, audacious, almost insane yet powerful and effective, as to have no precedents, it seems to me, in the great social agitations of ages past. Where does this new race come from? Who produced it? Who made it so effective? Who perpetuates it? For we are still facing men like this, although circumstances are different, and they have left their descendants throughout the civilized world. My mind wears itself out in trying to conceive a clear notion of this object and looking for ways to describe it. Beyond everything that can be explained in the French Revolution there remains something unexplained in its spirit and its acts. I sense where this unknown object is, but try as I may, I cannot lift the veil that covers it. I grope as if across a foreign body that prevents me from quite touching it or seeing it.[42]

Tocqueville never succeeded in fashioning an explanation of the 'monstrous' revolutionary spirit that seemed so bewildering to contemporaries and that he believed would continue to bedevil French political practice. That spirit remains a shadowy presence in his historical writing, as does the original Revolution: a mysterious interlude that links the eighteenth century's incubating democratic despotism with the nineteenth century's more openly and efficiently centralized regimes.

In his discussions of this revolutionary spirit, Tocqueville still wavered between two contrary and competing impulses. As in *Democracy in America*, he denied the Revolution itself any lasting legacy, yet he found in it the source of an insane modern hubris that disturbed him so deeply that his analytical powers quailed before it. In *Democracy*, in his 1836 essay on French history, and implicitly throughout *The Old Regime*, Tocqueville portrays the Revolution as the most powerful, rapid, destructive, and creative in history. But it only regulated, coordinated, and legalized the effects of a great cause, rather than itself being such a 'great cause'. The Revolution created a multitude of secondary and accessory things, Tocqueville argues, but it was merely transitional.[43] Hence, the ideas of the French Revolution that spread into other countries did not themselves cause revolutionary events, but rather provided the light that enabled the seeds of social revolution (if they existed) to flower. According to this view of things, the Revolution may have caused long aftershocks, but it did not itself generate norms or patterns of behaviour. Indeed, the underlying premiss of *The Old Regime* was that the anarchic element in the Revolution, its bias against all authority, was a temporary aberration masking the transformation of the old social structure into a society that was more, rather than less, receptive to authoritarian rule.

These explanations of the Revolution as a transitional phenomenon recur throughout Tocqueville's writing on the subject. They fail to account, however, for its generation of a powerful and long lasting revolutionary 'spirit'. It is this phenomenon for which Tocqueville has no adequate explanation. His experiences in 1848 crystallized the need to understand the revolutionary mentality, and in the *Souvenirs* he half-heartedly speculates that the French readiness to take to the barricades could be a sign of decadence: 'intermittent anarchy . . . is well-known to be the chronic incurable disease of old peoples' (S, 83). But more often he views revolutionary behaviour as a series of unnatural acts in which people overstep the boundaries that make them human and enter an alternate mental universe in which the rules of human logic are suspended.

Tocqueville believed that all widespread democratic ideologies have a universalistic, abstract form. What differentiates revolutionary dreaming from radically reformist ideologies is the lack of any lasting connection to the possibilities inherent in the 'social state'.

For Tocqueville the realistic social alternatives of the modern age exist on a continuum bounded by equality in freedom or equality in servitude. In his view, however, revolutionary utopias, particularly as they developed into socialist ones, did not even exist on this continuum. They seemed to him to inhabit an anti-universe in which the laws of reality do not apply. Things that are wholly inconsistent with one another in any rational universe—freedom and the abolition of private property, freedom and atheism, or freedom and the appearance of women as actors in the public sphere—become simultaneously objects of desire. When he views the revolutionary impulse from this perspective, then, Tocqueville abandons the effort to 'ask the inhabitants to point out the road', since he cannot fathom their responses. Instead he retreats into his spiritual intuitions that religion, property, and ordered domesticity provide 'natural' barriers against collective insanity. Insofar as the French Revolution seemed to have spawned a semi-permanent attack on these institutions, he feels himself truly faced with a 'grim terrific force of nature . . . red of tooth and claw'. He fights back not with the cool half-light of analysis, but with warm intuitions 'of the heart'. Those intuitions form the subject of the next chapter.

Notes

1 On Tocqueville's political career and absorption in French affairs, see André Jardin, *Tocqueville, (1805–1859): A Biography*, trans. Lydia Davis with Robert Hemenway (London: Peter Halban, 1988) 279–461 and Edward Gargan, *Alexis de Tocqueville: The Critical Years, 1848–1851* (Washington, DC: Catholic University of American Press, 1955). For Tocqueville's continuing thoughts on American affairs, see the interesting article based on Tocqueville's American correspondence by Hugh Brogan, 'Alexis de Tocqueville and the Coming of the American Civil War', in *American Studies: Essays in Honour of Marcus Cunliffe* (New York: St. Martin's Press, 1991), 83–104, and Françoise Mélonio, 'Tocqueville et les malheurs de la démocratie américaine (1831–1858)', *Commentaire*, 38 (1987), 381–9.

2 Jardin, *Tocqueville*, 481.

3 See his projected outline of the work written in Dec. 1850, OC 2:2, 301–4.

4 Ibid. 319.

5 See Melvin Richter, 'Tocqueville, Napoleon, and Bonapartism', in Abraham Eisenstadt (ed.), *Reconsidering Tocqueville's 'Democracy in*

America' (New Brunswick, NJ: Rutgers University Press, 1988), 125. In the drafts of *Democracy in America* in the Yale archives, James T. Schleifer finds the following unpublished passage in a discussion of the distinction between 'general' causes in history (those he takes up in the *Democracy*) and 'secondary' causes (individual influence and accidents): 'The destiny of a people may be modified or changed by the accidental influence of a powerful man, such as Napoleon, I suppose. Or even by an accident of chance such as a plague or the loss of a battle.' Quoted in Schleifer 'Tocqueville as Historian', in Eisenstadt, *Reconsidering*, 149.

6 Tocqueville to Paul Clamorgan, 17 Apr. 1842, OC 10: 221.

7 'Discours de réception à l'Académie Française', OC 16; 263.

8 Ibid. 264–5.

9 For a discussion of the genesis of the *L'Ancien Régime*, see Françoise Mélonio and François Furet, 'Introduction' to *The Old Regime and the Revolution*, trans. Alan Kahane (Chicago: University of Chicago Press, 1998), 1–12.

10 Quoted in Jardin, *Tocqueville*, 506.

11 Tocqueville speculates that part of the reason for English exceptionalism was the high level of 'civilization' of the Norman conquerors. Since feudalism had been introduced to France by relatively civilized Normans, rather than primitive tribes, they left a more enlightened legacy to their heirs (the English nobles). Tocqueville seems to take some comfort from this attribution of English liberties to his own Norman ancestors. *État social et politique*, OC 2:1, 50.

12 For Whig historians' consciousness of the indigenous character of English political development, and in particular the contrast with France, see J. W. Burrow, *A Liberal Descent: Victorian Historians and the English Past* (Cambridge: Cambridge University Press, 1981), 11–35.

13 Jardin, *Tocqueville*, 493.

14 *État social et politique*, OC 2:1, 56.

15 AR, 223, n. 1; cf. Tocqueville's claim that dissatisfaction with localism in the late Middle Ages causes countries to begin to communicate in order to seek a wider law, *État social et politique*, OC 2:1, 33, and his observation that kings were singularly helped in centralizing tendencies by the 'légistes', ibid. 57.

16 AR, 224, n. 2; cf. *État social et politique*, OC 2:1, 57: 'A people in whom the social state is becoming democratic almost always proceed by centralizing power in the prince alone, later, if they find the energy and power, they shatter the instrument and transport the same prerogatives into the hands of an authority that depends on themselves.'

17 In his 1836 sketch of French history, for example, he notes the incongruities of the Old Regime conception of the Third Estate, a term that

included both the wealthy cultivated bourgeois and the poor ignorant peasant: *État social et politique*, OC 2:1, 44.

18 Ibid. 49; cf. AR, 23–5.

19 He does, however, condemn those among the nobility who claimed to be motivated by an honourable code that forbade intermarriage with lesser beings—a code both foolish and unjust—but then breached their own principles for money: *État social et politique*, OC 2:1, 42.

20 In that sense Tocqueville perceives a connecting thread between the earlier philosophes and the eclectic spiritual ferment that characterized the end of the Old Regime, the 'feverish agitation of the human mind . . . that immediately preceded the French Revolution everywhere in Europe and that manifested itself as Illuminism, the Rosicrucians, Freemasonry, and Mesmerism': Tocqueville to A. de Circourt, 12 Jan. 1857, OC 18, 362.

21 *État social et politique*, OC 2:1, 48.

22 Again he cites the comparative cases of Germany and England, where scepticism is espoused by an elite but never catches on—even among the privileged classes—as well as the case of America, profoundly imbued with both religion and the rights of man (AR, 149, 153–4).

23 Tocqueville notes that officials and privileged classes spoke in front of peasants about their wrongs as if *le peuple* could not hear or understand; similarly, administrative authorities each publicly blamed the other for the plight of the peasants (AR, 181–2).

24 See Tocqueville's long discussion of the noble *cahiers* in AR, 262–72 (n. 44).

25 Tocqueville's opposition to determinism in history can perhaps best be followed in his correspondence with Arthur de Gobineau. See esp. OC 9, 199–201.

26 Georg Wilhelm Friedrich Hegel, *The Philosophy of History*, trans. J. Sibree (New York: Dover, 1956), 427, 429.

27 'The German Constitution', in *Hegel's Political Writings*, ed. Z. A. Pelczynski, trans. T. M. Knox (Oxford: Clarendon Press, 1964), 147.

28 Ibid. 205.

29 AR, 75; Hegel, 'Proceedings of the Estates Assembly in Wurtemberg', in *Political Writings*, 274.

30 Hegel, ibid. 257.

31 Hegel, 'The English Reform Bill', in *Political Writings*, 297.

32 Ibid. 299.

33 Ibid. 300.

34 Hegel, 'Proceedings of the Estates Assembly in Wurtemberg', 250.

35 'The extensive jumble of English private law which even Englishmen master their pride in their freedom sufficiently to call an Augean stable, might well afford grounds for hoping for some tidying up': 'English Reform Bill', 310.

36 *Philosophy of History*, 429–30.

37 Tocqueville reminds the reader that the French population has risen by 25 per cent since 1790.

38 In 'Tocqueville as Historian' Schleifer cites a long unpublished discussion by Tocqueville of the uses of statistics from the Yale drafts of the 1835 *Democracy*. I think it is too strong to conclude, as Schleifer does, that Tocqueville here exhibited a 'distaste for numbers' and a 'suspicion of their mystique' (p. 165). Rather, he seems to caution against exaggerated hopes for what statistics could add to social science. Tocqueville points out that statistics merely establish 'facts'; they do not provide reasons or explanations. Reasons are discernible 'only to the mind's eye', but nevertheless it is from facts that one must begin to think. Hence his own efforts to use the 'facts' to frame almost every argument.

39 Unpublished letter from Tocqueville to Freslon, 20 Sept. 1856, quoted in Jardin, *Tocqueville*, 514.

40 See below, Chapter five, pp. 227–32.

41 Tocqueville to Beaumont, OC 8:3, 522, quoted in Jardin, *Tocqueville*, 515; cf. unpublished letter to Freslon, quoted in ibid. 514.

42 Tocqueville to Kergolay, May 16, 1858, OC 13:2, 337–8; translation from Palmer, *The Two Tocquevilles*, 241–2.

43 *État social et politique*, OC 2:1, 65.

4

Social Science and Moral Duties: The Secrets of the Heart

Implicit in Tocqueville's discussion of the social and political tendencies of his time is a subtly shaded Jekyll-and-Hyde portrait of democracy and of the historical emergence of its two faces: one despotic, one free. Tocqueville saw himself as the unbiased anatomist of this strange case, but also as a guide to its moral paradoxes. Beneath his painstaking attempts to clarify the instincts and tendencies of a democratic social condition lies a set of ethical intuitions, 'secrets of the heart' that give his works the aura of prophecy as well as science (DAI, 293). The connection between Tocqueville's analytical and prophetic voices, however, is difficult to elucidate, at least in part because that connection arises from a set of spiritual anxieties that have become strange to us. In this chapter, I turn to the spiritual subtext of Tocqueville's work, evident not only in his vague religious yearnings but also in his ambiguous uses of the terms 'natural' and 'unnatural', his spontaneous admiration for justice and rights, and his idealization of democratic domesticity. One can say of Tocqueville what he said of the Americans: 'it is not a question of sterile beliefs bequeathed by the past and vegetating rather than living in the depths of the soul' (DAI, 293). Tocqueville's moral beliefs lived in the depths of his soul, nourished by instinctive reactions to what he perceived as the ultimate horrors of his time. Yet he did not attempt a principled defence of these values; rather he offered a particular mix of allusion to transcendent norms and appeal to collective self-interest that has always been a challenge to his interpreters.

Tocqueville recognizes and at times deliberately reflects on his own philosophical silences. In the second *Democracy*, he offers this extended analysis of the function of dogmatic beliefs among democratic peoples, worth quoting at length because in it he not only characterizes the habits of democratic times, but also confesses his own intellectual sins.

man has to accept as certain a whole heap of facts and opinions which he has neither leisure nor power to examine and verify for himself, things which cleverer men than he have discovered and which the crowd accepts. On that foundation he then builds the house of his own thoughts. He does not act so from any conscious choice, for the inflexible laws of his existence compel him to behave like that. No philosopher in the world, however great, can help believing a million things on trust from others or assuming the truth of many things besides those he has proved. Such behavior is desirable as well as necessary. Anyone who undertook to go into everything himself could give but little time or attention to each question. He would keep his mental faculties in a state of perpetual excitement, which would prevent his going deeply into any truth or being firmly convinced of anything at all . . . . some beliefs must be accepted without discussion so that it is possible to go deeply into a few selected ones for examination. (DAII, 434; cf. 433)

It is hard not to see in this commentary a projection of Tocqueville's own decision to accept many beliefs without discussion. Moreover, the matters that Tocqueville chooses for 'deep examination' are rarely matters of abstract right. 'I am one of those', he writes, 'who think that there is hardly ever absolute right in any laws.'[1] Rather than explicating universal ideas of morality, he prefers comparing concrete cases. In his contrast between notions of honour in democratic and aristocratic times, for example, he acknowledges 'universal standards' characteristic of all humanity, but quickly adds, 'Nothing is so unproductive for the human mind as an abstract idea. So I hasten to consider the facts. An example will make my meaning clear' (DAII, 617). His rueful assessment of his shortcomings as a politician gives us a useful formulation of his peculiarities as a moralist: 'for me truth is something so precious and rare that once I have found it, I do not want to risk it in the hazard of an argument; I feel it is like a light that might be put out by waving it to and fro' (S, 104).

Among Tocqueville scholars there are two ways of dealing with this failure to wave 'to and fro' the light of truth underlying his many evaluative judgements. One is to ignore the issue as peripheral to what is of permanent importance in his work, namely the innovative comparative political sociology and cultural history that we have examined in the previous two chapters. These interpreters simply decline to discuss the more philosophical aspects of his thought.[2] A variation on this strategy recognizes that Tocqueville often based his interpretations on unacknowledged moral preconceptions, but argues that such prejudices—or moral clichés—are merely the inevitable biases that make true impartiality impossible for any theorist. They can therefore be dismissed as unimportant and theoretically uninteresting.[3] On the other hand, those who deliberately set out to give a wider and more complete picture of Tocqueville's thought, or who are themselves more interested in questions of moral and political philosophy, are forced to provide the context that Tocqueville omits. These scholars elucidate Tocqueville's views by comparisons with a host of other contemporary writers or various traditions of political thought.[4]

This chapter takes a slightly different tack. Like the former commentators on Tocqueville, I shall argue that Tocqueville's ethical judgements are in one sense merely prejudices. These prejudices are theoretically uninteresting, however, only if one thinks of them as residual idiosyncratic biases. If one is concerned with the changing moral and cultural assumptions of political argument, with the ways in which notions that are accepted as beyond analysis in one period become contested and vulnerable in another, Tocqueville's particular group of preconceptions is significant and illuminating. In his moralizing moments, he reveals not just his own anxieties but, inevitably, something about the way his generation connected moral malaise to political argument. Like those who take his moral theory seriously, then, I think that his reverence for certain values— spontaneity, honour, authentic passion, true human dignity, and self-mastery through heroic renunciation—is worthy of careful analysis.

Tocqueville alerts us to his spiritual intuitions by changing the emotional register of his prose, as in this sentence, which follows a description of the possibility that democracy will generate despotism: 'when I conceive a democratic society of this kind, I fancy myself in some low, close, and gloomy abode where the light which breaks in from without soon faints and fades away. A sudden heaviness overpowers me, and I grope through the surrounding darkness to find an opening that will restore me to the air and to the light of day' (DAII, 456). Sometimes intimately drawing in the reader by revealing a personal reaction, sometimes flattering by assuming that his own intimations of sublimity will be shared, Tocqueville often reveals this attraction to 'higher things' in connection with a discussion of divine providence or of human actions that rise above self. But one finds a similar alteration of tone in other contexts as well: in his discussion of place and landscape, in his speculations on the meaning of time, and in his discussion of family and the character of women.

The organizing principle of this chapter is to consider together the subjects that apparently tap into this emotional undercurrent in Tocqueville, and that are likely to evoke admiration or revulsion. Rather than contextualizing his normative judgements by situating them among the discussions of other contemporary thinkers who presumably said more explicitly what he intended, I consider the significance of the particular set of notions that trigger his elegiac moods. Understanding this sensibility and its place in his analyses helps us to make sense of arguments that often may seem implausible or contradictory. And recognizing the unique conjunction of concerns that either exalt or terrify Tocqueville tells us something about the cultural assumptions of his liberalism and his usefulness as a guide to our own moral paradoxes. One way to approach these underlying preconceptions is to probe his admiration for the 'natural'. Perhaps even more revealing is to reflect on his revulsion from the 'unnatural'.

The Natural and the Unnatural

Tocqueville uses the term 'natural' with almost wanton disregard for its potential ambiguities. As with other key concepts, however, he stays within a range of possible meanings that can usually be gleaned from the context. I find at least four possible meanings of 'natural' in Tocqueville's texts. Of these, one is more or less devoid of moral connotations, while three involve implicit references to God's purposes for men and women on earth. I want to consider first the neutral quasi-positivistic sense of 'natural' by reviewing some characteristic examples from the two *Democracies* (emphases added).

Therefore, in the first part of this book I have endeavored to show the *natural* turn given to the laws by democracy, when left in America to its own inclinations with hardly any restraint on its instincts . . . (DAI, 19).

Each type of government harbors one *natural* vice which seems inherent in the very nature of its being: the genius of a lawgiver consists in discerning that clearly. (DAI, 137)

[In America] the people prevail without impediment; there are neither dangers to fear nor injuries to revenge. Therefore in America democracy follows its own inclinations. Its features are *natural* and its movement free. (DAI, 196)

This tendency [of aristocracies towards abstract truth and democracies towards immediate practical applications] is both *natural* and inevitable (DAII, 463)

I think that in the dawning centuries of democracy individual independence and local liberties will always be the products of art. Centralized government will be the *natural* thing. (DAII, 674)

In these passages Tocqueville means 'natural' in something like the sense that objects naturally fall unless another force intervenes to counteract gravity. We may assume that a tendency will produce a particular effect, if unopposed by some other force. Speculating about such 'natural' tendencies of democracy forms a large part of Tocqueville's analyses of democracy in both America and Europe.

Tocqueville rarely speculates further about overarching laws of social science that subsume or govern the 'natural' tendencies that he observes. Indeed, when he uses the term 'natural law' *tout court*, he usually invokes a more traditional conception of the moral law, divine in origin and available to humans through reason. 'There are some universal and permanent needs of mankind on which moral laws are based; if they are broken all men everywhere at all times have connected notions of guilt and shame with the breach. *To do wrong* meant to disregard them, *to do right* to obey them' (DAII, 616–17; cf. 627). This residual use of older natural law imagery is Tocqueville's second characteristic employment of 'natural'. It connotes the idea of basic equity and justice that is the same for all because implanted in all by a benevolent deity. There is, of course, a tension between natural tendencies in the first, largely descriptive, sense and natural law in the second, prescriptive one. We find a similar tension in many Enlightenment moralists, as well as in Montesquieu, whom Tocqueville recalls here as elsewhere.[5]

A third Tocquevillian use of 'natural' denotes that which is pure and spontaneous in human nature as against that which is socially and historically constructed. This employment of 'natural' to mean the pure promptings of the human heart, which Tocqueville recognizes in all races and all historical periods, differs from his first use of 'natural' (social or psychological regularities flagged by the scientific observer) or the second (faint imprints of natural justice). Rather, he here suggests spontaneous upsurges of sentiment that are the proximate sources of truly human qualities. He often signals this use of 'natural' by a variation on the phrase 'rooted in the human heart'.[6] Consider the following references to 'natural' passions (emphases added).

In America I found passions like those familiar in Europe; some were due to the *very nature of the human heart* and others to the democratic state of society. (DAI, 310)

It depends on the laws to awaken and direct that vague instinct of patriotism which *never leaves the human heart*, and by linking it to everyday thoughts, passions, and habits, to make it a conscious and durable sentiment. (DAI, 94)

Having nothing but ... the *spontaneous instincts of his nature* against our profound designs, he [the American Indian] fails in the unequal contest. (DAI, 320)

there was something particularly touching in the scene I have just described [of a Native American and an African slave woman attending a European child]; here a bond of affection united oppressors and oppressed, and *nature bringing them close together* made the immense gap formed by prejudices and by laws yet more striking. (DAI, 320)

I saw him [a slave owner who realized that his own son by a slave woman would become a commodity] a prey to the agony of despair, and then I understood how *nature can revenge the wounds made by the laws*. (DAI, 328)

Religion, therefore ... *is as natural to the human heart* as hope itself. It is by a sort of intellectual aberration, and in a way, by doing moral violence to their own nature, that men detach themselves from religious beliefs; an invincible inclination draws them back. (DAI, 296–7)

It was not man who implanted in himself the taste for the infinite and love of what is immortal. These sublime instincts are not the offspring of some caprice of the will; their foundations are *embedded in nature*; they exist despite a man's efforts. (DAII, 535)

In these passages Tocqueville betrays his kinship with Rousseau. Prepared to acknowledge that natural passions are amoral rather than either moral or immoral, he nevertheless celebrates instincts that are 'natural' because authentic and free from wilful distortion by civilization. Such passions are the fragile shoots of human sociability. Carefully nurtured, they may grow into fully ethical tendencies. Unattended, they are easily denatured through the process of social development itself. Tocqueville observes in his highly sympathetic portrait of the character of Native Americans in *Democracy in America* that there was something in their proud emotions 'which seizes the heart [of the observer] and carries him away in spite of reason and experience' (DAI, 331). This third use of 'natural' refers to those human qualities that have the power to seize Tocqueville's own heart and carry him away.

Finally, Tocqueville sometimes employs 'natural', in a usage closely linked to the Rousseauian notion just identified, to designate a sphere of spontaneous social interaction distinct from both the civil and the political spheres. He refers to communal or tribal groupings and the patriarchal family, associations that result from relatively unmediated 'promptings of the human heart', as natural associations. According to Tocqueville, local communes or townships are a feature of all societies. 'The township is the only association so well rooted in nature that wherever men assemble it forms itself. Communal society therefore exists among all peoples, whatever be their customs and their laws; man creates kingdoms and republics, but townships seem to spring directly from the hand of God.'[7] He pays particular attention to the favourable social conditions and human artfulness that may cause these spontaneous communal groupings to flower into free civic institutions, as well as to the unfortunate circumstances and bad choices that undermine their independence and cause them to give in to the inexorable pull of centralizing powers. But, whatever their fate, there is an aura of authenticity that clings to communes because of their quality as natural human formations.

A second example of natural association—the family—also springs everywhere 'from the hand of God'. Tocqueville's general argument about the effects of democracy on the family takes for granted a fundamental distinction between the 'natural' ties of family life and the civil and political ties that prevail in society. 'Democracy loosens social ties, but it tightens natural ones. At the same time as it separates citizens it brings kindred closer together' (DAII, 589; cf. DAI, 291). Families—intimate and interdependent occasions for selflessness—are not just empirically frequent but morally praiseworthy. The contrast between nature and art implicit in Tocqueville's insistence that some human impulses are rooted in the heart, while others are constructed by society and history, also pervades his notion of natural associations, whether communal or familial. These human groupings, though shaped by their histories, are born not made. 'The sovereignty of the [American] Union is a work of art. That of the states is natural; it exists on its own, without striving, like the authority of the father in the family' (DAI, 167).

At least three of the ways in which Tocqueville employs the term 'natural', then, refer to ideas, passions, and instincts that constitute the indelible marks of a higher human nature—however subsequently smudged or refined by social development. Harking back to an older natural law tradition, but more frequently evoking a romantic sense of the authentic law of the heart, Tocqueville refers to a number of passions and behaviors as 'natural'. Considering the matter from the opposite point of view brings more clearly into focus the constellation of concerns that animates his thinking here. When he labels an instinct, or pattern of behaviour, or idea 'unnatural', he not only expresses repugnance and distaste but also implicitly decries the absence of certain moral virtues. The phenomena that elicit this condemnation most frequently are slavery and 'permanent revolution'. The unnaturalness of these social practices lies not in their rarity—they are all too apparent in Tocqueville's world—but rather in their presumed perversion of natural ideas, instincts, or associations. Slavery intensifies and thus deforms relationships of social inequality, whereas permanent revolution disfigures equality of social conditions. But the conjunction of misfortunes is the same in both cases: the distortion of religious impulses; the inability to form stable notions of right, especially of property right; and irregular or vicious sexual habits.

Slavery

Tocqueville clearly distinguishes modern race slavery from a hereditary caste society such as European feudalism, a system also based on unequal social conditions. His few references to the 'unnaturalness' of hereditary aristocratic societies do not really constitute a complete moral condemnation of such societies. Consider, for example, his judgement that an aristocracy 'cannot last unless it is founded on an accepted principle of inequality, legalized in advance, and introduced into the family as well as into the rest of society—all things so violently repugnant to natural equity that only constraint will make men submit to them' (DAI, 399). Contrary to nature because they offend against the sense of equity and fairness that results from adopting a God's-eye view of the world, aristocracies must have been founded by force; people would never have 'naturally' accepted them. But Tocqueville also frequently praises the moral *strengths* of aristocracies, in particular their achievements in having stimulated and perfected what is best in man's nature. He openly values the ability of aristocracies to shape human impulses into a fully formed capacity for religious devotion, human loyalty, proud independence, lasting association, and, above all, a sense of honour and personal freedom that scorns petty self-interest.[8]

Tocqueville, then, gives us at least two contrasting perspectives on the moral worth of aristocracies. His discussions of slave societies manifest no such moral ambivalence. 'There is one evil which has percolated furtively into the world: at first it was hardly noticed among the usual abuses of power; . . . it was cast like an accursed seed somewhere on the ground; it then nurtured itself, grew without effort, and spread with the society that accepted it; that evil was slavery' (DAI, 340). Modern race slavery grows like a pernicious weed in the soil of democracy.

During their legislative careers, Tocqueville and Beaumont were closely associated with questions surrounding the abolition of slavery in the French colonies. Although Tocqueville's writings on slavery employ a range of rhetorical arguments for abolition (including prudential assurances that sugar production would not fall with the use of free as opposed to coerced labour), his underlying belief in the injustice of slavery as an institution, and in particular his condemnation of modern slavery based on race, never wavered.[9] Not only did he think slavery unnatural in the sense that it transgressed the most basic laws of equity (which might also be said of aristocracy, as Tocqueville himself recognized in the example already quoted), but it was unnatural in the sense that it extinguished in the hearts of slaves those spontaneous instincts that alone assured their potential humanity. 'In one blow oppression has deprived the descendants of the Africans of almost all the privileges of humanity': loss of ties to homeland, incapacity for religion and family life, and loss of all interest in their own fate (DAII, 316–17). Moreover, slavery fostered no compensating virtues among the masters. Indeed, it degraded them by making them complicitous in an institution widely contested as illegitimate, but accepted on grounds of expediency (namely that emancipation was impractical).[10]

Tocqueville reacted quite differently to the relationship between master and serf, in which he saw a kind of lost idyll.

These men [serfs] were in a situation like that of our colonial slaves, although they played their role with more liberty, dignity, and morality. Their means of subsistence was almost always assured; the interest of the master coincided with their own on this point. Limited in their desires as well as in their power, without anxiety about a present or a future which was not theirs to choose, they enjoyed a kind of vegetative happiness. It is as difficult for the very civilized man to understand its charm as it is to deny its existence.[11]

Whatever delusions may lurk beneath this judgement, it is clear that Tocqueville thought modern slaves belonged to a category quite different from these allegedly happy serfs; the institution of black chattel slavery had not only inequitably appropriated their labour but had almost obliterated their humanity.

Tocqueville's indictment of slavery relies on the same association of ideas that supported his judgement that democracy could reach a free equilibrium if certain psychological tendencies characteristic of people living in equal social conditions were properly cultivated. *Democracy in America* argues that religion, respect for rights, and a pure family life are among the most important social *mœurs* that sustain the habits of free political action. These are precisely the practices denied to slaves. Without the capacity for independent action, and the hopes and fears it engenders, a slave cannot develop the moral virtues that in turn support the practice of liberty. Therefore, emancipation is necessary to 'enlighten [his] religion, regularize his morals, constitute a family for him, extend and strengthen his intelligence so that he may conceive an idea of the future and live in anticipation of it'.[12] According to Tocqueville, an enslaved person's religious instincts are blunted or perverted, he is utterly without a conception of the rights and wrongs attaching to respect for property, and his (or her) licentious sexuality resembles that of a depraved child or beast.[13] Although Tocqueville relies on contemporary accounts of slavery in America and the Caribbean to bolster these opinions, his position is hardly based on an empirical reconstruction of the psychology of actual slaves. Rather, it is in great part a projection of fears and anxieties surrounding the linked notions of religion, private property, and family that he placed at the core of any recognizably human morality. To deny people access to these social practices was not just a case of extreme despotism; it was an unnatural abomination.

Permanent Revolution

The other social case to which Tocqueville applies the epithet 'unnatural' is that of a society which has succumbed to the temptations of permanent revolution. This alarming spectre—*l'esprit révolutionnaire*—periodically haunts Tocqueville's analyses of French political culture. It is to be distinguished from his dread of a stagnant and spiritless despotism. Although he fears and despises such a democratic despotism—a historical possibility that he brilliantly diagnosed as the bastard offspring of the marriage of democratic individualism to administrative centralization—he does not generally characterize it as 'unnatural' in the sense I have been discussing. The legacy of revolution, however, can literally unhitch people from their human moorings if it should become engrained in their political culture. In the introduction to the first *Democracy*, Tocqueville offers this characterization of the strange confusion of French democracy.

I search my memory in vain, and find nothing sadder or more pitiable than that which happens before our eyes; it would seem that we have nowadays broken the natural link between opinions and tastes, acts and beliefs; that harmony which has been observed throughout history between the feelings and the ideas of men seems to have been destroyed, and one might suppose that all the laws of moral analogy had been abolished. (DAI, 16)

Although in the 1835 *Democracy* Tocqueville characterizes the effects of revolution as inseparable from France's painful transition to democracy, in his later writings the impulse to revolt appears less transitory than permanently inscribed into the rhythms of France's collective life.

Revolutionaries of a hitherto unknown breed came on the scene: men who carried audacity to the point of sheer insanity; who balked at no innovation and, unchecked by any scruples, acted with an unprecedented ruthlessness. Nor were these strange beings mere ephemera, born of a brief crisis and destined to pass away when it ended .... They were already here when we were born, and they are still with us. (AR, 157)

The Revolution of 1848 suggested to him that the French had managed to institutionalize disorder itself. Those who 'silently, methodically' hacked down trees in anticipation of street fighting were perverse reflections of the normal activities of democratic industry: 'it looked exactly like some industrial undertaking, which is just what it was for most of those taking part; an instinct for disorder had given them the taste for it, and experience of past revolutions had taught them the theory' (S, 48). Revolutionary patterns of behaviour had become internalized in the psyches of French men and women where they lay dormant, awaiting the trigger of *ressentiment*.

Revolutionary excitement, however, produces grave disturbances in the natural tendency to believe in God, to limit oneself through established right, and to form stable families. These diminished capacities endanger not only liberty but, in Tocqueville's more pessimistic moments, the concept of stable social life itself. If slaves cannot grasp the elements of religion because their circumstances preclude the idea of hope, people in revolutionary times run amok through an excess of hope and desire. What led the French to commit such 'singular excesses' in the Revolution was not moral callousness or debased standards so much as a complete upset in 'mental equilibrium' (AR, 156). 'In the French Revolution . . . men's minds were in a state of utter confusion; they knew neither what to hold on to, nor where to stop' (AR, 157). The collapse of old religions introduces a chronic restlessness that leaves people open to grotesque and absurd forms of religiosity. If the capacity for religious transcendence withers in the slave from a lack of the opportunity to exercise any forethought at all, the revolutionary spirit overstimulates religious instincts and prevents them from being channelled. Tocqueville describes the following scene observed at the 'Festival of Concord' in his *Souvenirs*: 'One tall young woman stepped aside from her companions and, standing in front of Lamartine, recited an ode in his honour. Gradually, as her recitation went on, she got so excited that her expression became alarming, and her face went into terrible contortions. I have never seen enthusiasm look so like epilepsy' (S, 161).

Just as revolutionary enthusiasm can pervert the natural capacity for religious feeling, so the endless contestation and calculation of revolutionary activity can obliterate the conception of stable rights. For if the very idea of a right is meaningless to a slave, who owns nothing, the notion of a system of rights for all is meaningless to a revolutionary, who feels entitled to everything (DAI, 239). Again in his *Souvenirs*, Tocqueville writes bitterly that the French should not have been surprised that the notion of property itself, the very 'foundation of our social order', should eventually have been repudiated by deprived and depraved individuals. The outbreak of a bout of revolutionary dispossession is like a fever that indicates a deeper malady in the social body. Reflecting on the influence of socialist writers, Tocqueville notes that a 'natural restlessness in the minds of the people, with the inevitable ferment in the desires, thoughts, needs, and instincts of the crowd, formed the fabric on which the innovators drew such monstrous and grotesque patterns' (S, 95). Tocqueville muses that such times bring forth a new political type: a mixture of demagogue, madman, and knight: 'a type who would never come into prominence except in a society as sick and distracted as ours' (S, 148).

This restlessness of mind, finally, is also endemic to households and families in revolutionary times. Men and women routinely break their marriage vows and turn infidelity into a way of life. Evoking the vicious circle of reciprocally reinforcing passions that allegedly emerges between the natural sphere and the civil and political spheres in revolutionary times, Tocqueville contrasts Europe, with its poisonous revolutionary legacies, to America, with its gift of having been born equal without the pain of becoming so:

in Europe almost all the disorders of society are born around the domestic hearth and not far from the nuptial bed. It is there that men come to feel scorn for natural ties and legitimate pleasures and develop a taste for disorder, restlessness of spirit, and instability of desires. Shaken by the tumultuous passions which have often troubled his own house, the European finds it hard to submit to the authority of the state's legislators. (DAI, 291)

Conversely, excited by unstable revolutionary aspirations in the civil and political spheres, they find it difficult to remain quietly at home.

The revolutionary spirit, then, disconnects people from their normal humanity; unchecked, this expansion of human desire can burst the bounds of nature in a kind of collective insanity. Then, perversely, a 'state of semi-madness is not out of place and often leads to success' (S, 152). In some ways the mirror image of institutionalized slave societies, such anarchic situations are equally frightening and unnatural. Indeed, in Tocqueville's mind these opposites exist in uneasy symbiosis and tension. The slave, incapable of supporting absolute repression, at times breaks out in bursts of unregulated savagery. Revolutionary society, exhausted by its own excesses, periodically falls back into lethargic despair. But the earmarks of such unnatural societies remain the same: the frustration of authentic religious experience, the lack of a true conception of rights, and the prevalence of sexual confusion and licence. These are moral disorders with a long pedigree in writings on republicanism, but the self-evident immediacy of the threats they posed for Tocqueville suggests a sensibility exquisitely attuned to the fragility of the moral order and the absence of shared social purpose. Examining more closely Tocqueville's instinctual reactions to the demands of God, the rights of man, and the duties of woman reveals a peculiar interplay between moral apprehension and social analysis in these arguments 'from the depths of the heart'.

The Demands of God

According to Tocqueville, Christianity sustains free democratic *mœurs*.[14] He offers a number of separate arguments for this belief, including direct affinities between the intellectual demands of salvation religions and the demands of free politics, the compensatory psychological effects of stable beliefs, and the structural benefits of separating church and state. In all these arguments his point is to demonstrate the positive relationship between Christian beliefs and the psychological dispositions necessary to sustain liberty. This sociological analysis—or, as Tocqueville puts it, consideration 'from a purely human point of view'—responds in a particular way to a wider problematic of his generation, namely the need for a psychological *point d'appui* that would inspire independent and confident judgements, but would at the same time facilitate self-restraint.[15] But one should not be misled into thinking that this analysis was cynical, or even formulated in any simple way from the stance of an unbeliever. In Tocqueville's case, an insistence on the utility of religion is linked to an obscure recognition of God's claims on him.

The question of Tocqueville's religious beliefs and temperament has long been a matter of historical controversy, complicated by his admission of a loss of faith coupled with such regretful statements as 'I am not a believer, though I am far from celebrating that fact'.[16] Brought up in a pious Catholic milieu and educated by a Jansenist-leaning abbé to whom he was firmly attached by ties of sympathy and respect, Tocqueville did not lose his faith lightly. Although he managed to achieve an admirable intellectual equilibrium after his reading of Rousseau and Voltaire destroyed his naive religious beliefs, he never truly regained his moral and spiritual ballast. In a famous confession to Madame Swetchine near the end of his life, he relates that this early religious crisis left him prone to black periods of doubt and despair, moods in which he seemed to thrash about in a void.[17]

Looking at the problem of human existence, I am both absorbed and overwhelmed. I cannot penetrate this mystery; neither can I stop looking at it. It excites and depresses me by turns. In this world, I find human life inexplicable; in the other world, it is terrifying. I firmly believe in an afterlife because God, who is supremely wise, has given us an idea of it; and that good will be rewarded and evil punished, because God has allowed us to tell them apart and has given us the freedom to choose; beyond those clear notions, everything outside of this world seems shrouded in darkness which terrifies me.[18]

Tocqueville always clung to a belief in a benevolent deity, in an afterlife in which God would reward the just, and in the moral superiority of Christianity. These convictions, however, brought no serenity. Unlike Pascal, whose writings he knew intimately and returned to frequently, Tocqueville could neither leap into faith nor find any permanent respite from his doubts. Indeed, the closest he came to an authentic religious experience was a sense of fear and awe when abruptly confronted by his own inadequate powers of comprehension. These fleeting experiences of powerlessness did not sustain Tocqueville spiritually, but they apparently confirmed his instinct to accept certain matters 'without discussion' (DAII, 434). They served as psychological evidence of his own—and by extension humanity's—capacity for transcendence of the mundane. They also fortified his suspicion that true religious experience was humbling; it held one back from limitless experimentation.

Intimations of a hidden spiritual world were frequently triggered in Tocqueville by natural landscape and by evidence of the inexorable passage of time. These themes are already present in Tocqueville's earliest writing—for example in the travel diaries of his trip to Sicily in 1827. Unlike some other romantic souls, however, he responded to nature neither with ecstatic contemplation nor a mystical sense of wholeness or release. Instead he experienced premonitions of nothingness and abandonment. 'Standing on this burning rock in the middle of the sea . . . we had a feeling of abandonment and isolation that weighed heavily on our imagination and crushed it.'[19] The terror of human insignificance overcomes him in the shadow of Mount Etna, in the surreal light of a single lantern held up against the darkness of an ancient Sicilian forest, and in the experience of utter helplessness on shipboard during a fierce storm. In the midst of the storm he observes:

I will remember all my life the profound impression I experienced, when, in a moment of calm, I heard nearby a certain number of muffled voices repeating the responses of a psalm. I looked for the source of the voices and I saw that they were rising from under a canvas where ten or twelve poor passengers had taken refuge. Where is the philosopher, however sure of his systems, who has not been tempted to do likewise at the sight of this terrible manifestation of divine power?[20]

Tocqueville could never bring himself to join those under the canvas, but he always envied their ability to react with spontaneous piety.

The spectacle of human efforts effaced by the passage of time or by the reclaiming powers of nature moved Tocqueville in similar ways. Italy, so filled with ruins of the past, constantly recalled to him the fragility of human things. And the most personal and revealing passages both in the published volumes of *Democracy in America* and in his travel diaries are those which record his reaction to landscapes, and to the power of 'nature' in the face of human efforts to influence it. The immensity and silence of the virgin forest, rather than any interaction with America's people or institutions, called forth passages of transparent feeling. The ruins of a house being rapidly overtaken by vegetation on an uninhabited island on Lake Oneida, he reports, moved him more profoundly than anything else in his American travels.[21]

Similar images of extinction—the slipping away of human purpose and meaning—emerge in Tocqueville's poignant discussions of the plight of native peoples in America. The thought of lost civilizations, obliterated from collective memory, oppressed his imagination. The present Indian inhabitants, whom he explicitly compared to the barbarian ancestors of European aristocrats and whose nobility of spirit he openly admired, were themselves doomed to a similar fate. They could not prevail against the forces of civilization and were in any case too proud to try.[22] Tocqueville gives this account of the dispossession of the Choctaws, which he witnessed in 1831.

I saw them embark to cross the great river [the Mississippi], and the sight will never fade from my memory. Neither sob nor complaint rose from that silent assembly. Their afflictions were of long standing, and they felt them to be irremediable. All the Indians had already got into the boat that was to carry them across; their dogs were still on the bank; as soon as the animals finally realized that they were being left behind forever, they all together raised a terrible howl and plunged into the icy waters of the Mississippi to swim after their masters. (DAI, 324)

The plaintive howl of the dogs evokes the shattered link to the Indians' birthplace and that of their ancestors, a tie that Tocqueville thought arose naturally in the human heart. Not the least of the many tragedies associated with race slavery and the forced evacuations of Indians in America was the wrenching displacement that occurred when a people was forcibly evicted from its 'ancestral fields' (DAI, 323).

Although Tocqueville at times describes patriotism, the tie to one's homeland, as an extension of individual self-interest, his deepest inclination is to pit patriotism against calculations of material self-interest.[23] For this reason his heart was drawn to the Canadian peasant who, unlike his southern neighbour, tilled his own fields without restless thoughts of moving on to more fertile land. When Tocqueville asked such a farmer why he stayed at home, he retorted, 'Why do you love your wife best, even though your neighbor's has more beautiful eyes?' Tocqueville 'found that there was a real and profound sentiment in this response'.[24] Typical also is his appreciation of the Indians' first reaction to European offers to purchase their lands. 'We will not sell the spot which contains the bones of our fathers' (DAI, 323). Images of ancestral bones, entombed forever in the soil where their descendants would also live and die, exerted a powerful pull on Tocqueville. They countered his fears of the rootlessness of democratic peoples and symbolized a reverent attraction to birthplace that was obscurely but tightly intertwined with religion, family, and all the truly human instincts. 'There is a patriotism which mainly springs from the disinterested, undefinable, and unpondered feeling that ties a man's heart to the place where he was born. This instinctive love is mingled with a taste for old habits, respect for ancestors, and memories of the past; those who feel it love their country as one loves one's father's house' (DAI, 235). Disinterested patriotism of this sort is a natural antidote to the petty activities that consume daily life in a democracy.

Two incidents, separated by twenty years, suggest the romantic nature of attachment to place in Tocqueville's emotional makeup. When travelling in Sicily as a young man, he observed by chance a fisherman's family near the shore. The sight of them doting on the baby of the family caused a piercing homesickness. 'Never in my life, as in that moment, had I understood the horror of exile and the reality of those feelings for one's native land which bring you back home from so far away, in spite of all the obstacles and dangers. The memory of France and of everything that this word includes descended on me like a prey.'[25] '[P]oor dear Tocqueville', his ancestral chateau in Normandy, provoked similar flashes of undefinable feeling. He leaves us this account of his stay there during the Second Republic: 'This was the first time I had been back there since the revolution [of 1848] and I was perhaps going to leave it forever. On entering the house I was flooded with such an intense and peculiar sadness that the memory of it still remains firmly engraved on my mind' (S, 118).

Such passages from Tocqueville's diaries and memoirs as well as from his published works suggest a nature prone to infusions of intense, inchoate longings. But what connects this sensibility to his determinedly earthbound analyses of the useful functions of religion or patriotism? When considered from the point of view of Tocqueville's spiritual malaise, these analyses 'from the human point of view' appear to exhibit the humility of a penance. If he cannot find peace himself, he will nevertheless use the gift of his intelligence to make the utilitarian case for God's plan, which is both the only standpoint left to him and the only one likely to move his listeners. But it is the evidence of Tocqueville's own soul that both convinces him of men's natural religious instincts and fuels his arguments for the compatibility between democracy and Christianity. His utilitarian arguments constitute a species of offering to a God that he can no longer wholeheartedly embrace.

Tocqueville, then, responds to his fitful experiences of the transcendent with terror at the approach of a smothering darkness and a resolve to stand his watch to the best of his ability. These responses frequently appear as well in his discussion of the providential and inexorable march of equality. The same images that convey his intimations of a divine presence in nature—darkness and light, constriction and expansion, terror and hope—convey his intimations of a divine presence in history. The revolution taking place in the social condition, laws, ideas, and feelings of men, he tells us, is so overwhelming and sudden that '[t]he past throws no light on the future, and the spirit of man walks through the night' (DAII, 702; cf. 456, 463, 464, 487). Characteristically, he reacts to the prospect of this dark journey with exhortation to steadfast efforts: 'Let us, then, look forward to the future with that salutary fear which makes men keep watch and ward for freedom, and not with that flabby, idle terror which makes men's hearts sink and enervates them' (DAII, 702). In the introduction to the 1835 *Democracy* he offers this account of his motivation in undertaking such a vast intellectual task as describing the shape of the democratic future.

> This whole book has been written under the impulse of a kind of religious dread inspired by contemplation of this irresistible revolution advancing century by century over every obstacle and even now going forward amid the ruins it has itself created. God does not Himself need to speak for us to find sure signs of His will; it is enough to observe the customary progress of nature and the continuous tendency of events; I know, without special revelation, that the stars follow orbits in space traced by his finger. If patient observation and sincere meditation have led men of the present day to recognize that both the past and the future of their history consist in the gradual and measured advance of equality, that discovery in itself gives this progress the sacred character of the will of the Sovereign Master. In that case effort to halt democracy appears as a fight against God Himself, and nations have no alternative but to acquiesce in the social state imposed by Providence. (DAI, 12)

Much has been written about Tocqueville's invocation of providence in passages like these; in part he is attempting to counter rhetorically those who based their anti-democratic arguments on religion. But this passage is more than strategic rhetoric; it also faithfully reflects Tocqueville's conception of a spiritual duty to justify God's mysterious ways to the world despite his own fears and contrary inclinations.

At the very end of the second *Democracy* Tocqueville again refers to the need to overcome human weakness in order to accomplish a difficult spiritual and intellectual task.

> I see that this pleasure [in contemplating the glories of aristocracy] arose from my weakness. It is because I am unable to see at once all that is around me that I am allowed thus to select and separate the objects of my choice from among so many others which it pleases me to contemplate. It is not so with the Almighty and Eternal Being, whose gaze of necessity includes the whole of created things .... I therefore do all I can to enter into understanding of this divine view of the world and strive from thence to consider and judge the affairs of men. (DAII, 704)

For Tocqueville, judging the affairs of men from the standpoint of the divine *means* striving to make out the new logic of democracy, the new grammar of its psychology and culture. After this passage on the need to imitate the divine 'gaze', he abruptly changes his tone and reassumes his analytical persona. 'No man on earth can affirm, absolutely and generally, that the new state of societies is better than the old, but it is already easy to see that it is different' (DAII, 704).

That Tocqueville breaks the rhythm of his prose after a self-revelatory passage, switching from poet to analyst, is significant substantively as well as stylistically. A paragraph on the disappearance of the type of servant characteristic of the old European aristocracy, for example, builds to this sentence: 'They are slipping from our sight and daily merging into the darkness of the past with the social state that bore them.' Tocqueville then begins a new paragraph with the brisk 'Equality makes new men of servant and of master and establishes new connections between them', repeating the word 'new' and taking the reader back to present descriptive time. This disjunction of affect, this moving back and forth between evaluative standpoints, creates a style of multiple irony in which the reader is always in the position of appraising incongruities. The cumulative effect of such layering is to induce an awareness of Tocqueville's moral intuitions, and of the moral struggle behind his apparently objective analyses, without requiring him to defend his religious or ethical views in any straightforward manner. To ignore the force of these textual elisions is to risk misunderstanding the context of his 'functional' theorizing. Jack Lively, for example, arguing (with good reason) against those early commentators who tried to make Tocqueville into a closet son of the church, notes that they failed to see that 'it is possible (if disconcerting) to appreciate the social or even psychological value of a religion without believing in its truth'.[26] But Lively fails to see that his construction in its turn creates a false impression of Tocqueville's indifference to religious claims. Both Tocqueville's views on the natural religious instincts and his strenuous intellectual attempts to demonstrate the social and psychological utility of religion were ultimately dependent on his own spiritual intuitions.

Tocqueville, then, forces himself to make the case for the democratic masses because God has allowed him enough 'light' to glimpse the justice of their claims, if not enough real illumination to allow him to embrace democratic justice with his soul.[27] Contrast this Tocquevillian self-image with his judgement on the eighteenth-century philosophes, whom he indicts for intellectual and political hubris.

To be accurate, it must be said that the human intellect which some of these philosophers adored was simply their own. . . . I could mention several who despised the public almost as heartily as they despised the Deity. Towards the latter they evinced the pride of rivals—the former they treated with the pride of parvenus. They were as far from real and respectful submission to the will of the majority as from submission to the will of God. (AR, 281)

Unlike these *philosophes*, who thought that religion and political progress were antithetical, Tocqueville viewed the qualities of character necessary for submission to God and for submission to democracy as fused and inseparable. In neither case did this submission happen without moral effort on his part, nor was it achieved without continual discipline. Indeed, the similar efforts at psychological self-mastery involved in serving God and serving the public apparently reinforced the connection between religion and democracy in Tocqueville's own mind and hence fuelled his intellectual efforts to persuade contemporaries of religion's utility. Because he did not experience his intellectual efforts at justification by consequences to be in conflict with the spiritual task God had set for him, he was not deeply troubled by the possibility of an ultimate contradiction between utility and right. His efforts arose from a will to believe that not even his own loss of conventional faith could shake.

The Rights of Man

If Tocqueville strove in the first instance merely to describe and analyse social relations, we have seen that certain 'natural' instincts nevertheless wrung from him spontaneous and unqualified approval, and that such emotional responses profoundly shaped his thinking. Among these instincts was respect for the 'beautiful' idea of rights. But to revere rights was not necessarily to revere the 'natural rights of man'. Tocqueville shared the pervasive post-revolutionary distaste for the ideology of abstract individual rights, which he associated with the naivety of the first French revolutionaries and the excesses of their successors. Moreover, his own intellectual gifts for historical discrimination, comparison, and contrast led him away from a philosophical defence of rights as they had led him away from a theological defence of religion. He completely distanced himself, for example, from the phrase 'sovereignty of the people' insofar as it connoted the idea that the people have an absolute *right* to self-rule. Almost every use of this phrase is qualified by the words 'the dogma of', 'the principle of', or 'so-called'. These locutions are determinedly descriptive. When Tocqueville says, 'The dogma of the sovereignty of the people came out from the township and took possession of the government', he is reporting that the practice of local self-government in America facilitated the development of an idea of self-rule on the national level.[28] Like the dogma of divine right, the dogma of the sovereignty of the people is simply a collective opinion to be judged by its effects and the company it keeps: 'It is a great puzzle to decide if one is more false than the other; but what is very certain is that neither is true.'[29]

If Tocqueville recoiled from some kinds of rights talk, he nevertheless insisted that nothing so elevates people in their mutual relations as the notion of fixed unbreachable limits to human action. He discusses this notion from two points of view, which parallel the normative uses of 'natural' described above: from the vantage-point of natural justice and from that of a set of admirable instincts that contribute to a truly human life. His use of the traditional language of natural justice is evident in the following passage, which defines justice as those rules deriving from the 'sovereignty of the human race'.

There is one law which has been made, or at least adopted, not by the majority of this or that people, but by the majority of all men. That law is justice. Justice therefore forms the boundary to each people's rights. A nation is like a jury entrusted to represent universal society and to apply the justice which is its law. Should the jury representing society have greater power than that very society whose laws it applies? Consequently, when I refuse to obey an unjust law, I by no means deny the majority's right to give orders; I only appeal from the sovereignty of the people to the sovereignty of the human race.[30]

The phrase 'unjust law' in this passage presumably refers to a law that contravenes the most basic notions of justice, such as prohibitions of murder and false dealing. These prohibitions can never be set aside by the sovereign's claims because higher law 'forms the boundary to each people's rights'. Tocqueville may also intend to include other basic rights under this rubric of justice, since one also finds him occasionally labelling certain civil rights respected in free democracies as 'natural', e.g. 'The most natural right of man, after that of acting on his own, is that of combining his efforts with those of his fellows and acting together. Therefore the right of association seems to me by nature almost as inalienable as individual liberty' (DAI, 193). In an unpublished gloss on the Declaration of the Rights of Man, Tocqueville apparently added a list of indispensable liberties that the original declaration had never managed to protect: procedural guarantees against preventive arrest and home searches, the responsibility of government agents to the proper authorities, religious liberty, freedom of association and press, and freedom of elections.[31]

Although one can find such scattered natural rights language in Tocqueville's works, it is difficult to discern any consistent use of it other than a vague deference to natural justice. His judgements on the place of specific freedoms in structuring the relations among people in society are much more characteristically relative and contextual. But there is another sense in which rights are fundamental to human existence. From this point of view what is transcendently valuable is not any particular set of rights, but the very capacity to form the idea of a right and to abide by it. This capacity calls forth humanity's highest faculties because, like religious impulses, it simultaneously promotes energetic action and self-restraint. When the idea of untouchable rights is embodied in institutions and behaviour, it both establishes channels for action and creates limits. 'By means of the idea of rights men have defined the nature of license and of tyranny. Guided by its light, we can each of us be independent without arrogance and obedient without servility' (DAI, 238). Slavery and permanent revolution are unnatural more because they injure the precious capacity to form rights and the motivations necessary to respect them than because they suppress any civil rights in particular. Here Tocqueville is very close to Burke in his perception that respect for rights and law-abidingness come from long practice. 'It cannot be repeated too often; nothing is more fertile in marvels than the art of being free, but nothing is harder than freedom's apprenticeship' (DAI, 240). Unlike Burke, however, Tocqueville saw no other recourse in democratic times than to equalize access to civil and political rights. His analysis of the strongest psychological tendencies associated with a democratic social condition had convinced him that tendencies towards individualism could not be uprooted, but they could be combined in new ways with the idea of untouchable rights.

The example of property illustrates Tocqueville's lack of interest in a philosophical defence of rights and his bent towards a contextual analysis of how rights actually function in aristocratic and democratic societies. More important for the purposes of the present discussion, however, it also reveals his assumptions about what was morally at stake in a democratic world, since attacks on the general idea of rights to private property touched on a core fear: a society in which literally any transgression was thinkable. Underlying Tocqueville's analysis of the social and moral effects of private property is an article of faith: private property and the family structure that it supports are inextricably tied to any conception of civilized freedom. He nowhere suggests that there is an absolute right to private property; indeed, his argument in *Democracy in America* on beliefs in the general right to property parallels his argument about the belief in popular sovereignty. Just as Americans derive the idea that they have a right to rule themselves from the fact that they do rule themselves in local assemblies, so they derive the general idea of the legitimacy of property from the fact that everyone has (or can realistically be expected to own) some property. But these observations on the social construction of property rights do not suggest that Tocqueville himself was prepared to question the right to property or to condone such questioning. The intrusion of his comparative sensibilities into the issue of property's *legitimacy*, in contrast to the variety of its functions, was rare and tentative.[32] Tocqueville himself could never seriously conceive of a civilized order that did not recognize an individual's exclusive property claims. For him the notion of property was fundamental to the rule of law itself.

There is a curious passage in the *Souvenirs* when Tocqueville, apparently without irony, likens the hysterical closing of all ranks against the socialists to the heroic last stand of a family: 'the richest were the elder brothers and the less prosperous the younger; but all thought themselves brothers, having a common inheritance to defend' (S, 109). He saw clearly that such an alliance was temporary, motivated solely by despair and fear of the loss of worldly goods. It was nevertheless praiseworthy because it held back the barbarian hordes of misguided levellers. For Tocqueville, as for others in 'respectable' society, the defence of a notion of individual property rights that was the legacy of the Revolution and enshrined in the Civil Code had become a clear line in the sand. Arrayed on one side were those who could still think more or less rationally about social order; on the other was the mob led by men whose minds had become unhinged. He recalls his first glimpse of Blanqui in the following terms.[33]

It was at that moment that I saw a man go up onto the rostrum, and, although I have never seen him again, the memory of him has filled me with disgust and horror ever since. He had sunken, withered cheeks, white lips, and a sickly, malign, dirty look like a pallid, mouldy corpse; he was wearing no visible linen; an old black frock coat covered his lean, emaciated limbs tightly; he looked as if he had lived in a sewer and only just come out. (S, 147)

Tocqueville judged socialist attempts to appropriate the language of rights into such areas as state aid to the poor or the right to work to be perversions of a democratic social order, rather than derivations from its liberal sensibilities. He constructed a slippery slope from the recognition of any such claim to the final disaster of revolutionary social chaos.[34]

It is, of course, possible to envision social rights in the opposite light: not as a slide into Armageddon, but as a bridge from civil democracy to social democracy. Whatever the arguments for or against such an expansive notion of civil rights, it does not seem that the move from civil to social rights is conceptually incoherent.[35] But in Tocqueville's rhetorical world, the gulf was impassable and the idea of rights contained no such exploitable ambiguities.

There is nothing which, generally speaking, elevates and sustains the human spirit more than the idea of rights. There is something great and virile in the idea of right which removes from any request its suppliant character, and places the one who claims it on the same level as the one who grants it. But the right of the poor to obtain society's help is unique in that instead of elevating the heart of the man who exercises it, it lowers him.[36]

Concerned about the potential abuses of a state bureaucracy administering any system of state aid, Tocqueville was even more worried about the moral dangers of recognizing a legal right to aid. To claim such a right would be to avow weakness and to undermine the virtues leading to independence. Moreover, state charity would shatter the voluntary relationship between giver and receiver without putting another social context in its place. Voluntary charity at least created the admirable feelings of responsibility and gratitude, while a system of state aid, on the contrary, 'ranges [rich and poor] each one under a banner, tallies them, and, bringing them face to face, prepares them for combat'.[37] Tocqueville's fears of tampering with the legal bases of property— beyond the equitable adjustment of some taxes—blinds him to other possible ways in which the idea of 'right' might function in the public sphere. John Stuart Mill, for example, speculates that the legal recognition of a subsistence right might symbolize a new spirit of altruism consistent with moral progress and mutual respect, or even foster a new associational relationship between employer and employed.[38]

As in the case of religious opinions, Tocqueville clearly recognized that under some circumstances scepticism could successfully undermine the belief in the legitimacy of private property. In both these areas, however, Tocqueville could hardly conceive of any compensating good that might result from such interrogation of religion or property. These were topics that provoked strong pre-monitions of slipping into a confusing darkness in which 'the spirit of man walked through the night'. The same can be said of attempts to abridge 'the oldest inequality of all, that between men and women' (S, 98).

The Duties of Woman

Tocqueville's deeply gendered conception of society and politics and his portrait of women in democracy reveal both his particular preconceptions and his method of argument when social anxieties are brought near to the surface. It is odd, then, that the subject should occasion so little systematic commentary by Tocqueville scholars.[39] A partial exception is Jon Elster, who, in the context of examining Tocqueville's prejudices and their impact on the pattern of his thought, has recently puzzled over his unwavering approval of 'masculinity'. Elster notes that although Tocqueville sometimes exhibits spontaneous respect and affection for aristocracy and monarchy, those subjects could also trigger a bracing realism. 'By contrast, his innumerable references to the 'male and virile' vir-tues are not counterbalanced in his writings by any criticism of male domination or questioning of female submission.'[40] Accord-ing to Elster, however, Tocqueville's gender prejudices turn out to be uncharacteristic blind spots which impede the progress of his reasoning, but do not affect the way in which we read him as a whole. Theoretically, then, these prejudices are something of a curiosity.

In these remarks, Elster seems to make both too much and too little of Tocqueville's views on the status of women. On the one hand, he mistakes the significance of Tocqueville's praise of manli-ness. It is certainly true that, while other Tocquevillian terms have potentially contradictory meanings, *manly* and *virile* are synonyms only for the praiseworthy qualities of independent judgement, self-respect, and the capacity for voluntary autonomous action. But in context *virile* and *manly* are always distinguished from *servile* or *slavish*; Tocqueville does not explicitly or implicitly contrast them to *feminine* or *womanly*. Consider these characteristic uses (emphasis added):

Each man having some rights and being sure of the enjoyment of those rights, there would be established between all classes a *manly* confidence and a sort of reciprocal courtesy, as far removed from pride as from servility.   (DAI, 14)

There is indeed a *manly* and legitimate passion for equality which rouses in all men a desire to be strong and respected. This passion tends to elevate the little man to the rank of the great. But the human heart also nourishes a debased taste for equality which leads the weak to want to drag the strong down to their level and which induces men to prefer equality in servitude to inequality in freedom.   (DAI, 57)

I like this natural demeanor of democratic government and the inner authority which goes more with the office than with the official, and more with the man than with external symbols of power, for there is something admirably *virile* therein.   (DAI, 203)

It seems to me that such men [white men who agree temporarily to serve others for wages] carry into domestic service some of those *manly* habits which are born of freedom and equality.   (DAII, 578)

There is no need for me to say that this universal and uncontrolled desire for official appointments is a great social evil, that it undermines every citizen's sense of independence and spreads a venal and servile temper throughout the nation, that it stifles *manly* virtues . . .   (DAII, 633; cf. DAI, 258; DAII, 568, 593, 601; AR, 208)

These texts do not construct masculinity as against femininity, or implicitly uphold male domination over women. Rather they reveal Tocqueville's fixation on the contrast between classes in aristocracies and democracies. In the former only nobles could be independent *vires* with the psychological characteristics such independence encourages, but in the latter all citizens were potentially so.

On the other hand, there is something deeply puzzling and potentially more significant about Tocqueville's arguments about women over which Elster does not linger. Tocqueville's consideration of women in democracy, unlike his discussion of slaves, native Americans, or French peasants, almost never dwells empathetically on women's perspectives or psychology; he relegates them uncompromisingly to the realm of domesticity, using a singular chain of argumentation that has the unmistakable ring of a *parti pris*.[41] Considered in the company of the other parameters that, in his view, prevent a people from swirling into collective excess and transgression, Tocqueville's belief in the need to confine women within the family looks less like discrete prejudice and more like part of a larger web of cultural apprehension. As in the cases of religion and rights, particular fears cloud his arguments about women's natural place in a well-ordered democracy. The perceived nearness of a terrifying unnatural alternative strengthens his determination to work out a convincing brief for democratic freedom, and lends an inexorable quality to his combination of moralism and pragmatism.

Tocqueville's categorization of social interactions in America divides them into civil, political, and natural. In America, he tells us, women inhabit the natural sphere exclusively. Men, in their capacities as heads of families, also live in natural associations, but they step outside of these to act as citizens. Tocqueville thus espouses the quite conventional view that the equality existing among democratic men—all capable of serving the same functions, having the same rights and duties, and sharing the world of work, pleasure, and public affairs—is inappropriate for women. 'It is easy to see that this sort of equalization forced on both sexes degrades them both, and that so coarse a jumble of nature's works could produce nothing but feeble men and immodest women' (DAII, 601). What is of particular interest, however, is not this garden-variety prejudice, which was hardly remarkable for the time, but rather Tocqueville's peculiarly charged arguments about why the presence of women ought literally to be expunged from civil and political relations.

In arguing against allowing women into the public sphere, Tocqueville relies surprisingly little on evidence about the physical and mental differences between men and women. Here, as elsewhere, he shuns arguments based on physiological difference that would seem to downgrade the existential value of human choice.[42] And he specifically sets aside Montesquieu's argument that climate affects the status of women as a 'cheap way of getting out of the matter' (DAII, 594). Nor do his arguments arise out of close analysis of women's actual roles in America, despite his famous observation that women are the primary conduit of religious influence in America and thus a crucial influence on mores. Religion, Tocqueville says, 'reigns supreme in the souls of the women, and it is women who shape mores' (DAI, 291). And again: 'There have never been free societies without mores, and as I observed in the first part of this book, it is woman who shapes these mores. Therefore everything which has a bearing on the status of women, their habits, and their thoughts is, in my view, of great political importance' (DAII, 590). One would expect from these comments to find some consideration of women and religion, or a discussion of women as educators and socializers of citizens. In all of these areas, there

192

would have been much to observe.[43] Tocqueville, however, tells us nothing about them, and very little at all about women's habits or thoughts in democratic society. Indeed, his references to women are overwhelmingly directed to a different issue: how the seclusion of married women in the family, that is, their subjection to a strict sexual code and lack of social contact with men not their husbands, helps to inoculate democracy against its potential dangers.

What Tocqueville wishes to account for and to advocate above all is the connection between 'purity of morals'—by which he means absolute sexual fidelity for women and men's avoidance of extramarital affairs with respectable women—and equality of social conditions.[44] In order to shape his American material to this theoretical end, Tocqueville rejects the possibility that Americans' attitudes towards sexual morality were mostly derived from causes associated with America's *point de départ*, in particular its English and Puritan origins. In a diary note of 21 September 1831, he gives five causes for chaste American morals: physical constitution ('They belong to a northern race'), Puritan religion, preoccupation with business, special attitudes towards marriage, and the education and character of American women.[45] By the time of the writing of the first *Democracy*, he would emphasize only the last three, which could be construed as tendencies arising from democracy itself.

No doubt this great strictness of American mores is due partly to the country, the race, and the religion. But all those causes, which can be found elsewhere, are still not enough to account for the matter. To do so one must discover some particular reason. I think that reason is equality and the institutions deriving therefrom. Equality of conditions does not by itself alone make mores more strict, but there can be no doubt that it aids and increases such a tendency. (DAII, 595)

A very instructive contrast to this generalizing argument can be found in his discussion of American art and literature. Tocqueville disdained American efforts in literature, poetry, art, and history as ignorant and philistine. But he was at some pains to argue that there was no culture in America not because America was democratic, but because it was American (DAII, 454–8). The Americans were in an exceptional situation and 'a thousand special causes' fixed their minds on practical objects. In particular, the legacy of Puritanism and the continued identification with aristocratic England (which supplied ready-made cultural notions to American elites) inhibited the growth of an indigenous art and literature. But other societies need not follow this pattern. Democratic culture will be different from aristocratic culture, but not necessarily devoid of merit and feeling. Tocqueville in fact believed that the coming of democracy had not impeded human capacities for profound literary and artistic expression in Europe, even though that expression had so far come in revolutionary form.[46] Tocqueville could have made a similar argument about sexual attitudes in America; he could have asserted, and with more basis, that strict notions of sexual morality in America obtained not because America was democratic, but because it was American. But in this matter Tocqueville wished to make the Americans exemplary for Europe, whereas in the matter of artistic culture he wanted to render them irrelevant.

What, then, are the elements of this exemplary sexual model that can be espied in American experience? Tocqueville's argument proceeds in two stages. First, he shows how the coming of democracy has broken down the formal structure of the aristocratic family and hence transformed the context in which the natural relationships of kinship develop. Next he demonstrates the allegedly stabilizing mechanisms that unfold along with those new relationships, among which the most important is an unexpected affinity between democracy and purity of morals.

Tocqueville begins with the Roman law conception of the patriarchal family, which, he argues, has lost its *raison d'être* because of the rise of democracy. It should be noted, however, that the crucial chapter of the second *Democracy*, 'Influence of Democracy on the Family', chronicles the death of the inegalitarian family by analysing relations only among fathers, sons, and brothers. Tocqueville never even mentions mothers, wives, or daughters until he has examined the crucial matter of the dominance of fathers over sons, in his view the heart and soul of patriarchy. His point is to show how a combination of democratic influences, of which the most important is division of patrimonies, undermines the aristocratic father's influence over his sons' lives and the consequent hierarchy among brothers. The father's political and legal function as the link between past and present, between sovereign and subject, disappears entirely and he is left 'only a citizen older and richer than his sons' (DAII, 586). 'So at the same time as aristocracy loses its power, all that was austere, conventional, and legal in parental power also disappears and a sort of equality reigns around the domestic hearth . . . The master and magistrate have vanished; the father remains'

(DAII, 588–9). Similarly, the pre-eminence of the first-born brother dissolves and brothers face each other as equals.

These powerful forces of equality cannot help but affect relations between the sexes as well. 'I think that the same social impetus which brings nearer to the same level father and son, master and servant, and generally every inferior to every superior does raise the status of women and should make them more and more nearly equal to men' (DAII, 600). Indeed, the breakdown of the patriarchal family frees daughters from parental influence in ways that parallel the release of sons. Here Tocqueville uses the example of American girls, who have experienced to a greater degree the effects of a completely democratic social condition: 'Before she has completely left childhood behind [the young American woman] already thinks for herself, speaks freely, and acts on her own' (DAII, 590). The system of arranged marriages, weakened in Europe, has broken down totally in America. Pairing by choice is the rule for daughters as well as sons.

Dissolution of the patriarchal power that formerly connected natural to civil and political society might be thought to presage great disorder. On the contrary, Tocqueville argues, democracy gives birth to its own stabilizing tendencies and to the possibility of a new congruence between family and societal patterns. He considers first the challenge of a new relationship between fathers, sons, and brothers. When the special legal and political status of the aristocratic family disappears, its members' natural ties are strengthened because their hearts are now 'free to unite' (DAII, 589). They lend each other trusty support and are united by a new affection and intimacy. While the dissolution of aristocratic corporate bodies may be a cost to society, in that bulwarks against despotism are eroded, Tocqueville believes that on balance the individual gains. A new sweetness pervades daily life and replaces the coldness and formality of familial relationships under aristocracy. Sons do not have to struggle for freedom, but are quite naturally launched into the world; consequently, 'one sees none of those hateful, disorderly passions which disturb men long after they have shaken off an established yoke' (DAII, 595). Tocqueville's analysis of new forms of association in *Democracy in America* suggested that damage to society caused by the new democratic family—loss of corporate identity among aristocratic citizens—is not necessarily irreparable. His discussion of paternal and fraternal relations in democratic families is in fact an unexpectedly romanticizing text. In many of the other moral contrasts he draws between aristocracy and democracy, Tocqueville idealizes aristocrats as honourable, loyal, and selfless, while he judges democratic citizens more severely as cold calculators—whether egoistic or enlightened. Here he turns the tables completely. He depicts relations in aristocratic families as 'cold' and 'rigid'; brothers are held together largely by a common interest in promoting family fortunes. In democracy, however, 'not interest . . . but common memories and the unhampered sympathy of thoughts and tastes' draws brother to brother (DAII, 589).

The issue of democratic relationships between fathers and daughters, and between husbands and wives, is inherently more difficult to resolve. If Tocqueville were to adopt the reasoning that he has used elsewhere, he might speculate—even were he to disapprove—that women brought up to think and act and speak on their own would also seek independent roles on the intellectual and public stage. After all, many of his arguments about democratic practices are based on the 'spillover' effect, the notion that habits and sentiments contracted in one sphere of social life spread into others. But Tocqueville constructs a very different trajectory for the democratic woman's life, a narrative that owes more to a particular cultural disquiet than to observation of American practice or clear-eyed analysis of democratic tendencies. His chapter 'Education of Girls in the United States' constructs a special heroic destiny for women. If Tocqueville sentimentalizes the relations among men in the new democratic family, he romanticizes in quite a different way the fate of women in those families.

Democracy inclines all individuals to depend on their own powers of reasoning and judgement. Americans encourage this tendency among women as well as men. Exposed to the conflicting demands and passions of the world at a young age, girls must and do develop self-reliance and self-restraint and the habit of taking responsibility for themselves and their futures. Educated to choose a compatible mate, they are left entirely free to make that choice. It is at this point that Tocqueville's story takes a surprising and implausible turn. Upon her marriage, a woman suddenly vanishes from civil society and retreats into a wholly private existence as a devoted wife and mother: sexually faithful and consumed by the petty details of domestic economy. The American woman thereafter 'never leaves her domestic sphere and is in some respects very dependent within it' (DAII, 603). I will return to this *deus ex machina*. But first, let us consider the functions of the wife's domestic role in Tocqueville's conception of the ideal workings of democracy 'itself'.

In classical republican political theory, the strict confinement of women to the household and the enforcement of female chastity were thought to be directly related to the success of the republic. Since men must deliberate together in the public arena as equals, they must trust one another. But women—the objects of men's deepest passions and the instruments of their immortality through their role in producing children and heirs—are necessarily the causes of quarrel and mistrust. Therefore, even if technically free by law, women must be highly circumscribed by custom. Women's absence from the public sphere is a condition of men's collective presence there.[47] There is certainly more than an echo of this classical republican argument in Tocqueville. But there are also new elements, reflecting his particular awareness of the challenges of democratic self-rule under modern conditions, as well as the general discourse of domesticity that had begun to transform discussions of family life and the status of women.

Tocqueville argues that chastity in private life becomes a point of democratic honour, analogous to aristocratic attitudes towards virtue in the conduct of war. Just as feudal codes of honour helped to stabilize a society where armed conflict was the norm, so 'purity of morals' stabilizes a restless and potentially anarchic democratic society where commerce fills daily life. On the one hand, the lack of opportunities for sexual intrigue keeps men focused on the 'search for well-being', while their absorption in commercial life 'crowds out' the practice of adultery (DAII, 598). On the other hand, a regular family life prevents this necessary search for well-being from getting out of control. Care for the welfare of a wife and family provides a fixed goal, which serves as a tether on restless acquisitive instincts and transforms potentially destructive self-interest into controlled prudence. Furthermore, the seclusion of women within marriage and family life allows them to buffer the psychological shocks and reverses associated with industrial life. Not themselves responsible for acting in civil society, they moderate the disappointments and exhilarations that must result from what Tocqueville calls 'the natural instability of [democratic] desires', that is, 'the disposition to think of sudden and easy fortunes, of great possessions easily won and lost, and chance in every shape and form' (DAII, 548). How do wives themselves experience such instability? 'American women', Tocqueville asserts, 'face such upheavals [the gain and loss of private fortunes] with quiet, indomitable energy. Their desires seem to contract with their fortune as easily as they expand.'[48]

Tocqueville assigns to women, then, a complex steadying and empowering function within the psyches of democratic men; like religion and rights, they both hold back and push forward.[49] Finally, women's confinement in the family means that they will not complicate or impede the development of a public culture of cooperation and trust. When democracy comes in a revolutionary form, policing women's morality and confining them to domestic roles apparently becomes even more urgent. In such a society men are touchy and mistrustful; bitter memories, unsettled customs, and internalized instincts of disorder add to the normal causes of division. If such men also lead licentious private lives—in Tocqueville's view the inevitable result of women moving freely in civil and political society—they 'come to feel scorn for natural ties and legitimate pleasures and develop a taste for disorder, restlessness of spirit, and instability of desire'. Spilling over into political society as a whole, these tastes inhibit civil and political discipline (DAI, 291). Tocqueville interprets American women's frequent attendance at political rallies and speeches as the apparent exception that proves his point. In America women are so securely insulated from civil and political life that they may be safely trusted to view politics as harmless spectacle.[50]

This relentlessly one-sided portrayal of the advantages of female domestication betrays more than hidebound and 'unenlightened' views about women. Tocqueville, like many of his contemporaries, judged women's presence in the civil and political spheres to be not only inappropriate or unnecessary but dangerous and deeply destabilizing. Such fears suggest that behind general arguments erasing women from public life lies a particular perception of their presence there. Indeed, even a cursory consideration of women in French politics in the previous century reminds us that 'public' women had become potent symbols of transgressive politics. In the French Old Regime, aristocratic women were both pawns and major players in the scramble for place and patronage at court. Granted a certain amount of sexual freedom, and occupying a role in intellectual life that amazed English and German observers, the aristocratic French woman had become liberated from a domestic-centred life. But her independent role at court and in salon life indelibly marked her with the corruption of the Old Regime. In ways that became obvious during the Revolution, the sexually avaricious aristocratic woman became the defining image of a degenerate aristocracy unfit to join the nation.[51]

If the corrupt aristocratic woman symbolized the antithesis of republican virtue, the politically active woman of the middle and popular classes was fast becoming a symbol of the Revolution's own excesses. The presence of such women in revolutionary clubs, demonstrations, and trials, as well as their exercise of more traditional roles as backstage brokers of revolutionary politics, were lightning-rods for criticism of one faction by another. As the Revolution spun out of control, the activism of women—reflected in both popular violence and the ever-maligned female 'intrigue'—became a ubiquitous marker of a frightening disorder to republicans of every stripe.

Intrinsic to the final break from the Old Regime, then, was the deliberate and explicit exclusion of women both from politics and from parts of civil society for the first time. They were not temporarily overlooked in the constitution of the new order, but were deliberately deprived of citizenship. Paradoxically, at the height of what some have seen as the first modern moment in democratic politics, came the decree in the fall of 1793 prohibiting all women's political associations and banning the exercise of political rights by women. Moreover, the Civil Code inscribed this inferior status in what became the sacred text of post-revolutionary France.

This cultural and political history permeates Tocqueville's views on the necessity of female retirement. It is not just that they must be removed from social view because they incite sexual jealousy and disorder, as classical republicans would have it. Nor is it merely that their absorption into domesticity makes functional sense in a commercial and industrial society. Women's presence in civil and political society is a veritable moral reproach. Their social visibility had become identified with both the 'worst' excesses of the Old Regime and those of the Revolution. It excites—in Tocqueville as well as many others—an involuntary frisson of revulsion. Those men (and women) who wished to learn from history apparently learned one lesson very well. If the precarious psychological balancing act required for democratic citizenship required that women steady the ropes, they must do so from a well-hidden position off the public stage.

Let me return now to the curious moment of transformation in Tocqueville's account of the democratic woman's life: that moment when she renounces a life of freedom to enter the domestic cloister. One might well expect to encounter at this point some assertion of the suitability of domestic life to woman's nature, or perhaps a discussion of her superior ability to sympathize or nurture. One finds nothing of the kind. Indeed, Tocqueville's great appreciation of the sweetness of democratic family life among male family members apparently does not extend to relationships between husbands and wives. The very education which teaches a girl to restrain her passions and to look on all the disorder inseparable from democratic society 'with firm and quiet gaze' introduces a necessary calculating quality into her behaviour that Tocqueville notices with some distaste. 'She, like the European girl, wants to please, but she knows exactly what it costs' (DAII, 591). Women are pure in America, just as men are good citizens, out of a kind of enlightened self-interest. Tocqueville's assessment of the costs and benefits of democratic gender relations in fact contrasts starkly with his judgement of the relations among men in the new democratic family. In the case of fathers, sons, and brothers, society's loss of corporate solidarity is more than compensated for by the individual's gain in personal happiness; in the case of men and women, society's gain is balanced by the individual's loss.

I know that such an education has its dangers; I know too that it tends to develop judgement at the cost of imagination and to make women chaste and cold rather than tender and loving companions of men. Society may thus be more peaceful and better ordered, but the charms of private life are often less. But that is a secondary evil which should be faced for the sake of the greater good.[52]

Tocqueville argues, then, that women's democratic education deprives men of the personal pleasure of delightful companions. But what of the women themselves? If men lose the charms of private life, women lose the opportunity to satisfy the democratic instincts that they—as well as their husbands—now possess. Public opinion and law prevent them from participating in the freedoms of democratic life. More important, however, they embrace this yoke freely. 'Often it is simply their own will which imposes this sacrifice on them' (DAII, 593). It is this renunciation that engages Tocqueville's imagination and provokes a singular moment of supreme sympathetic identification with the 'woman's point of view'. The American girl with an eye to the main chance becomes a tragic heroine who deliberately sacrifices her happiness for the social and political health of the republic.

Although Tocqueville recognizes that religious beliefs and

industrial habits combine to form a powerfully constraining opinion in favour of a purely domestic existence for women, this inevitable bowing to convention does not excite his approval. Such conventional pressure is, after all, a rather obvious example of tyranny of majority opinion. Rather, he conveys his belief in the 'rightness' of women's banishment from civil life by inviting the reader to share his intuitive appreciation of this voluntary submission, which becomes an exemplary model of democratic sacrifice. He portrays the young wife not as a shrewd calculator of her own happiness, as one might expect from his description of the confident unmarried girl who knows exactly what she is doing, but as a heroic suppressor of her own inclinations and passions for the common good. This moment of martyrdom resembles a warrior's right of passage; it helps to steel the democratic wife for an austere and lonely existence in which she will be called on to withstand the trials of life in a democratic society marked by extreme restlessness and constant shifts of fortune. Tocqueville's description of an American woman who has undergone the severest experience—moving to the wilderness—becomes a particularly striking symbol of the resigned *tristesse* that allegedly marks the inner life of all democratic women.

A woman was sitting on the other side of the hearth, rocking a small child on her knees. She nodded to us without disturbing herself. Like the pioneer, this woman was in the prime of life, her appearance seemed superior to her condition, and her apparel even betrayed a lingering taste for dress; but her delicate limbs were wasted, her features worn, and her eyes gentle and serious; her whole physiognomy bore marks of religious resignation, a deep peace free from passions, and some sort of natural, quiet determination which would face all the ills of life without fear and without defiance. Her children cluster around her, full of health, high spirits, and energy; they are true children of the wilds; their mother looks at them from time to time with mingled melancholy and joy; seeing their strength and her weariness, one might think that the life she has given them exhausted her own, and yet she does not regret what they have cost her. (DAII, 732; cf. 594)

Tocqueville rarely personalizes Americans in this way; his perception of a deliberate self-sacrifice by this unnamed woman betrays his own emotional responses to the coming of democracy. What prompts this sentimentalizing portrait of a wasted, 'delicate' woman who draws comfort from the health and happiness of her children? At least two parallels present themselves immediately, and neither has much to do with American mores. One is to the experience of French aristocratic women during the revolutionary period. The other is to the moral stance that he himself takes towards the choices posed by democratic society.

Contemporary sources echo—and subsequent demographic studies confirm—Tocqueville's account of the change in the structure of families in western Europe during the eighteenth and nineteenth centuries. Middle-class models of domesticity gradually spread into both the working classes and aristocratic elites. But in the case of the French aristocracy, this adoption of domesticity was peculiar in several ways: it was abruptly accomplished within one generation, it was politically motivated, and it was based in part on conscious choice and 'conversion experiences'.[53] Dramatic changes in the behaviour of French noblewomen are noticeable from the 1790s, when for economic reasons these women became personally responsible for domestic management. Emigré women in particular were thrust into a totally different existence by life in exile. But the changes in the lifestyles of aristocratic women were consolidated only after the Revolution, when economic necessity and the exigencies of life in another country no longer played the same constraining roles. One popular explanation for this embrace of new roles—which involved deep changes in patterns of education, age at marriage, and, most important, social and political roles after marriage—was that noblewomen had discovered the joys of intimacy. But though many letters and memoirs do speak of a new appreciation for children, there is also much evidence that these women experienced high levels of tedium and hardship. They clearly began to centre their lives on the household rather than on the court or salon for reasons other than personal fulfillment.

Much evidence indicates that these changes in the lives of aristocratic women arose from a combination of moral suasion, public pressure, and political strategizing. Fully aware of the barrage of criticism of their intellectual and social roles in the eighteenth century, noblewomen *en masse* turned against Enlightenment thought and embraced a reformed Catholicism that preached 'conjugal fidelity and filial respect'.[54] The aristocracy in fact waved domesticity as a flag to symbolize the reformed and purified status of the class as a whole. They did so to counter middle-class criticism, to forestall a full triumph of the bourgeoisie under the new post-revolutionary order, and to assuage their own guilt for having helped to precipitate the destruction of the monarchy. For their class, for France, and for their immortal souls, women like the Marquise de la Tour du Pin became convinced of the need for a purposeful revolution in the aristocratic way of life. Such a revolution required in particular a transformation in the character of women of the upper classes. She recommended that they face new political realities, retreat to their *foyers*, and support the quests of their husbands and fathers for public recognition and power. From the day that she realized that the pernicious example of the court aristocracy had encouraged the subsequent moral excesses of the lower classes, the Marquise wrote, 'my life was different, my moral outlook transformed'.[55]

What Tocqueville identifies as the two democratic tendencies forcing American women into an existence centred on the household—a relentless public opinion and an admirably clear-eyed embrace of domesticity by women themselves caused by their particular democratic education—are in fact the major reasons for fundamental changes in French aristocratic families. The chapter of the second *Democracy* entitled 'How Equality Helps Maintain Good Morals in America' strengthens this conclusion that Tocqueville was thinking of French noblewomen rather than of American democratic women when he demonstrated a necessary link between strict morality and stable democracy. In that chapter he asks why equality has not had the same beneficial effects on private morality in Europe as in America. He answers, as usual, that revolutionary social upheaval has perverted European experience; the beneficial effects of equality have not yet had time to show themselves. Paradoxically, however, there is one exceptional case that proves the general rule of an affinity between moral purity and democracy. That case is the French aristocracy. Not having experienced 'revolutionary passions' and 'anarchical excitement', they have been spared the pernicious effects of those experiences and have become exemplary models of democratic morality through the effects of equality *tout court*.

No one denies that the eighteenth-century French aristocracy was very dissolute. . . . On the other hand, we can all agree that the relics of this same aristocracy now exhibit a marked austerity of principles, whereas lax morals have spread through the middle and lower classes. Thus those very families that were most lax fifty years ago now set the best example, and it would seem as if democracy had improved the moral standards only of the aristocracy. . . . One can therefore conclude, surprising though this seems at first sight, that in our day it is the most antidemocratic element in the nation which gives the best example of the moral standards one can rationally expect from democracy. (DAII, 600)

The American woman who treks into the wilderness, devotes herself totally to hearth and home out of duty rather than egoism, and gazes with quiet determination and religious resignation at the next generation who will reap the benefits of her sacrifice is more French than American, more aristocratic than democratic.[56] More precisely, she is a romanticized distillation of the experience of the French nobility, held up as a reproach to the petty individualism and lax morality that Tocqueville saw infecting democratic social life in Europe.

A second resonance of Tocqueville's image of the resigned but melancholy heroine is his own existential experience of moral choice in a democracy. In the key decisions of his life—his oath of allegiance to the new bourgeois dynasty, his selection of a middle-class English wife without great fortune against the wishes of his aristocratic family, his commitment to an imperfect democratic process, and, most important, his strenuous intellectual efforts to clarify the 'shape' of democracy and to reconcile his own class to its demands—he resolutely turned his back on his ancestral past. But neither did he gain any compensating sense of righteousness, or new fellowship, or any lasting joyfulness. Rather he experienced at most a fleeting tranquillity, ever subject to new periods of restlessness and depression.[57] For him the stillness of the frontier woman's deep peace, her 'quiet determination which would face all the ills of life without fear and without defiance', represents successful equanimity in the face of a continual suppression of one's spontaneous inclinations for a higher purpose. Like Tocqueville himself, she had made a 'manly' sacrifice (DAII, 601).

Tocqueville's discussion of the place of women in democracy, then, both hovers close to the psychological roots of his thought and resists comprehension apart from the larger historical context in which those roots were entangled. He exorcises the culturally disturbing images of women in public life through an implausible projection onto women of a purifying sacrifice. This self-denial exemplifies the steadfast resolution that he enjoins on all citizens to abandon immediate gratification in favour of building a democratic future. If Tocqueville's assumptions about the threats that women pose in democracy strongly influence the shape of his exemplary narrative, he characteristically tells that story in the form of an objective argument about the tendencies inherent in democracy itself. A final comparison with Montesquieu, whose views on women in republics and whose historical and sociological bent as a theorist were so close to Tocqueville's own, is particularly illuminating in this context. Despite their similarities, there is a great gulf between Tocqueville's examination of the 'woman question' and that of Montesquieu, a gulf that illustrates a vast historical shift in moral and cultural sensibilities on certain questions associated with social order.

Despite his suggestions about the determinative influence of climate on women's natures, his frequently stated belief in the social significance of their physical differences from men, and his conviction that 'it is against reason and against nature for women to be mistresses in the house', Montesquieu was fascinated by the variety of customs that marked relations between the sexes.[58] It is much more literally true of Montesquieu than of Tocqueville that he derived great political importance from 'everything which has a bearing on the status of women, their habits, and their thoughts' (DAII, 590). The place of women in social and political life, however, did not arouse Montesquieu's anxieties about the cultural bases of freedom, but rather served as a liberating mechanism by which to discuss that very culture. His treatment of the question of women's 'freedom', as well as his willingness to play theoretically with the critical point of view inherent in the female perspective, differs in fundamental ways from Tocqueville's impulse to shield civil life from these potentially disturbing influences.

Montesquieu's comparative framework was essentially tripartite; he explored the spirit of the laws under republics, monarchies, and despotisms. Of these, the freest governments (republics) and the most unfree (despotisms) confined women within tight limits, whereas monarchies drew women into society and created for them key social roles. Montesquieu gives various functional reasons for female seclusion under republics, but it is clear from his recourse to parody and irony that he does not necessarily approve of it.[59] He was more interested, in any case, in the contrast between despotism and monarchy, and hence in the modes of exercising power in those regimes. The status of women served as a symbolic marker of the difference between those modes of power: 'the despotism of the prince is naturally united with the servitude of women; the liberty of women, with the spirit of monarchy.'[60]

What most interested Montesquieu, and what he endorsed as more suitable to modern politics than the utopian, if admirable, discipline of republics, was the civilizing function served by women's relative freedom in aristocratic monarchies. Although he recognized that the court was a corrupting influence on both men and women, the positive effects of women's presence in public life more than compensated for this corruption. In monarchies such as the French, 'Our connection with women is founded ... also on the desire to please them because they are quite enlightened judges of a part of the things that constitute personal merit.'[61] Montesquieu wished to validate precisely that sphere of *politesse* that provided not only pleasure and interest to social life, but also a public space with norms of communication and reciprocity. Such a public space was an invaluable resource for the development of the taste and judgement that were required to refine the 'spirit' of a regime. Montesquieu likened intellectual commerce with women to commerce in general: both were civilizing functions that increased personal freedom.[62]

The satirical *Persian Letters* exhibits in more exuberant form Montesquieu's interest in the theoretical uses to which a discussion of woman's status could be put. In this text he skilfully juggles several narratives at once: the sceptical commentary on France of Usbek, an Eastern nobleman on a grand European tour; Usbek's correspondence with his many wives, duplicitous on both sides; and the true story of harem life, recounted through the intelligent and passionate eyes of the women imprisoned there.[63] *Persian Letters* is less a unified philosophical tale than a series of provocative sketches, by turns satirical, ironic, farcical, and tragic. What is of interest in the present context is not so much Montesquieu's complex portrait of the culture of despotism as his willingness to explore this theme through the analogue of the despotism of gender. This 'novel' deploys a number of subversive perspectives on patriarchal power, including an ironically idyllic incestuous union, homosexuality, forced celibacy, full-blown female rebellion, and the subtle resistances of salon society. Montesquieu's free-wheeling use of the subjective viewpoints of secluded women and castrated men to discuss the delicate relationships between self-control and social control could not be further from Tocqueville's narrowed and shuttered construction of a polarity between purity and corruption, harmony and chaos, liberty and license.

Tocqueville drew deeply on Montesquieu, not only for his general methodological approach but also for his discussions of the plural sources of resistance to centralizing governments (fundamental law, intermediary bodies, legal elites, and local assemblies). He was deaf, however, to Montesquieu's implication that the social freedom of women promotes public liberty, contributes to the adaptability of modern societies, and impedes the drift towards centralized despotism.[64] Montesquieu believed that the loss in private morality

SOCIAL SCIENCE AND MORAL DUTIES

occasioned by women's participation in society was worth the gain of a public space for criticism and judgement. In contrast, under the shock of the democratic revolution in France, Tocqueville adapted classical republican notions of the need for surveillance and control of women—ideas described rather than endorsed by Montesquieu— to bolster his intuitions that women's freedom would turn the moral world upside down.

The World Turned Upside Down

Montesquieu's brilliant exploitation of the ambiguities of sex roles in Europe, his willingness to envision the reversal of the natural order, and his graphic portrayal of subversion and rebellion in the seraglio suggest that he was playing sophisticated riffs on certain popular themes and images that created laughter and reduced social tensions by standing the social world on its head. A brief consideration of what cultural historians identify as the nightmare of the world turned upside down may thus be useful in concluding the arguments of this chapter that a particular unease about what made the world right side up—the 'secrets' of Tocqueville's heart— disproportionately shaped his analysis of the cultural conditions of democratic stability.

Images such as the fool crowned king, the henpecked husband riding backward on a donkey, or the artisan turned magistrate pervade French popular culture from the late medieval period. Part of many carnivalesque activities and the visual representations associated with them, these images have provided cultural historians with a window onto presuppositions about order and hierarchy.[65] By their very nature, representations of the world turned upside down served contradictory functions. They defused underlying social tensions and thus reaffirmed traditional order, but they also provided a space for the potential escalation of discontent into riot. Such images presumably had the power to cause laughter only if they remained powerless to alter a seemingly permanent reality, and if they kept deep anxieties from rising to full consciousness. The cultural historian Roger Chartier has studied depictions of the world turned upside down by printmakers in France from the end of the Old Regime to the mid-nineteenth century, that is, during Tocqueville's cultural 'time'.[66] While he finds many continuities with earlier themes

during these years—the prey still stalks the hunter, the child forever corrects the parent—there are also some striking differences
that bear on the account of Tocqueville's fears that I have been
developing.

Reversal of sex roles, in earlier times often tinged with violence or
absurd hilarity, remained a theme during this later time period, but
with a significantly different inflection. Popular prints throughout
the century continued to lampoon the traditional functions of the
sexes, perhaps because complementary tasks within family groups
formed the very conditions of survival for the popular classes to
whom these prints were addressed. As the century progressed, however, the scenes of butchery or violence that the motif had contained
in the traditional world turned upside down were eliminated. The
Réformes du ménages (Household Reforms) sold by Pellerin, for
example, manipulated images to render sex-role reversal within a
future time that made the reforms seem improbable and ridiculous,
but took away the immediate shock of contemporary reversal. These
images were far from the iconography of the Revolution, with its
evocation of violent transgressive women 'excited by the furies' and
'drunk with the prospect of blood'.[67]

Even more significant, there was a sharp reduction in traditional
images involving the exchange of social roles in general—for
example, the rustic teaching scholars, or the king on foot as the
peasant goes on horseback. While peasants lording over lords had
been a staple of earlier representations of a world turned upside
down, these images almost totally disappeared in the first half of the
nineteenth century. Even after the theme of social role reversals
returned (at the end of the century), the industrial worker never
moved into the place that the peasant had occupied for centuries.
Chartier concludes: 'The *imagiers* censor out of their production,
consciously or unconsciously, anything that might threaten the
delicate balance of the social order, even when offered in jocular
fashion. . . . It seems as though the image merchants did not want
to risk having their images misunderstood: taken literally, they
might be an invitation to subversion.'[68] These omissions occurred,
then, not because no one thought seriously to question the legitimacy of social roles, but because the social order had become so fragile
that symbolic reversals produced intolerable anxiety rather than
consoling merriment.

At the same time as wild women and presumptuous peasants were
losing their ability to reduce social tensions, there was a relative

increase in another kind of traditional reversal: animals (usually domestic) putting people at their mercy and ruling over them. In numerous prints donkeys and sheep enslave millers and shepherds; farmers pull ploughs or carry sacks and baskets. This imagery is marked above all by the ferocity of the reversal. A pig that a farmer would have butchered obsessively hacks the man to death; turkeys roast farmers; geese stew the human cook in a pot. What is the meaning of such bloody and fearsome images? They seem to suggest a generalized cultural fear of letting loose animal forces that have been mastered only with great difficulty. Worrisome notions of an unnaturally upset power ratio are conjoined with the fear of loss of human qualities.[69]

These examples from recent studies of popular print images of the early nineteenth century remind us of the larger shifts in cultural sensibilities that, as it were, support and surround social and political argument. In the early nineteenth century, a number of subjects were no longer joking matters. The moral sensibility underlying Tocqueville's analysis of the challenges and opportunities presented by democratic social conditions is marked by a similar sense that a delicate balance might be upset by too open an exploration of things that deeply moved him, but that no longer elicited automatic social approval: the truth of Christian dogma, the worth of instinctive patriotism, the legitimacy of property rights, and the 'natural' confinement of women to the *foyer*.

It is not that Tocqueville does not have many subtle, complex, and sometimes contradictory trains of thought involving religion, property, and family, but in these areas there is a hidden moral anxiety that draws his arguments more deeply into the realm of apologetic. When his intellect and bent for comparison would nudge him in the direction of awkward questions—might religious doubt be a natural result of civilization? might we be convinced of the naturalness of private property because we know nothing else? might democracy mean freedom for women?—he smothers these questions in an urgent train of counter-argument driven by his conviction that there are sacred moral limits beyond which no human can safely pass. Atheists, socialists, and 'scribbling women' bring too close the terrifying possibility of breaking the remaining threads that allow democratic individuals to live dignified and independent lives. Tocqueville does not even attempt to weave these remaining threads together into an intelligible theology or philosophy. Rather, they are legitimated by his own language of the heart veiled in functionalist rhetoric. Perhaps it is the ultimate Tocquevillian irony that he should uphold the quintessential bourgeois virtues with an aristocrat's obstinate conviction that it must be honourable to defend with all the means at our disposal what God has bred in our bones.

Notes

1 DAI, 18. Cf. *Voyages en Angleterre, Irlande, Suisse et Algérie*, OC 5: 2, 38. There is 'no absolute truth in human affairs'; and *État social et Politique*, OC 2:1, 42: 'To judge of [men's] conduct, we must place ourselves at their own point of view, and not at the point of view of abstract truth.'

2 e.g. Pierre Birnbaum, *Sociologie de Tocqueville* (Paris: Presses Universitaires de France, 1970); Gianfranco Poggi, *Images of Society: Essays on Sociological Theories of Tocqueville, Marx, and Durkheim* (Stanford Calif.: Stanford University Press, 1972); Irving M. Zeitlin, *Liberty, Equality, and Revolution in Alexis de Tocqueville* (Boston: Little Brown, 1971).

3 Jon Elster, *Political Psychology* (Cambridge: Cambridge University Press, 1993).

4 See, among the vast literature on the subject of situating Tocqueville among other thinkers, Jean Claude Lamberti, *Tocqueville and the Two Democracies*, trans. Arthur Goldhammer (Cambridge, Mass.: Harvard University Press, 1989); Roger Boesche, *The Strange Liberalism of Alexis de Tocqueville* (Ithaca, NY: Cornell University Press, 1989); George Armstrong Kelly, *The Humane Comedy: Constant, Tocqueville and French Liberalism* (Cambridge: Cambridge University Press, 1992). Much of this contextualization of Tocqueville is invaluable to an understanding of his ideas, and I have hazarded my own such 'situation' of his moral thought in Chap. 1. I have chosen in this chapter, however, to approach the question of the moral suppositions of his thought from a more textual perspective.

5 On Montesquieu and Tocqueville, see Melvin Richter, 'Comparative Political Analysis in Montesquieu and Tocqueville', *Comparative Politics*, 1(2) (1969), 129–60, and 'The Uses of Theory: Tocqueville's Adaptation of Montesquieu', in Richter (ed.), *Essays in Theory and History: An Approach to the Social Sciences* (Cambridge, Mass.: Harvard University Press, 1970), 74–102.

6 Tocqueville's disregard for terminological consistency now becomes particularly striking. That which is socially and historically constructed is from this third point of view 'artificial'. Tocqueville, however, also described the social psychological forces that *caused*

those artificial constructions as occurring 'naturally' (in the first, positivistic sense described above). As against those sorts of positivistic 'natural' tendencies, he often valorizes the practical 'arts' of freedom, thus investing artificial with a positive connotation.

7 DAI, 62; see also AR, 48; and 'Seconde lettre sur l'Algérie', OC 3:1, 149 (on the tenacity of tribal structure in Algeria).

8 See e.g. DAII, 507: 'So people living in an aristocratic age are almost always closely involved with something outside themselves, and they are often inclined to forget about themselves.'

9 OC 3:1, 41–126. On Tocqueville and slavery, see Seymour Drescher, *Dilemmas of Democracy: Tocqueville and Modernization* (Pittsburgh: University of Pittsburgh Press, 1968), 151–95; François Mélonio, 'Tocqueville et les malheurs de la démocratie américaine (1831–1859)', *Commentaire*, 38 (1987), 386–9.

10 Tocqueville himself was not free of complicity, as in this passage: 'When I see the order of nature overthrown and hear the cry of humanity complaining in vain against the laws, I confess that my indignation is not directed against the men of our own day who are the authors of these outrages; all my hatred is concentrated against those who, after a thousand years of equality, introduced slavery into the world again' (DAI, 363). Tocqueville had some sympathy for the quandary of the American slave-owner, since emancipation, he thought, would leave the Southerner faced with a race war.

11 'Memoir on Pauperism', in *Tocqueville and Beaumont on Social Reform*, ed. and trans. Seymour Drescher (New York: Harper & Row, 1968), 6. The differences, in Tocqueville's mind, seem to include modern slavery's racial basis, its reliance on the pure profit motive, and its embeddedness in an otherwise democratic social order.

12 'Rapport fait au nom de la commission chargée d'examiner la proposition de M. de Tracy relative aux esclaves des colonies', OC 3:1, 43.

13 See ibid. 44, 53–6, 59, 88, 94, 97, 117.

14 See above, Ch. 2, pp. 95–101.

15 DAII, 445; see above, Ch. 1, pp. 34–9, 40–1.

16 Tocqueville to Gobineau, 2 Oct. 1843, OC 9, 57; See André Jardin, *Tocqueville (1805–1859): A Biography*, trans. Lydia Davis with Robert Hemenway (London: Peter Halban, 1988), 528–33, for a discussion of the controversy over whether Tocqueville died 'in the faith'. For general accounts of Tocqueville and religion, see Doris Goldstein, *Trial by Faith: Religion and Politics in Tocqueville's Thought* (Amsterdam: Elsevier, 1975), and Françoise Mélonio, 'La religion selon Tocqueville', *Études* 360(1) (1984), 73–88. See below, Ch. 5, n. 58.

17 Tocqueville to Mme Swetchine, 11 Feb. 1847, OC 15:2, 309.

18 Tocqueville to Mme Swetchine, 26 Feb. 1857, OC 15:2, 314–15.

19 *Extraits du voyage en Sicile*, OC 5:1, 48.

20 Ibid. 38.

21 *Voyage en Amérique*, OC 5:1, 162; cf. *Voyage au Lac Oneida*, ibid. 336–41. On the episode, see George Wilson Pierson, *Tocqueville and Beaumont in America* (New York: Oxford University Press, 1938; repr. Baltimore: Johns Hopkins University Press, 1996), 197–205.

22 *Voyage en Amérique*, OC 5:1, 225.

23 See Michael Hereth, *Alexis de Tocqueville*, trans. George Bogardus (Durham, NC: Duke University Press, 1962), 161, for a discussion of patriotism in connection with Tocqueville's policy on Algeria.

24 *Voyages en Amérique*, OC 5:1, 216.

25 *Voyages en Sicile*, OC 5:1, 49.

26 Jack Lively, *The Social and Political Thought of Alexis Tocqueville* (Oxford: Clarendon Press, 1965), 183.

27 For a perceptive reading of the links between democratic and Christian equality in Tocqueville, see Peter Augustine Lawler, *The Restless Mind: Alexis de Tocqueville on the Origin and Perpetuation of Human Liberty* (Lanham, Md.: Rowman & Littlefield, 1993), 156–8.

28 DAI, 59; cf. DAI, 33, 58, 60, 61, 66, 67, 181, 183, 397; AR, p. xi; *Voyages en Amérique*, OC 5:1, 182.

29 Ibid. 184

30 DAI, 250; cf. DAII, 616: 'Public opinion employs two very different standards in judging the actions of men; in the one case it relies on simple notions of right and wrong, which are common to all the world; in the other it assesses them in accordance with some very exotic notions peculiar to one age and country.'

31 Roland Pierre-Marcel, *Essai politique sur Alexis de Tocqueville*, 183, cited in Jean-Claude Lamberti, *Tocqueville and the Two Democracies*, trans. Arthur Goldhammer (Cambridge, Mass.: Harvard University Press, 1989), 78.

32 On occasion Tocqueville considered the possibility that 'what are called necessary institutions are only institutions to which one is accustomed, and that in matters of social constitution the field of possibilities is much wider than people living within each society imagine' (S, 96). Cf. Tocqueville to Harriet Grote, 24 July 1850: 'Who can therefore affirm that one form of society is necessary, and that another cannot exist?', Quoted in Seymour Drescher, *Tocqueville and England* (Cambridge, Mass.: Harvard University Press, 1964), 147. But in that same letter to Harriet Grote Tocqueville notes that whatever one might think of the property question in the abstract, 'The duty of honest men is nonetheless to defend the only one [society] that they understand, even to die for it, until a better one has been shown'. For him, respect for property was the basis of a civilized society: *Voyages en Angleterre*, OC 5:2, 59. One

of the best guides on the issue of Tocqueville's fear of the social question is Drescher, *Tocqueville and England*, 125–51.

33 Louis Auguste Blanqui (1805–81). French revolutionary and radical; prominent in every revolutionary upheaval in France during his lifetime; leader of the Central Society that was powerful in the Revolution of 1848.

34 'Memoir on Pauperism', 25.

35 T. H. Marshall was the fruit of a long line of such thought in England, with roots in J. S. Mill as well as in English socialism. See Cheryl B. Welch, 'Liberalism and Social Rights', in Welch and M. Milgate (eds.), *Critical Issues in Social Thought* (London: Academic Press, 1989), 173–9.

36 'Memoir on Pauperism', 17.

37 Ibid. 18.

38 Mill, 'The Poor Laws', in *Collected Works*, xxiii: *Newspaper Writings: August 1831–October 1834* (Toronto: University of Toronto Press, 1986), 686; and 'On the Claims of Labour', in *Collected Works*, iv: *Essays on Economics and Society, 1824–1845* (Toronto: University of Toronto Press, 1967), 380.

39 Delba Winthrop has offered a probing reading of Tocqueville on women very different from the one offered here. See 'Tocqueville's American Woman and "the True Conception of Democratic Progress" ', *Political Theory*, 14(2) (1986), 239–61. Beginning from a similar recognition of Tocqueville's neglect of 'natural differences', Winthrop argues that Tocqueville's main point is that at least some citizens should be protected from the banality of democratic politics.

40 Elster, *Political Psychology*, 107; cf. 114: 'the only case in which he seems to be completely and consistently the prisoner of prejudice is in the case of women'. I find it curious that Elster should emphasize Tocqueville's spontaneous affection for monarchy, since it is aristocratic *loyalty* to the monarch that Tocqueville has a tendency to romanticize, rather than monarchy itself. While aristocrats have made tragic mistakes, the monarchy has committed 'crimes'. Elster could better have pointed to Tocqueville's religious prejudices; there are very few passages, for example, condemning Christian religious intolerance or fanaticism.

41 Haydon White has characterized Tocqueville's style as marked by a particular turbulence that has its source in two emotions: 'an overriding capacity for sympathy for men different from himself, and a fear of the destruction of those things he valued most in both the past and the present': *Metahistory: The Historical Imagination in Nineteenth-Century Europe* (Baltimore: Johns Hopkins University Press, 1973), 192. In the case of women, Tocqueville's fears almost completely inhibit his capacity for sympathetic identification and thus limit the range of his political psychologizing.

42 But see DAII, 601. During this period, medical literature was beginning to be filled with evidence purporting to prove differences between the sexes on which Tocqueville could easily have drawn.

43 Tocqueville's notebooks are filled with questions to his interlocutors about the status of women's sexual morality, but he does not exhibit much curiosity about other matters. For example, he could let the following sentence stand without modification in the published version of the second *Democracy*: 'You will never find American women in charge of the external relations of the family, managing a business, or interfering in politics; but they are also never obliged to undertake rough laborer's work or any task requiring hard physical exertion. No family is so poor that it makes an exception to this rule' (DAII, 601). Women's religious roles, and women as socializers of the republic, were matters of general interest in Tocqueville's time, and have occasioned much recent research. See e.g. Nancy Cott, *Bonds of Womanhood: Woman's Sphere in New England, 1780–1835* (New Haven, Conn.: Yale University Press, 1977); Nancy Hewitt, *Women's Activism and Social Change: Rochester 1822–1872* (Ithaca, NY: Cornell University Press, 1984); Mary Ryan, *Cradle of the Middle Class: the Family in Oneida County, New York, 1790–1865* (Cambridge: Cambridge University Press, 1981).

44 The phrase 'pure morals' almost always has this meaning of sexual fidelity. See DAII, 588; OC 5:1, 61; OC 5:2, 32.

45 Cited in James T. Schleifer, *The Making of Tocqueville's 'Democracy in America'* (Chapel Hill: University of North Carolina Press, 1980), 65.

46 DAII, 486. See 482–7 on poetic inspiration in democratic times. All his examples (Byron, Chateaubriand, Lamartine) are European. Of course it is Walt Whitman, as many commentators have noted, who most vindicates Tocqueville's view that democratic poetry will celebrate not the 'external appearance and palpable fact' but the democratic soul itself.

47 See Paul Rahe, *Republics Ancient and Modern: Classical Republicanism and the American Revolution* (Chapel Hill: University of North Carolina Press, 1992), 31–8. Rahe argues that the emergence of the classical Greek polis coincided with a restriction in the personal freedom and independence of women; its decline occasioned an improvement. He does not find much influence of this classical position on male and female republican 'virtue' in America, but it was clearly important in the European republican tradition. On the misogyny of French revolutionary republicanism, see Joan Landes, *Women and the Public Sphere in the Age of the French Revolution* (Ithaca, NY: Cornell University Press, 1988).

48 DAII, 594. See Elster's discussion of this point in *Political Psychology*, 177. He argues that women might be thought capable of performing this adaptive function because they would be only reacting to circumstances

rather than being responsible for them. It is difficult, however, to see why a response of stoic serenity is any more psychologically plausible than sullen acquiescence or passive resistance.

49 Tocqueville uses the same imagery of 'loosening and tightening' with reference to the effects of democracy on moral (i.e. religious) ties and natural (i.e. family) ties. Cf. DAII, 58 and DAI, 294.

50 Cf. his very different view of women in the Revolution of 1848; their presence in the 'mobs' is a natural result of the loose morals in society as a whole and a frightening confirmation of the unnaturalness of revolution (S, 170).

51 See Lynn Hunt, *The Family Romance of the French Revolution* (Berkeley: University of California Press, 1993), 89–123, for ways in which Marie Antoinette becomes a lightning rod for this feeling.

52 DAII, 598. Among the necessary costs to individuals when respectable women are chaste is also the 'deplorable . . . wretchedness' caused by a system of prostitution. But still 'a lawgiver must fear prostitution much less than intrigues'.

53 Margaret H. Darrow, 'French Noblewomen and the New Domesticity: 1750–1850', *Feminist Studies* 5(1) (1979), 42. My analysis relies on Darrow; for another view that somewhat downplays the political motivations of these women, see Cissie Fairchilds, 'Women and Family', in Samia I. Spencer (ed.), *French Women and the Age of Enlightenment* (Bloomington: Indiana University Press, 1984), 97–127.

54 The phrase is from Louis-Gabriel-Ambroise, Vicomte de Bonald, 'Des lois et des mœurs considérées dans la société en général', in *Œuvres* (Paris: J.-P. Migne, 1859), 2: 202. For Bonald's views on the education and public role of women more generally, see also 'Législation primitive considérée dans les derniers temps par les seules lumières de la raison', in *Œuvres Complètes, 1: 1398–1402*.

55 Quoted in Darrow, 'French Noblewomen', 41.

56 The 'aristocratic' ideal of a totally self-effacing woman who nevertheless helps bring out the best rather than the worst in democratic society by her recognition of the needs of the public has its counterpart in several unflattering portraits of French bourgeois women, e.g. Tocqueville's sister-in-law Alexandrine, a bourgeois heiress. He leaves us this account of her behaviour in 1848: 'Characteristically, my sister-in-law had lost her head. . . . What made me most impatient was that my sister-in-law had no thought for the country's fate in the lamentations she poured out concerning her dear ones. There was neither depth of feeling nor breadth of sympathy in her demonstrative sensibility. She was, after all, very kind and even intelligent, but her mind had contracted and her heart frozen as both were restricted within the narrow limits of a pious egotism, so that both mind and heart were solely concerned with the good God, her husband, her children and especially her health, with no

interest left over for other people. She was the most respectable woman and the worst citizen one could find' (S, 51). Tocqueville implicitly contrasts this to his own wife's 'staunch spirit' (S, 107). Mary Mottley was, of course, not an aristocratic woman, though Tocqueville seems to have thought that his wife's 'loftiness of soul' made her exceptional (Jardin, *Tocqueville*, 50). Note also Tocqueville's unflattering portrait of the women of the people in 1848: 'these women carried the preoccupations of a housewife into battle: they counted on victory to bring easy circumstances for their husbands and help them to bring up their children. They loved this war much as they might have enjoyed a lottery' (S, 170).

57 Letter to Mme Swetchine, 11 Feb. 1847, OC 15:2, 309.

58 Baron de Montesquieu, *The Spirit of the Laws*, trans. Anne Cohler, Basia Miller, and Harold Stone (Cambridge: Cambridge University Press, 1989), 7.17 (111); on women and public life, see 7.8–17 (96–111); 16 (264–78); 27 (521–31).

59 See e.g. ibid. 16.9 (270). For a discussion of this point, see Pauline Kra, 'Montesquieu and Women', in Spencer, *French Women*, 281.

60 *Spirit of the Laws*, 19.15 (316).

61 Ibid. 28.22 (561).

62 Ibid. 19.6 (311). My understanding of Montesquieu's view of women's functioning in the public space in monarchies has been influenced by a stimulating article by Michael A. Mosher, 'The Judgmental Gaze of European Women: Gender, Sexuality, and the Critique of Republican Rule', *Political Theory*, 22(1) (1994), 25–44.

63 *Lettres persanes* (Paris: Garnier-Flammarion, 1964).

64 *Spirit of the Laws*, 7.9 (104): 'In monarchies, women have so little restraint because, called to court by the distinction of rank, they there take up the spirit of liberty that is almost the only one tolerated.'

65 See e.g. Emmanuel Le Roy Ladurie, *The Peasants of Languedoc*, trans. J. Day and G. Huppert (Urbana: University of Illinois Press, 1984); Natalie Zemon Davis, *The Return of Martin Guerre* (Cambridge, Mass.: Harvard University Press, 1983).

66 Roger Chartier, 'The World Turned Upside-Down', in *Cultural History: Between Practices and Representation*, trans. Lydia G. Cochrane (Ithaca, NY: Cornell University Press, 1988), 115–26.

67 Originally quoted by Dominique Godineau, *Citoyennes tricoteuses: les femmes du peuple à Paris pendant la Révolution française* (Aix-en-Provence: Alinéa, 1988), 137; cited in Hunt, *Family Romance*, 118.

68 Chartier, 'World Turned Upside-Down', 122.

69 Ibid. 123.

5

Tocqueville in
Our Time

Tocqueville assuaged his own acute social anxieties by setting implicit limits to the boundless transformative processes of democratization that he perceived in modern Europe and America. Disciplined yet empowered by religion, the market, and a severely gendered 'natural' order, democratic citizens, Tocqueville thought, might yet withstand the psychological onslaught of egalitarian culture and create a democratic form of freedom. History, however, has not respected those limits in democratic aspiration. And with new struggles have come new forms of social anxiety about exploding democratic sensibilities as well as about the alleged need to channel democratic desire. In this context, Tocqueville's complex mixed messages of dire warning and hopeful counsel have continued to find receptive readers. Today the urge to converse with Tocqueville and to seek his blessing on a bewildering range of projects, both theoretical and political, exerts a pull across the political spectrum. That theoretical pull forms the subject of this chapter.

Tocqueville wrote to Eugene Stoffels in 1835, 'I please many persons of opposite opinions not because they penetrate my meaning, but because, looking only to one side of my work, they think they find in it arguments in favour of their own convictions.'[1] Part of Tocqueville's contemporary appeal continues to be this ease with which he can be appropriated for rhetorical purposes. He has become a surprisingly central figure in contemporary discussions of politics

and society because he continues to 'please many persons of opposite opinions' who use him only to bolster their own convictions. Yet
Tocqueville also attracts those—perhaps more today than in the
past—who attempt seriously to 'penetrate [his] meaning'. Indeed,
the French aristocrat whose idiosyncratic intellectual odyssey
swerved around the questions that defined classical social theory
has recently been termed 'the greatest political thinker of the
nineteenth century'.[2]

I have argued in preceding chapters that Tocqueville provides us
less with a general theory of modern democracy than with a set of
prescient psychological insights into the democratic *mentalité*
(drawn from his fruitful juxtaposition of France and America) and
with a provocative, contextually bound account of the historical
emergence of one modern democracy (drawn from his meditations
on the destiny of France). I have tried to show, in fact, that these
accounts draw their power from Tocqueville's ability to combine
grounded description with empathetic intuition, and that they
resist too great an abstraction from the phenomena with which
he was concerned. At the same time, however, Tocqueville's particular combination of sociological, historical, and moral insight
has played a unique role in uncovering certain fault-lines in contemporary democratic life. In this concluding chapter I wish to
reflect explicitly on his role in stimulating reflection on democratic
dilemmas by public intellectuals in the latter part of the twentieth
century.[3] My discussion of these turns to Tocqueville—both rhetorical and real—revisits topics that have preoccupied us in previous
chapters: the historical constraints and possibilities inherent in
moving from the Old Regime to the New (Chapter 3), the place of
associations in the 'shape' of democracy (Chapter 2), and the
paradoxes involved in discussing democracy's need for spiritual
foundations (Chapters 2 and 4). Confrontations with Tocqueville's
discussions of these themes, I shall argue, reveal a set of concerns
peculiarly characteristic of a democratic world in which we are often
said to be 'all liberals now': the viability of liberal alternatives to
revolutionary change in past and present; the role of intermediate
associations in creating a functional democratic culture; and,
finally, the question of democracy's need for a unifying core of
moral beliefs.

I shall explore these issues primarily by considering Tocqueville's
presence in French and American debates, a limitation that may at
first seem rather arbitrary. His major works were translated almost

immediately into English, German, Spanish, and Italian, and they have continued to generate important scholarly discussions, especially in England and Germany. Tocqueville of course felt a special affinity for England, particularly at the end of his life when he lived in spiritual exile from imperial France. Moreover, English history and politics stimulated the development of his ideas in important ways and served as an instructive counter-history to the French path to democracy.[4] Many English liberals, for their part, welcomed him as a kindred spirit. But despite this kinship, or perhaps because of it, his work never entered deeply into ongoing debates about the history and politics of national identity in Britain. In the nineteenth-century English political and intellectual landscape, his texts immediately occupied familiar territory. Liberals found an important and insightful ally in their attempts to understand the tensions between liberty and democracy. But this influence—like that of English liberals whose fears were primarily focused on the dangers of democratization and the advent of universal suffrage—waned as England negotiated these processes without apparent catastrophe.[5] Similarly, Tocqueville had and has many readers in Germany, and he has inspired exemplary German scholarship.[6] Yet he has not become a 'German' writer in the sense of entering deeply into debates over Germany's democratic identity.

In his own country and in America, however, the case has been quite different. Tocqueville's choice of subject ties him intimately to the questions of democratic national identity and political self-understanding that have preoccupied French and American thinkers throughout the histories of their republics. Yet in both cases he speaks from a perspective that was (and is) outside the discourses that have most decisively shaped those preoccupations. Hence he has been perpetually available to critics and commentators for fresh beginnings. 'As Tocqueville said' has been a perennial trope for those who wish to contest the terms of existing debates or to invoke authority for a new reading of history and politics. The combination of centrality of subject-matter and ex-centrality of perspective has magnified his power both to provoke fundamental discussion about democracy and to confer intellectual authority.[7] This chapter will briefly review the history of Tocqueville's place in French and American intellectual debates from the publication of *Democracy in America* through to the mid-twentieth century: his immediate reception, eventual eclipse, and surprising revivals. But its real focus is on more recent appropriations, and on Tocqueville's role in throwing into relief a set of concerns about democracy with particular resonance in the second half of the twentieth century.

Receptions, Eclipses, Revivals: Two Histories

The waxing and waning of Tocqueville's importance in French and American intellectual debates exhibit some rough parallels. In both cases he enjoyed an enthusiastic initial reception, a long period of prominence, an even longer eclipse—almost total in France, only partial in the United States—and, finally, a series of overlapping revivals from the 1930s to the present in which he is celebrated as a uniquely insightful observer of the dynamics of democracy. These similar trajectories, however, mask important substantive distinctions. The most obvious of these is the nature of his prescient 'voice'. Both the French and the American Tocqueville write from an authoritative distance, but their tones are quite distinct. In France Tocqueville speaks as the estranged insider who reveals family secrets buried in collective memory, whereas in America he speaks as the empathetic outsider who pierces through the surface of daily life to reveal the inhabitants to themselves. In the first case the appearance of objectivity arises from alienation, in the second from alienage. Listening attentively to these distinctive voices can alert us to some important differences in both the initial receptions and later appropriations of his texts.

In France, Tocqueville immediately staked out an unusual political and intellectual position. Although he participated actively in French public life for most of his career and was an acknowledged member of the political *notables* who ruled France in the July Monarchy, this quintessential insider held a view of politics that was not premised on the characteristic opposition between Jacobin democracy and liberal individualism. His particular understanding of republican self-rule, an understanding that cloaked itself in the guise of an American counter-democracy, evoked at once participatory democracy and defensive liberalism. In nineteenth-century France these views made him a continual critic of French politics, an historian with a difference, and eventually a spiritual exile. Today many French readers find in Tocqueville an eyewitness account of France's transition to democracy that continually reminds them of the consequences of a road not taken. Evoking forgotten genealogies,

Tocqueville offers new perspectives on the strange and sometimes monstrous phenomena that European society has spawned in the twentieth century, the progeny of its nineteenth-century political evolution. Part of Tocqueville's appeal in France, then, has come from the perception that he can redirect debate and open up the question of France's political future in a way that jars entrenched sensibilities on both left and right.

Tocqueville's authorial liminality in America has a different cause and a different effect. Not a fellow-countryman unearthing buried secrets, but rather a clairvoyant foreigner demonstrating second sight, Tocqueville initially appeared to Americans as an outsider who possessed the power to explain them both to themselves and to the outside world:[8] for Americans trying to understand who they were and why they acted as they did [Tocqueville was] a brilliant discoverer ... '[9] Even today, in scholarly works that chronicle his theoretical ambiguities and that subtly recreate his multilayered intentions in writing *Democracy in America*, this admiration for Tocqueville as a psychological seer persists.[10] His work was and remains a medium in which to discuss the ambiguities, contradictions, and complexities of America's national character and of its particular democratic culture. On a popular level, quotations from Tocqueville have ornamented American speechifying and journalism from the mid-nineteenth century to today's culture wars. In more serious works, he has launched many intellectual odysseys into the American political soul. The celebration of the 150th anniversary of Tocqueville's voyage to America only reinforced the apparently ineradicable tendency to genuflect before *Democracy in America* before entering into any extended discussion of American politics and culture.

The First Hundred Years

Although Tocqueville's claims to distanced objectivity have influenced his reception in both France and America, the stance of estranged compatriot has made his relationship with French readers a particularly complicated affair. Though immediately acclaimed in his own country both as the definitive guide to the new American democracy and as a nineteenth-century Montesquieu, Tocqueville was nevertheless often misunderstood or read superficially. The French left commended his republicanism and the right his affirmation of religion, but neither fully understood his model or his

method.[11] Closer to the liberal Doctrinaires in politics, he nevertheless caused offence with his criticisms of the bourgeoisie.[12] Many
readers seem to have missed both his central argument about the
connection between the progress of individualism and the extension of central power and his unique version of the doctrine
of enlightened self-interest.[13] The second *Democracy*, with its critique of modern individualism and dearth of material specifically on
America, caused even more confusion.

Like the two *Democracies*, *The Old Regime* immediately became
a lightning-rod for partisan confrontations, since revolutionary history was always an ideological battleground in nineteenth-century
French politics. Tocqueville's *Old Regime*, however, struck a deeper
chord in French readers than had either of the *Democracies*. In the
final years of the Second Empire, it became a symbol of the need
to repudiate the tainted legacy of absolutism and helped to make
Tocqueville the focus (soon posthumous) of the liberal opposition to
the Empire. After his death in 1859 Tocqueville enjoyed his greatest
period of influence, both as the interpreter of America—this was the
height of the 'American school' in French politics—and as the
author of an historical classic that had exposed the dangers of tutelary despotism. A chorus of praise for decentralization, civic virtue,
the rule of law, and communal institutions infused the new liberal
opposition and drew on Tocqueville as moral authority. This period
of prominence appears even more striking when viewed from the
standpoint of his subsequent fall from grace, a fall that coincided
with the consolidation of the Third Republic and was to last until
that regime itself collapsed.

Tocqueville's influence in France waned for many reasons. Ironically, liberals invoked *Democracy in America* most successfully as a
reproach to French politics at the very time that Tocqueville's portrait of America was becoming demonstrably false to the facts. In the
late nineteenth century Tocqueville's United States—a brilliant
intellectual reconstruction but never an authentic picture—seemed
to lack any resemblance to the industrializing, urbanizing nation
that was accepting waves of southern and eastern European immigrants. Thus Tocqueville lost his primary role as the interpreter of
the New World. More important, however, he never became a founding father of republican institutions in the Old World. The French
Third Republic took a different route: centralized, increasingly
welfare-oriented, and held together by a civic culture based on universalism, positivism, and *laïcité*. The newly emerging academic

disciplines, moreover, divided up Tocqueville's intellectual subject-matter and acknowledged him as a master in none.[14] Never acclaimed as a founder of the Third Republic, hence missing from the powerful iconography of French republican nationalism, and never claimed as a forerunner of the social science disciplines, hence missing from the academic canon, Tocqueville fell into dusty oblivion by the end of the nineteenth century. His *Democracy* saw only two reprintings between 1870 and 1945, a period in which his claim to literary fame in France rested more on *The Old Regime and the Revolution*, which never quite lost its status as a historical classic, than on his famous travel book.[15] Only recently have French scholars fully acknowledged *Democracy in America* as a 'philosophical' work.[16]

Seymour Drescher, among others, has pointed to a more general, and perhaps more long-lasting, barrier to a sympathetic hearing for Tocqueville's American morality lessons in France. To accept Tocqueville's prognosis, with its didactic reliance on the superiority of Anglo-Saxon liberties, would have been an unimaginable blow to French self-esteem in the nineteenth century. From its role in creating Christian civilization in the Middle Ages to its awe-inspiring revolutionary and imperial regimes, France viewed itself as a world-historical nation. 'Did one really need to go to the land of the Philistines in search of redemption? Was Paris bereft of prophets?'[17] It is not accidental that Tocqueville's contemporary revival in France is linked to the need to come to grips with a certain decentring of France's place in Europe and the world.

Tocqueville's initial reception in America was quite different, though equally circumscribed by his potential relevance to the political issues that preoccupied American elites. Not least among those issues was a need to validate their republican experiment in the eyes of Europe. Accustomed to European disdain for their society—one recent commentator has noted that most European visitors attempted to 'quarantine' America, refusing it a place in western culture because of its violence, incivility, and barbarousness—Americans naturally welcomed Tocqueville's laudatory account.[18] Initial reviews particularly praised its balanced analysis of the ways in which Americans maintained both freedom and order, an unsurprising reaction if one considers that these early readers came from the same conservative republican elite as the Federalist interlocutors and informants who had shaped Tocqueville's view of the United States.

After the first American edition in 1838, *Democracy in America* was constantly in print; it became an important textbook on American political institutions used in schools throughout the country. Commentators frequently pointed out certain errors of fact or judgement, such as an allegedly excessive fear of the tyranny of the majority or of the power of the presidency. In general, however, the first *Democracy* rapidly attained the status of a classic. The second *Democracy*, with its darker tone and even greater focus on democracy 'itself' rather than on American institutions, proved less successful. As in France, Tocqueville's long 'digressions' on democratic social psychology sometimes baffled readers. *The Old Regime and the Revolution*, on the other hand, could not fall out of favour because it never attracted much notice in America. Even today American commentators, with some important exceptions, rarely roam beyond the two volumes of the *Democracy*; almost exclusively they read Tocqueville as an analyst of American politics and culture—as an American author.[19]

The primary cause of Tocqueville's decline in the United States was neither a change of political regime nor the institutionalization of the social science disciplines, but rather the obvious transformation of America itself. Daniel Coit Gilman, in his introduction to the 1898 edition of the *Democracy*, admitted that westward expansion, urbanization, industrialization, immigration, the growth of cultural and educational institutions, and increasing diversity had made Tocqueville's great work less relevant as a guide to republican practice, but he termed it still valuable for its positing of fundamental questions about the future of democratic society in America.[20] Tocqueville's initial appeal to Americans, then, never quite faded. Perhaps the most consistent aspect of that appeal has been the impression that Tocqueville miraculously addresses the reader's own time 'whether 1838/40, 1862, 1898, 1945, 1966, or 1981.'[21]

World War and Cold War: Tocqueville versus Marx

The current revival of interest in Tocqueville in America is usually dated from the publication of George Wilson Pierson's masterful study *Tocqueville and Beaumont in America* (1938), which has recently been reissued in paperback (1996). Since the late 1930s there has been a steady stream of American scholarly material on Tocqueville, punctuated by waves of more general interest. In

France, on the other hand, Tocqueville disappeared more completely and re-emerged more dramatically. Not until after the Second World War, when many sought to validate the freedom of the West as against the communist East, was Tocqueville dusted off and partially reclaimed as a standard-bearer in the Cold War. In Germany, Italy, and England, as well as in France, his texts were reprinted as part of the effort to shore up anti-Marxist liberalism. His contemporary importance on the Continent, then, began with his anointment as counter authority to Marx, and his work has never totally escaped that theoretical space. Contemporary theorists still read Tocqueville—explicitly or implicitly—against the backdrop of an apparently discredited Marxist project.

During the 1950s and 1960s Tocqueville's analysis of democracy in fact emerged on both sides of the Atlantic as an alternative to historical materialism, and as a stimulus to comparative reflection on societies that seemed to be increasingly less defined by class. Postwar prosperity appeared to be ushering in a society of equals that was 'post-' rather than 'pre-' industrial. In this context Tocqueville's attention to the complex mentality of an egalitarian society struck social and political thinkers as more relevant than Marx's insistence on structural economic conflict. There were, however, significant differences in these American and French castings of Tocqueville as the anti-Marx. In America that role was both more immediately obvious and less important, since Marxism itself was less rooted in the academy. Tocqueville's classic discussion of equality in America quickly became a touchstone for the consensus school of democratic pluralists such as David Truman and Robert Dahl, as well as for Hartzian historians of hegemonic liberalism in America.[22] It is hard to overestimate the lasting resonance of Louis Hartz's work, a brilliant recasting of Tocqueville's thesis that America was exceptional because its lack of a feudal past inoculated it against class warfare. This perspective has served as a stimulus to numerous counter-arguments about ways to theorize political conflict in America, especially for those on the left. Even today the term 'Tocquevillian' is often used as shorthand for mainstream views that privilege the notion of a liberal consensus as the most suitable framework from which to analyse American politics and political history. Rogers Smith, for example, in his recent attempt to shift attention to a multiple-traditions view of political ideology in America, uses Tocqueville and Tocquevillians as foils for his own views because 'these sorts of accounts . . . are still cited as authoritative by a wide range of scholars and their premises are often echoed even in works that appear to present quite different views'.[23]

At the same time that Tocqueville was lending his name to social scientific projects that implicitly accepted liberalism as normative in America, he emerged as an anchor of a new discipline known as 'American Studies'. As the United States struggled to come to terms with its emergence from the Second World War as both a superpower and the world's largest liberal democracy, its intellectuals became increasingly self-conscious about exploring America's particular expressive life: its culture high and low. Tocqueville's *Democracy in America*—always a beginning for the study of American life—was one of the founding texts of this discipline; indeed, 'if there is any orthodoxy in the study of American civilization, it is some sort of Tocquevillian one'.[24]

Tocqueville's simultaneous praise for America's political culture and barely veiled disdain for its literature and art had put American intellectuals on the defensive from the beginning. One response, perhaps the dominant one, has been to adopt a detachment and reserve that mimics Tocqueville's own: to live within democracy but remain detached from its popular life, to judge American life from the standpoint of some higher culture, and to defend civilized values and individual distinction against the corrosive workings of egalitarianism. Henry Adams, Henry James, and William Santayana may be said to have taken this particular path.[25] This ambivalent stance allows intellectuals to rally around America's espousal of economic and political freedom, yet remain distant from its culture. It has been an enormously seductive position, with many parallels to the appeal of the political philosopher Leo Strauss, whose followers rehearse classical debates about the tension between the true life of the mind and the daily necessities of ruling and being ruled in a democracy.[26] Tocqueville's appropriation by students of American Studies tended to cement his emergence as a fixture on the American cultural right, although the appeal of both American Studies and Tocqueville himself was, of course, far broader than that. But to a great extent the postwar American Tocqueville was not just a theoretical alternative to Marx, but also a potential rallying-point for those suspicious of popular culture and a free-wheeling cultural left.

These postwar 'Tocquevillian' orthodoxies—the linked assumptions that America was a model of pluralist liberalism and that its institutions should provide a normative political, if not cultural, ideal for the free world—were not readily exported. In the eyes of most European postwar thinkers, American politics and culture remained the peculiar products of American exceptionalism, unreflective of the ideological spectrum that dominated debates in Europe. Hostility to liberal theory, generated by a century of polarized conflict that had succeeded in marginalizing liberal discourse, permeated much of intellectual life, especially in France. Many participants in democratic politics viewed liberal institutions as practical (and sometimes demeaning) accommodations to an imperfect reality, rather than as accomplishments desirable in themselves or worthy of being theorized. Critical theory dominated postwar thought in Germany and Italy, while academic Marxism and romantic collectivism held sway in France.[27]

It is true that maverick French intellectuals like Raymond Aron and Michel Crozier in the 1950s and 1960s began to use Tocqueville to question the paradigms that dominated French social science. Aron's admiration for the first *Democracy*, and his elevation of Tocqueville's work to the status of a sociology classic, has been termed the first wave of the French Tocqueville revival.[28] But Aron's use of Tocqueville to repudiate historical determinism, to search for the conditions of liberty, and to urge a soberly prudential politics was exceptional in the world of French public intellectuals. In postwar France, Marxism still presented an 'unsurpassable horizon' that marked the boundaries of political critique.[29] Only in the 1970s did the French awaken to the horrors of totalitarianism, a recoil that has in the past thirty years become the subtext of much contemporary thought. Reacting in part to the writings of Solzhenitsyn on the Gulag and to the massacres in formerly French Cambodia, French intellectuals began in those years to extricate themselves from their long attachment to Marxism.

This brief summary of Tocqueville's reception in the twentieth century reveals a similar pattern: as Western democracies became less preoccupied with the economic and social divisions that had defined the joint emergence of democracy and capitalism, Tocqueville's emphasis on the *mentalité* of liberal democracy, and on the social psychological mechanisms that potentially divide or unite a democratic people, exerted a greater pull. American writers and academics, exploring America's political identity as the 'leader of the free world' after the Second World War , used Tocqueville to discuss the underlying mechanisms, benefits, and costs of a stable pluralism based on a liberal ideological consensus. In France the rise of Tocqueville was linked even more closely to the decline of Marx.

When the French began to confront the problems of 'post-industrial' society, and at the same time to face the depressing political legacies of communism in Europe, Tocqueville's focus on the liberal potential of a political culture alternately buffeted by revolution and authoritarianism seemed newly compelling. Let me turn, then, to Tocqueville's role in prompting contemporary French theorists to dissect the historical legacies of revolution and to weigh the impact of these legacies on the possibilities of liberal democracy in the 'new Europe.'

Tocqueville and Liberal Alternatives to Revolution

The end of communism and the surrender of the illusion of an exemplary socialist 'other' has released in France—and indeed all of Europe—a flood of anguished, contradictory, and often divisive memories about the politics and culture of the recent past. Much contemporary political reflection has been taken up with this return of the repressed.[30] But French political thinkers have not so much become liberals as they have become interested in how liberal theory—especially submerged voices in their own intellectual tradition—might help them make sense of a 'world quite new'. What has replaced the horizon of Marxism is no single alternative theory, or even shared point of view, but rather a set of questions. If formal democratic freedom is not an ideological illusion, then what is it and how can it be justified? If totalitarianism is the poisonous fruit of modern democratic culture in Europe, then how do we understand this fateful turn in the history of modern politics? More important, how do we assess the possibilities for alternative outcomes both in western Europe and in the eastern countries newly admitted to the European zone of democratic 'peace and prosperity'?

This question of the roots and the fruits of modern democratic culture particularly troubled François Furet, the influential historian of the French Revolution who began in the late 1960s to use Tocqueville to uncover the ideological cracks inherent in France's particular democratic history. In his many works on the Revolution and its legacies, Furet self-consciously attempts to free French history—and particularly accounts of the Revolution—from the confines of a historiography that had absorbed the meaning of the Revolution into some variant of historical materialism. He both attributes a different logic to the course of the French Revolution and implies that this logic was not fated to prevail. By attempting to restore a sense of political contingency to the past, he implicitly restores indeterminacy and a sense of democratic possibility to the present. He terms this restoration of a sense of historical possibility the 'Tocqueville effect'.[31] This attempt to assess the contradictory trajectories inherent in current praxis by attending to democracy's particular *filiation*—its genesis in the past—most distinguishes the contemporary uses of Tocqueville in France from both the postwar and more recent American uses. In France, the Tocqueville of *The Old Regime*, the passionately engaged scholar who sought the destiny of France by rethinking her past, has a resonance that generally escapes American readers focused on the two *Democracies*.

François Furet began his career as a more or less orthodox French historian, a member of the *Annales* school who took for granted the relevance of historical materialism and class analysis to those who wished to write serious history. He ended as the author of several seminal works that reoriented the historiography of the French Revolution and pointed France in the direction of reclaiming its own liberal heritage as a way of understanding its current political dilemmas.[32] In *Penser la Révolution française*, rendered into English less powerfully as *Interpreting the French Revolution*, Furet explicitly takes his bearings from Tocqueville's *The Old Regime and the Revolution*. The hypothesis of *The Old Regime* is arresting for a person with Furet's objective of understanding the genesis of modern democracy. Tocqueville argues that the characteristics of French politics in the 1850s—its obsession with unitary sovereignty and its passion for equality—were implicit within the absolutism that emerged in France in the seventeenth and eighteenth centuries. He searches for the historical link between despotism and individualism in order to exorcise the satanic attraction that he observed in his own society between political centralization and social equality. Recovering and understanding the genesis of this historical dynamic, for Tocqueville, was necessary for any clear-sighted action in the world, for situating oneself as a political actor.

This drive to recover the hidden lessons of the past also inspires Furet's work, although he takes the Tocquevillian project in a slightly different direction. Tocqueville wrote *The Old Regime* in order to understand the debilitating political practices of the Second Empire. He dwells, therefore, on those aspects of the revolutionary decade that nurtured the despotic potential of the Old Regime and that facilitated Napoleon I's (and later Louis Bonaparte's) imposition of empire. Indeed, his argument is so past-determined and future-directed that the Revolution itself, as others have noted and I have argued above, appears as a somewhat strange interlude.[33] For Furet, interested above all in clarifying the difficult practice of democracy in the late twentieth century, this mysterious revolutionary transition becomes the dramatic focus. He finds in it, rather than in the Napoleonic state, the crucible of an identifiably modern culture.

Rather than viewing the Revolution as a sort of political epiphenomenon to be understood in relation to social forces, Furet finds in revolutionary praxis the birth of a troubling oscillation between liberty and repression that is the hallmark of our own age. On Furet's account, we can watch this new culture improvising itself as the Jacobins played out the ultimate logic of democratic politics for the first time. The Revolution takes on new immediacy in Furet's work because he suggests that we still live in its political shadow. Our struggles to negotiate the paths of liberal democracy, like those of the original revolutionaries, risk careening off into a terrorist skid (dérapage). Hence studying the culture of the French Revolution becomes the source of 'reflection on the ambiguity of modern democracy'.[34]

Through his sympathetic encounter with Tocqueville, then, Furet is drawn into a new perspective on the possibilities of contemporary democratic politics. Though he accepts Tocqueville's view that the institutions of modernity are partly a legacy of political absolutism, he argues that the transformative drama of the French Revolution itself—its rhetoric, its symbols, and its validation of the power of speaking, naming, and representing as sources of legitimacy—also plays a key role in creating modern political culture. Not just absolutism, but the legacy of revolutionary culture itself led to tendencies that constrict liberty in the present. According to Furet and his followers, the Revolution's political repertoire never made room for the legal expression of disagreement, much less conflict. When conflicts inevitably occurred, they could not be mediated but only suppressed by whoever spoke for the people. The Terror was an instrument to unify society surgically by removing all potential threats. This critique of a romantic attempt to create an authentic democratic politics that would deliver on the promise of the Revolution is also a critique of the revolutionary and democratic political tradition in Europe, of its hopeful messianism and its allegedly self-deluding propensity to separate the revolutionary gold from the terroristic dross. Furet finds in this republican political praxis not the possibility of authentic democratic representation but a deep-rooted dynamic of denial of difference that forms the 'matrix of totalitarianism'.[35]

Not only the Revolution but also the whole of nineteenth-century French history can be rethought in the wake of the Tocqueville effect. Without the sharp focusing lens of historical determinism or the comforting assumption that the Third Republic achieved republican closure after a century of false starts and temporary reversals, French nineteenth-century history again becomes uncharted territory. (The metaphor of uncharted seas was of course a favoured one among French thinkers in the nineteenth century.) The classic narrative historians of the nineteenth century, and especially Tocqueville, have regained a certain relevance in an era when the agenda is not to use France to exemplify a universal history, either of bourgeois hegemony or republican triumph, but rather to use France's 'singular' history to illuminate its current democratic malaise.[36] To explain a peculiar history is of course a formidable task. No history can be recreated solely from within, but to approach it from the outside often means contrasting it to an implicitly normal or typical development. Yet we have no such consensus on democratic normality.

The intellectual historian and Tocqueville scholar Françoise Mélonio has approached the task of reclaiming France's democratic history by focusing on the reception of Tocqueville himself, that is, by reflecting systematically on the 'quarrelsome conversation of the French with Tocqueville'.[37] By following the intellectual reception of a figure who was simultaneously inside and outside French political culture, she attempts to gain enough critical distance to see the nineteenth-century transition to democracy anew. Furet's approach to nineteenth-century history is ultimately a philosophical one; intrigued by the ways in which ideas beget ideas, he focuses on the texts in which those ideas take shape. Though Tocqueville was a crucial catalyst for his thought, his intellectual affiliations seem as much Hegelian as Tocquevillian. Mélonio, in contrast, approaches nineteenth-century history from a Tocquevillian concern with how the weight of inherited collective practices and the workings of political psychology combine to shape the politics of a society and its discourse. Her focus is not especially on texts, but on those political media (journals, newspapers, funeral orations, correspondence intended for publication) from which one gains a sense of the *mœurs* of political society. She treats ideas less as abstract positions than as historically and socially constructed artefacts.

Since the French shared neither one history nor one unified society in the nineteenth century, the story she tells is largely one in which ideas divide rather than unify. She shows, for example, how the first volume of *Democracy in America* had a restricted influence among those in power because it came to symbolize the tactical alliance of legitimists with the republican opposition, and was read largely through this suspicious haze. She shows how, even in the 1870s, the remembrance of things past inhibited political cooperation. And she shows how difficult it was to confront the French with a universalized America, since such an image contradicted a French prophetic rationalism that had been unconsciously assimilated—though in very different ways—by all heirs of the Revolution. Her story of democratic constraints and possibilities, in this akin to Tocqueville's own, is one in which political suspicion and distrust themselves become ingrained patterns of interaction, intensifying the fault-lines in civil society.

If Mélonio's account recalls the inexorable divisiveness of historical memory, it also reminds us of the role of choice and contingency in political history. Individuals may break the grip of a political psychology generated by past practice if they are able to recognize windows of opportunity. The decisive issue in such periods, as for example in France in the 1870s, is the fashioning of a new collective memory in which traditions are reinterpreted in order to legitimate a break with the past. Mélonio's use of Tocqueville, then, leads one to ask whether the opportunity to vindicate an experiment in political cooperation by giving it a legitimating ideological tradition can be successfully seized only with a simultaneous amnesia: that is, only if alternative traditions that feed divisive political psychologies are forgotten. Given the current political turbulence in societies attempting to create democratic cultures out of bitter historical divisions, her Tocquevillian portrait of the weight of the past in shaping French political psychology raises provocative questions and parallels.

French historians, then, have been using Tocqueville to probe the fissures in political culture that may open up under the contemporary practice of democracy, as well as to assess the possibilities of liberal recovery from the twentieth century's virulent strains of revolutionary despotism. *The Old Regime and the Revolution* is, after all, a classic study of how one political culture dies and another is born. Tocqueville's identification of an emerging pattern of despotism in the Old Regime prompts a series of questions about how social interactions become cultural patterns and then foster persistent behaviours, about how communal ties atrophy and are replaced by other forms of coordination, and about how the reasonable intentions of political actors lead to unintended and disastrous consequences. His discussion of imperial consolidation suggests yet another set of questions. How do we understand the decomposition of a revolutionary regime into corruption and cant? Why do people acquiesce rather than resist such regimes? If such a regime should end, where does one look for sources of civic revitalization?[38] These are questions that Tocqueville thought could be answered only by a historical anthropology of a national culture. After 1989 brought the end of so many regimes in Eastern Europe that had long lost the allegiance of their citizens, these Tocquevillian questions have seemed ever more urgent.

Particularly instructive in this regard were a series of conferences that took place in the early 1990s in Yugoslavia, Czechoslovakia, Romania, Bulgaria, Russia, and Poland, organized by the French minister of culture under the sponsorship of the École Pratique des Hautes Études. Several French scholars initiated an intellectual interchange with eastern European scholars as a contribution to the project of thinking through the cultural bases of a greater Europe. The occasion for these conferences was the publication in each country of a new edition of one of Tocqueville's works, which was then to form the focus of the conference in that country.

Tocqueville, the organizers thought, was rich and nuanced enough to serve as the basis of the most contemporary interrogations into democracy and to facilitate a shared language of intellectual exchange.[39] His work was particularly well suited to a discussion of the problems of democracy after the fall of communism because it was comparative, historical, and multidisciplinary. Thus it could help to sort out similarities and differences between West and East, provide perspective on the continuities and ruptures within political cultures, and appeal to disoriented elites in a time of upheaval in the organization of academic traditions in eastern Europe. Finally, Tocqueville's work was thought to be marked by a richness of vision that registered the tensions between liberalism and democracy. Hence his texts were capable of serving as a salutary warning of the dangers of substituting one ideology for another, i.e. of substituting *laissez-faire* for Lenin. The central preoccupation of Tocqueville's works—the difficulty of infusing liberal tolerance, restraint, and respect for rights into a majoritarian democratic political culture alternately seduced by revolutionary action and authoritarian order—thus came to be newly persuasive at the end of the twentieth century in a Europe confronting its own patterns of ingrained illiberalism.

If Europeans find in Tocqueville a stimulus to wide-ranging reflection on the liberal alternatives to the legacy of revolutionary democracy in past and present, Americans have been appropriating him, as they have in the past, to reflect on the particular social and institutional underpinnings of their own exceptional democratic experiment. And, as always, they focus almost exclusively on the two volumes of *Democracy in America*. Today, however, that scrutiny is less likely to lead to self-congratulation than to provoke lamentations over a failure to preserve the institutions of self-rule that so impressed Tocqueville in the early nineteenth century. American interest in Tocqueville in the last several decades has been concentrated on his diagnosis of the potential pathologies of full-blown democratic individualism, and his valorization of the psychological and moral benefits of association. If Tocqueville, for a number of reasons, offers nations formerly in the grip of communist discourse a sense of the liberal possibilities of their histories, he also offers a way to criticize the triumph of liberal individualism.

Tocqueville, Associations, and Civil Society

The lack of attention in America to Tocqueville's complex understanding of the weight of history and of the ways in which political actors are both constrained by that weight and free to shift its burdens, comes in part from the nearly exclusive focus on *Democracy in America*. For heuristic reasons Tocqueville there assumes—without much argument—that America's version of equality has no weighty history. Americans, in his famous phrase, were born equal rather than becoming so. And, as I have argued above, his purposes in *Democracy in America* were comparative and generalizing. He wanted to understand the democratic social and political state by delineating in ideal-typical fashion its most characteristic passions and motivations, and to show how these features allegedly reinforced each other in America to create a system that functioned without a traditional hierarchy. Tocqueville, then, was not primarily interested in how Americans came to be as they are. I do not mean to suggest that he was unaware of the importance of American history, but only that the genesis of American democracy was not his primary theoretical concern in *Democracy in America*. Nor do I mean to say that his work has been ignored by American historians, but only that he usually enters their field of vision as the author of a set of classic observations about Jacksonian America that present themselves for confirmation (or, more typically, for correction).[40]

There are hints in *Democracy in America* of the kinds of conceptual question that would have interested Tocqueville himself, had he approached America as he would later approach France in *The Old Regime and the Revolution*. And American historians who may not necessarily see themselves as Tocquevillian have in fact pursued these questions: When and how did Americans lose their semi-aristocratic attachment to ancient virtue and replace it with the modern virtue of self-interest well-understood? How did a set of disparate colonies come to be dominated and eventually defined by Anglo-American culture? What is the historical relationship between Puritan covenanting traditions and individualism? Those who follow out these issues, however, are sometimes speaking Tocquevillian prose without knowing it. Not historians, but sociologists, cultural critics, and (more recently) political theorists dominate the contemporary discussions of Tocqueville in America. Rampant privatization and widespread perceptions of the erosion of local and civic solidarities have at last produced an appreciative audience for the second *Democracy*, for Tocqueville's discussion of the virus of *individualisme* and its antidotes.

The second *Democracy*, published in 1840, reveals Tocqueville's dismay at what he saw as the *individualisme*, materialism, and corruption of the July Monarchy. The complex tension between the demands of markets and the demands of free democratic politics was, as we have seen, a constant theme in Tocqueville's work. When he was thinking of France, and of the bourgeoisie of the age of Louis-Philippe, he tended to stress the privatizing dynamic of the interaction between a market economy and the democratic state. As against that pessimistic portrait, he offered a picture of an exemplary society that had triumphed over the potentially negative social effects of commercial society by developing the techniques of political citizenship. Indeed, on Tocqueville's account, success in combating individualism—that 'calm and considered feeling which disposes each citizen to isolate himself from the mass of his fellows and withdraw into the circle of family and friends'—was the singular accomplishment of American democracy in the early nineteenth century (DAII, 506). The supposed erosion of that vital citizenship in the late twentieth century has been the focus of considerable theoretical debate and public hand-wringing in America. An invocation of Tocqueville in these debates immediately alerts the reader to an incipient discussion of a cultural crisis: the alleged decline of a healthy associational life and the consequent emergence of either anomic individuals, perverted extremist groups, or both at once. Those chapters of *Democracy in America* that discuss the poison of individualism and the science and art of association as its antidote take on new relevance in this context.

In America a certain litany of loss—that the nation has lost its associational fibre, that its citizens compete for the bottom line, 'bowl alone', and shirk public duties—has become a mantra among critics of American political culture on the left and the right. Against this frightening picture of self-absorbed narcissism, some American political scientists and political theorists hold up Tocqueville's idealized portrait of a vibrant civil society, filled with self-reliant individuals who practise the art of voluntary association for both private and public ends. These critics mourn the disappearance of this web of connection, of the spillover between civil and political association that is assumed to constitute the civic community. Robert Putnam, for example, takes his inspiration from Tocqueville in his study of civic traditions.

Probably the most illustrious example of the sociocultural tradition of political analysis (and one that is especially germane to our study) remains Alexis de Tocqueville's *Democracy in America*. Tocqueville highlights the connection between the 'mores' of a society and its political practices. Civic associations, for example, reinforce the 'habits of the heart' that are essential to stable and effective democratic institutions.[41]

Without association—the argument goes—habits atrophy, social capital shrinks, and the chances for effective democracy decline.[42] Political theorists also compare the current reign of the superficial sound-bite to a deeper Tocquevillian understanding of civic deliberation, thought to be facilitated by a society thick with voluntary associations that make possible public discussion and public decision. This lament for a lost associational culture transcends political divisions, because the alleged decline of associations may be attributed to radically different causes. On the left the villain is a capitalism so caustic that it tends to corrode not only inherited social ties but all new attempts to arrest its spread throughout society. On the right the culprit is the loss of individual moral fibre, muscle that was once developed by tough forms of capitalism as well as by traditional families and voluntary groups, but that has now gone flabby with the welfare state and self-indulgent popular culture. In neither case, however, does the appeal to Tocqueville for a contrasting vision of healthy democracy go much beyond rhetorical appropriation.

Participatory democrats seek to fill the void in civil society allegedly created by the decline of unions, old ethnic associations, and movement politics with new group players—a kaleidoscope of interest and identity groups who will create strong democracy and social justice.[43] In a broad reconsideration of civil society from a largely 'critical theory' perspective, for example, Jean Cohen and Andrew Arato enlist Tocqueville throughout as a fellow traveller in their efforts to conceptualize a democratic civil society that can both create 'particular identities' and help to 'actualize universalist, normative potentials'.[44]

We build upon the thesis of one of the most important predecessors of the pluralist approach, Alexis de Tocqueville, who argued that without *active* participation on the part of citizens in *egalitarian* institutions and civil associations, as well as in politically relevant organizations, there will be no way to maintain the democratic character of the political culture or of social and political institutions.[45]

Yet in their very long book there is no actual analysis of Tocqueville's work or reference to any specific textual passage. This embrace of Tocqueville, rather, signals a new tendency among democratic theorists in the critical theory tradition both to converge on liberal pluralism and to try to differentiate their approach from that of 'conventional' liberalism by pushing liberalism's conclusions in a more egalitarian direction. Tocqueville, with his emphasis on participatory associations and civil society, seems an obvious ally who cannot be ignored, though he is much more often cited than read.[46] For many theorists of participatory democracy, a nod to Tocqueville is a way both to acknowledge an indigenous strain of democratic radicalism and to distance themselves from the perceived bankruptcy of some versions of Marxism.

Even as the left mourns the decline of participatory associations, many on the American right keen the loss of families, churches, fraternal organizations, and neighbourhoods—all allegedly sacrificed not to markets, but rather to a runaway bureaucracy that saps individual initiative, and to rampant individualism that resists all discipline. Social conservatives hope to restore this lost sense of civic duty not by democratizing or empowering the organizations of civil society but by minimizing the role of government, strengthening family values, and promoting traditional voluntary groups. In support of this agenda, they too draw validation from *Democracy in America.*

In this context of a nearly universal invocation of a Tocquevillian theory of associations, it may be useful to review what Tocqueville actually said about groups and civil society in America. A number of his observations fit what has become a standard liberal view of the positive role of intermediary groups in democratic life: that they play a crucial part in articulating and bolstering individual interests, and at the same time form barriers against the encroaching centralization of the national state. This perspective presages the liberal pluralism that formed the dominant paradigm in American political science in the 1950s and 1960s. As I noted above, Tocqueville was acknowledged as a prescient forerunner by those who articulated the pluralist postwar consensus. But it is not this anticipation of interest group liberalism that attracts many to Tocqueville today. Rather, it is his view that the unintended social consequences of association combat isolating individualism and thus indirectly produce socialized and moralized citizens in the place of atomistic consumers. The phrase usually quoted is his observation that associations are spaces where '[f]eelings and ideas are renewed, the heart enlarged, and the understanding developed only by the reciprocal actions of men upon one another' (DAII, 515). A reference to Tocqueville, then, usually suggests the notion that Americans have squandered nineteenth-century social and moral capital, though there may be no agreement on the possibility of renewing that capital, or on the ways in which one should go about doing so. Tocqueville's relevance is that he allegedly identified something real—association—and appreciated its complex moral and political functioning in a liberal democratic polity. Contemporary political theory and rhetoric in America is marked by increasing debate over the place of groups, especially voluntary groups, in the moral life of liberal democracy.[47]

Pundits, theorists of left and right, and political scientists who stress the importance of social capital, then, all hark back self-consciously to a few key chapters in *Democracy in America*. Similarly, those who criticize these 'neo-Tocquevillians' usually accept this characterization of Tocqueville in order to use him as a theoretical foil for their own more nuanced views of the interaction between the state and associations. They object to Tocqueville's supposed neglect of the role of the state in the constitution of groups, or to his allegedly simplistic view that group interactions are always positive for political democracy.[48] These critiques illustrate the extent to which in America the term 'Tocquevillian' has become a shorthand substitute for the claim that associations have positive moral and social consequences for democratic politics, rather than a term that draws on any deeper appreciation of Tocqueville's work.

Those who criticize both Tocqueville and the neo-Tocquevillians for a naive faith in associations rarely acknowledge the extent to which Tocqueville himself theorized the other side of the coin, that is, the extent to which he considered the drawbacks of a certain kind of social capital and the importance of the state for the social 'investment climate'.[49] In *The Old Regime*, for example, Tocqueville sketches a democratic dystopia of group life gone awry: an intense associational culture within a state infrastructure that both deliberately and inadvertently made cooperation for larger ends impossible. His account of eighteenth-century France provides a model of democratic civil society that foregrounds the very factors that contemporary neo-Tocquevillians are charged with ignoring. *The Old Regime* might be read as a meditation on the crucial role of the state in impeding or fostering an atmosphere in which group life can become social capital available for investment in political democracy. It is not necessarily the case that this discussion of the French Old Regime would further the critical aims of the social capital critics, but their failure even to consider it reveals a certain shallowness in the contemporary Tocqueville revival in American political science.

Tocqueville's discussion of the potential pathologies of individualism, then, has struck a particular nerve in contemporary American intellectual life, and his identification of the complex functioning of associations in democratic civil society provides an important impetus for a renewed discussion of the benefits of pluralism. In France one also finds concern about the quality of democratic civil society. The freeing of markets, coupled with a decline in public culture and national sentiments, have led to deep worries about the phenomenon of individualism and the loss of social *solidarité* and discipline. Moreover, critical commentary on *Democracy in America*, with its deep-rooted worries about the place of individualism in egalitarian culture, has similarly become an important medium through which to analyse these concerns. By the 1970s and 1980s Tocqueville's *Democracy* had more readers in France than at any time since the mid-nineteenth century. The political culture in which French criticisms of individualism are embedded, however, is quite different from American pluralism, and the uses of Tocqueville in fact help us to see that difference. The appropriations of Tocqueville in American and French critiques of individualism betray very different national perceptions of the challenges of building a democratic civil society. Like a litmus test, reactions to Tocqueville—particularly to his advocacy of an associational civic culture—betray the persistence of entrenched patterns in democratic political thinking that seem to have been barely affected by the forces of globalization.

Let me take as one example of these differences in liberal political culture a controversial article by Gilles Lipovetsky analysing the meaning of May 1968 for French politics, an article that counters the typical class analyses of these discontents with an account based on Tocqueville's notion of the rise of democratic individualism.[50] Lipovetsky describes the student movement as ostensibly revolutionary, but in reality infected by the very privatism, hedonism, and search for personal gratification that Tocqueville had identified as the hallmarks of individualism. Lipovetsky stresses the search for personal and sexual fulfilment, the utopianism, and the non-serious nature of French student radicalism in order to suggest paradoxically that the permanent legacy of 1968—after the initial excitement had died down—was an intensification of apolitical withdrawal. What remained were 'microscopic, minority subversions: communes, squats, living on the fringes of society, psychedelic drugs, and unusual sexual practice'.[51]

My point here is not to assess the plausibility of Lipovetsky's argument, but to call attention to the character of his appropriation of Tocqueville to make that argument. First, Tocqueville's discussion of individualism is used as a theoretical marker, but not a marker that flags the role of associations in civil society. Rather the reference to the concept of 'individualism' suggests a methodology of social explanation. Not the language of Marxian dialectic, but the language of psychologized historical anthropology is what we should employ to understand May 1968.[52] Second, the implicit contrast to the dangers posed by marginalized, alienated groups with alternative lifestyles is not a normally functioning pluralistic social order in which a host of associations—ascriptive, voluntary, and political—integrate citizens into liberal democracy. Rather, Lipovetsky contrasts the strangeness and menace of new fringe groups in French political life to the implied normality of trade union and revolutionary party politics. That politics—however flawed—was in his view at least guided by a stable view of some future public good, a disciplined loyalty to party, and an implicit acceptance of 'the structures of society and the obligations it imposed'. Most striking to Lipovetsky is that '[t]he May movement did not demand of anyone the sacrifices and self-criticisms of the old revolutionary traditions'.[53]

The theme of the decline of a stable political culture in France is rarely tied to any functional analysis of group life other than recognition of the decreasing role of the army, schools, or, in Lipovetsky's case, older political traditions. Americans use Tocqueville—often superficially or merely for inspiration—to universalize the experience of sociological pluralism, forgetting that this view of liberal democracy, even if cast in the generalizing language of high theory and civil society, is quite parochial. 'From a comparative perspective [Americans] enjoy a deep historical reservoir of reciprocity between voluntary associations and democratic institutions' that is somewhat anomalous.[54] In France this focus on secondary associations as the symbolic nexus among the institutional, psychological, and social practices of liberal democracy is noticeably absent, and Tocqueville's discussion of the role of groups has no special resonance. For example, although there is some recognition of new interest groups in French political life—anti-racism groups, or groups asserting political ethnic identities—these groups are rarely viewed in the context of what Americans might characterize as a Tocquevillian civil society in which associations play a host of political, social, and moral roles. On the contrary, such groups are likely to be viewed only in their relationship to the French state, which has the primary responsibility for defining social membership.[55]

Claude Lefort's discussion of Tocqueville's portrait of civil society illustrates the difference I am attempting to draw between characteristically American and French appreciations of the 'art and science of association'. Lefort notes that Tocqueville is an important theorist for our time because he does not speak about democracy abstractly, but rather attempts to describe the tissue or the flesh (*la chair*) of democracy. Whereas an American might naturally turn to a discussion of the web of associations as constitutive of that *tissu*, Lefort grants associations no privileged place in this extended metaphor. Indeed after a short discussion of Tocqueville's view of civil and political associations, he notes:

> In our time, are we not still obliged to denounce the delusion of those who wish to screen the state administration from the effects of associations of all kinds, associations whose demands hinder its action and do not yield to the plans of experts; and likewise to denounce the opposite delusion of those who place all their hopes in strictly civil associations and who scorn 'politics'.[56]

The upshot of Lefort's posing these delusions as paired extremes—on the one hand the automatic defence of rational bureaucracy against the importuning of interest groups and on the other the desire to supplant the state completely by self-governing groups existing in civil society—is to privilege a more commonsensical median, in which the state profits from the input of interested groups but maintains its integrity as the sole arbiter of the social contract.

Although there may be worry in France about atomistic individuals who lack civic consciousness, this concern does not necessarily indicate any movement towards an American understanding of the relationships between social and cultural pluralism and the processes of liberal government. Tocqueville's discussion of civil and political associations has enormous resonance in America because it feeds into national obsessions with group life, but it remains almost as exotic in France as it did when Tocqueville wrote. The pull of his critique of individualism in France in fact reveals a rather different preoccupation: a fear that the collective national sentiments underlying republican legitimacy are being undermined by economic and political forces, and that French democracy will be cast adrift from its moral moorings.

French theorists are less likely to ponder the role of associations in democratic civil society than to ask whether citizens who do not share a desideratum of collective sentiment can agree to disagree productively in politics. I now want to turn explicitly to the question of democracy's need for a unifying core of moral beliefs, a question that has increasingly engaged theorists of democracy in the late twentieth century, and that has led many back to Tocqueville's discussion of the functions of religion in democracy.

E Pluribus Unum: *the Need for Stabilizing Beliefs*

Beyond the art of association, the most important antidote to the dangerous tendencies of democratic individualism discussed in *Democracy in America* is religion. Indeed, it was to religious belief, rather than to the art of association, that Tocqueville attributed Americans' avoidance of the worst consequences of individualism. As Peter Berkowitz has commented, however, this Tocquevillian premiss that religion forms a necessary background condition to the flourishing of liberal democracy is much less frequently explored in American debates over the preconditions of civil society than are the supposed benefits of association *tout court*.[57] The contrary is true in France. If contemporary French readers have not been especially moved by Tocqueville's praise of association, his discussion of religion strikes deeper chords, though not always in obvious ways. A consideration of Tocqueville's view of the relationship of religious belief to democratic viability has led theorists to question the need for foundational beliefs, and to raise the possibility that modern democracy must dispense with such transcendent supports altogether.

Tocqueville's opinion that religious belief was necessary to the successful practice of free mores was closer to the spiritual anxieties at the root of his thought than was his relatively dispassionate discussion of the functions of associations. I have argued that his complicated religious sensibility—compounded of a loss of faith and an incorrigible will to believe—drove these efforts to validate a role for religious faith in democracy. He simply could not envision the stable functioning of a democratic order without the psychological restraints produced by a widespread adherence to transcendent metaphysical certainties. For Tocqueville, religious beliefs anchored norms of liberal justice. In America this discussion of religion and politics has not 'spilled over' into more general intellectual debate about the nature of the necessary consensus on democratic values. Although there is a wide current of American public commentary that is likely to point out the role of religion and of traditional family life in producing the sorts of characters who can make democracy work, and although Tocqueville is sometimes cited in this context, his views on religion are rarely treated as an entrée into the challenge of grounding modern democracy in widely accepted norms of justice, an enterprise that uses a different vocabulary and has other theoretical inspirations.[58]

Tocqueville thought that an internalized sense of the rule of law, moderation in political life, and the practices of democratic reciprocity were not possible without belief in an unquestionable guarantee of justice, bolstered by religion. For him, one of America's most hopeful lessons was that religious belief was not contradicted by modernity. This presumption of the prima facie relevance of Christianity to debates about justice in democracy, however, has inevitably declined in a more diverse and more secular America.[59] One might argue that the space for debate and argument about guarantees of justice in America has shifted to a terrain that Tocqueville did not really foresee: to contentious debates about the connection between American constitutional norms and a philosophy of liberal justice. In these debates analytical philosophers have taken the field, and they have little reason to engage with Tocqueville. His historical and psychological preoccupations and lack of interest in foundational arguments make him a stranger to their concerns. His assertion of a necessary link between religious belief and democratic politics, therefore, does not generate much commentary in contemporary America among political thinkers who take as their subject the philosophical roots of liberalism or deliberative democracy. French intellectuals, on the other hand, have often taken just this route in order to identify the paradoxes and antinomies facing any theory of democracy.

Theorists as different as Pierre Manent, Marcel Gauchet, and Claude Lefort have recently turned to Tocqueville to illuminate the question of democracy's moral foundations, and in particular to explore the place of Christianity in the theory of western democracy. Before turning to some examples of this French discussion, however, I want to explore a rather obvious objection to my generalization that American debates about the unifying normative factors underlying liberal democracy tend to ignore Tocqueville. Those theorists influenced by the political philosopher Leo Strauss have in fact produced a body of serious and often illuminating work on Tocqueville, religion, and democratic thought.[60] What attracts Straussians to this aspect of Tocqueville?

Tocqueville and Strauss

Some of the most penetrating American scholarship on all aspects
of Tocqueville's thought has been produced by political theorists
who identify with Strauss's approach to the study of political philosophy. Such an attraction is not surprising, since Tocqueville,
like Strauss, manifests such ambivalence towards liberal democracy itself. Strauss believed that liberal democratic institutions
represent the best practical solution to the political realities of
modernity, but they do not promote the life of the mind, and may
even endanger it. Hence Straussians often turn to Tocqueville as
an ally in identifying the dangers to the cultivated life. 'But we
cannot help, with Tocqueville, but be dissatisfied with the medi-
ocrity and restless anxiety of a political liberalism.'[61] Tocqueville's
self-image as a philosophical social thinker who stood apart from
democratic culture in order to salvage the highest values of civilization and to instantiate them within a democratic regime is
indeed a Straussian stance. Moreover, his pervasive sense of loss
and of an imminent crisis of human value has obvious points of
contact with Strauss's overarching theme of the crisis of liberalism
and modernity.

Tocqueville's studied distance from Enlightenment rationalism,
his critique of historicism, his affinities with Aristotle as well as
Montesquieu, and his conviction that people of intellect and character have a duty to manage the unruly tendencies of democracy
both parallel and inspire the concerns of Straussian political theorists. James Caeser's recent book on Tocqueville, for example, illustrates a central affinity between the two on the definition of political
science. Caeser stresses the classical nature of Tocqueville's 'new
political science' and the important role of political knowledge and
insight—as opposed to simplistic scientistic generalization—in
helping to secure and maintain a reasonable political regime.[62] Political knowledge, on this view, needs to assist those elites who direct
society to 'choose well'. This emphasis on managing the dangerous
tendencies of the modern age fans out into a cluster of concerns
taken up by other theorists who identify themselves as indebted to
Strauss: the role of leadership in democracy, the role of education in
inculcating certain mental habits that foster social and political
restraint, the role of aristocratic and English common-law elements
in the American founding, and the dangers of rationalizing or
philosophizing the American constitution.[63]

Most important for my purposes here, Straussians take Tocqueville's views on religion seriously and see them as linked both to the roots of his thought and to his most profound insights into the conditions of political modernity. But this appreciation, I would claim, only confirms the point I wish to make about Tocqueville's ability to provoke a wide array of French thinkers— but fewer Americans—to confront the possibility that democratic practice might of necessity be unanchored to any larger theory of justice, and might be fated to coexist with uncertainty about its moral bases.

Straussians take Tocqueville's discussion of religion seriously, just as Strauss took seriously the political effects of the historical process of secularization, because they also fear the general effects of scepticism and disbelief. Like Tocqueville, they assume that religious belief is not merely sociologically useful in producing democratic consensus, but is crucial in blunting a philosophical nihilism that would doom liberal political culture if such nihilism were to become general. Indeed, Straussians have produced an important critical literature on Tocqueville, religion, and politics precisely because many of them share this judgement about the dangers of philosophical nihilism. As faith declines, moral relativism increases; as relativism increases, the political self-restraint induced by widely shared moral and religious norms dissolves. Hence, responsible intellectuals—even or especially atheists— should fear the decline of religion more than religion's potentially illiberal excesses, for only the precariously balanced political stability provided by liberal self-restraint permits true philosophical activity, rooted in disinterested study of the ancients, to continue. Such theorists are able to explore empathetically the tensions and contradictions involved in a position like Tocqueville's, which advocates the desirability of authentic belief from an ambiguous stance outside the conventional tenets of that belief. Yet precisely because religious belief is more widespread in America than in other liberal democracies, Tocqueville's worries fail to engage. Among American political and social thinkers interested in the question of normative restraints on democracy, these Straussian concerns represent a distinctly minority view: too detached from faith to engage many believers, yet too foreign to the philosophical languages and concerns of theorists of 'liberal justice' or 'democratic deliberation' to provoke a debate.

French scholars and philosophers who have taken part in the revival of liberal political theory over the past twenty-five years have largely avoided the idioms of Anglo-American analytical philosophy. But they have raised a similar underlying question: how are the political practices of modern liberal democracy connected to the moral life and to universal values? And like American Straussians, many have seen Tocqueville's discussion as a useful way to begin exploring these questions. Indeed, Strauss has important French disciples. A leading conservative voice in the revival of liberal political philosophy in France and the author of two important books on Tocqueville, Pierre Manent, has singled out Strauss—along with Raymond Aron—as an important influence on the formation of his thought.[64] Through his encounter with Strauss, Manent came to appreciate that Tocqueville's views on religion and politics could offer a particularly illuminating conceptualization of the project of modernity. According to Manent's reading of Tocqueville, modern democratic conditions unleash human wilfulness in a destructive cycle that continually undermines the natural order of human life. Manent's own understanding of that natural order, unlike that of Strauss, ultimately owes more to Thomism than to ancient rationalism. But like Strauss he pays attention above all to the constant tension between ways of institutionalizing noble and 'human' aspirations and the social and political processes that necessarily undermine these aspirations.[65]

In France this use of Tocqueville to explore questions of the relationship of unifying moral norms to democratic practice reaches beyond the circle of those rooted in Socratic philosophy or Catholicism. Thinkers like Marcel Gauchet and Claude Lefort, who believe that modern democracy entails a necessary philosophical journey away from consensus on fundamental principles into indeterminate uncharted territory, also find inspiration in Tocqueville. On these readings, Tocqueville instructs through his curious blind spots as much as through his insight. Using Tocqueville to identify the distinctiveness and restless destructiveness of modern democracy, then, does not necessarily mean endorsing attempts to dampen or contain democracy. Marcel Gauchet, for example, uses Tocqueville's very resistance to the idea of a normatively unanchored democracy as a way to introduce his own view that democracy is nothing but a set of 'infinite possibilities for questioning'.[66]

Tocqueville and the Question of Democracy's Moral Foundations

Tocqueville's discussion of religious *mœurs* in the second volume of *Democracy in America* sets the stage for Gauchet's contention that the essential nature of modern European democracy is an endless dispute over legitimacy. Gauchet begins from the 'compensatory' Tocquevillian arguments about religion that we have examined above: fixed notions about God, about the nature of the human soul, and about the duties of humanity can prevent humans from descending into revolutionary 'anarchy and impotence' (DAII, 443). Because the mind cannot reach these fixed notions on its own, Tocqueville believed it would be dangerous to leave their determination to the individual conscience. 'General ideas respecting God and human nature are therefore the ideas above all others which ought to be withdrawn from the habitual action of private judgment and in which there is most to gain and least to lose by recognizing an authority' (DAII, 443). Only a very few can 'let their minds float at random between obedience and freedom' (DAII, 451). He argued that in democratic times individual minds naturally compensate for this total lack of structure by gravitating toward a set of beliefs that are transcendentally based and beyond dispute. Without these beliefs, civil conflict can launch a devastating war of all against all, since anything—including annihilation of one's opponents—becomes thinkable. In this way Tocqueville linked the irreligion of the French Revolution to its degeneration into terror. It was the genius of the Americans, he thought, to have hit on a form of organization— separation of church and state in a society already moulded by religious opinion—that allowed religious beliefs to constrain human nature without antagonizing the principle of popular sovereignty. 'While the law allows the American people to do everything, there are things which religion prevents them from imagining and forbids them to dare' (DAI, 292).

Marcel Gauchet admires Tocqueville for discerning the link uniting social conflict with the 'extension of the human problematic'. He nevertheless accuses Tocqueville of a curious blindness in allowing himself to believe that political conflicts, which inevitably arise under democratic social conditions, can be avoided through the common acceptance of religious dogma. Tocqueville, on Gauchet's reading, was led astray by his own idealized portrait of America and the putative vision of a society reconciled with itself. Insofar as Tocqueville's vision of a democracy profoundly united by a consensus on republicanism and by a shared set of religious dogmas was a true picture of America, it could (and can) never present a picture of the more general future of democratic nations. According to Gauchet, Tocqueville needed to find a living intellectual unity in America analogous to those monarchical sentiments that formerly held together French aristocratic society. But Gauchet argues that Tocqueville failed to see that 'America's political novelty was essentially contrary to the normal march of modernity'.[67] The more typical path taken by democracy was in fact the European path, in which class and social conflicts were and are drawn into the political arena and there become the signifiers of democratic politics.

> To hold men together by means of their opposition, to engage them in an endless appraisal of the signification uniting them in society; in the final analysis, these are the crucial properties of democracy in the Old World, under the contradictory pressures of the revolutionary will and the republic's retrograde refusal to acknowledge equality.[68]

Not just the status antagonisms of the Old Regime, but also the class antagonisms of the New Regime became the stuff of democratic European politics. Paradoxically, according to Gauchet, this has meant not only a politics of interest, but a 'framework within which there developed an endless reconsideration of the reasons and the ends of human community'.[69] Tocqueville's paralysing fear of a generalization of the revolutionary political model caused him to cling to the potentially unifying functions of Christian belief. But on Gauchet's account this turn to religion is a kind of protective atavism that screens out the painful truth: 'everything is contestable, everything can be established or instituted otherwise than it is ... '.[70] Claude Lefort, who also argues that the works of Tocqueville can serve as a starting-point for rethinking the contemporary problems of democracy, makes a similar observation about the limitations of Tocqueville's intellectual resistance to the democratic unknown. According to Lefort, the essence of democratic regimes—as opposed to totalitarian ones—is the welcoming and preserving of 'indeterminateness', the sense of possibility that comes from a rich and contested history.[71]

Gauchet inserts his discussion of the Tocquevillian moment in democratic theorizing into a larger speculative history of the course of modern politics. On this view, modern European states insidiously usurped the jurisdiction formerly held by religious authorities, thus inspiring longings for reconciliation similar to those of the Christian religion from whence they came. These longings have manifested themselves both in the hubristic clashes of political parties preaching conflicting universalisms and in the perversions of totalitarian politics. What is to replace this old European practice in the new Europe? Gauchet's description of the character of modern democracy—like that of some other contemporary French theorists gingerly reconciling themselves to a 'liberalizing' project—is curiously vague. '[T]he problematic dynamics of democracy no longer imply the aggressive affirmation of an integral and exclusive representation of the good society. It is now taken for granted that life in society is legitimately subject to debate, and that the oppositions that make up the debate are inevitably affected by it.' We are witnessing 'the irresistible settling of societies into an interrogation about themselves'.[72]

Of course, citizens in democracies can engage in productive debate only by using mutually intelligible terms and concepts. What Tocqueville's texts appear to supply to some French readers today is just such a conceptual medium in which to 'interrogate themselves' about the future of democracy. The pull of Tocqueville's discussion of religion, the location where he connects democratic practice to restraining norms of justice, suggests not that his view is itself persuasive, but rather that the usual conceptual representations used to 'interrogate' the moral parameters of democratic practice—Marxism and republican positivism—have lost their authoritative purchase. The realities of life in the new Europe—the fall of communism, privatization, the spread of markets, serious debates over issues of national citizenship—have contributed not only to the decline of Marxism but also to a more general questioning of the republican nostrums that have anchored French politics since the consolidation of the Third Republic. The democratic legislature, the meritocratic bureaucracy, and the ideals of positivism and secular universalism bequeathed by the Third Republic together have provided standards—albeit always contested ones—to French political life. But it is precisely these traditional standards that seem so inadequate to a society buffeted by global markets, filled with non-European immigrants, and burdened by a tradition of *étatisme* that is being challenged from below by economic decentralization and from above by Europeanization. As commitments to traditional republican standards have eroded, and as the accepted Marxist languages of political critique have declined, theorists have turned to Tocqueville—among others—to help them find their historical and theoretical bearings and to address the question of what philosophical and moral resources democratic nations may draw on to mediate democratic conflicts.

Indeed, the ability of Tocqueville's texts to provoke fundamental questions about the normative bases of liberal democracy in France—and the relative neglect of that discussion in America—helps illuminate the current vulnerability of France's ideology of 'liberal' republicanism and the relative invulnerability (in the United States) of America's cult of the constitution. France has experienced in the final decades of the twentieth century an erosion of those certainties—and the political languages associated with them—that have defined its identity as a modern republic. Americans have not experienced a comparable *crise de conscience*.

When they speak of a crisis of liberal democracy, Americans often mean the loss of a moral attachment to the associations of civic life. For guidance in reinvigorating this civil life, they may turn to a communitarian or republican public philosophy from which they have supposedly strayed. Tocqueville is often invoked as an authority on 'the way we were', a theorist who can help reweave the threads of civic association that allegedly lie deep in the American past and in their constitutional traditions. Michael Sandel, for example, quotes Tocqueville on New England townships to illustrate a conception of situated liberty that he contrasts with the allegedly empty notions of the procedural republic.[73] Europeans also speak frequently of a democratic crisis of legitimacy. Indeed, in the case of France, the question of which principles should guide French democratic practice bedevils both regional party politics and philosophical debates. Yet there is little European nostalgia for lost habits of the heart. Contemporary French theorists turn to Tocqueville not because his texts point the way to a retrieval of social capital, but because they provoke a recognition of a dilemma that seems more real now than at any time since the foundation of the Third Republic: the lack of any widely accepted theory anchoring contemporary democratic practice and the difficulty of constructing such a theory given a contested history.

Modern democratic theory has struggled with the problem of grounding collective public life in something other than the human will since its inception in the late medieval period. These latest efforts to theorize the problem of democratic legitimacy in France by appropriating Tocqueville as foil constitute an attempt to reopen once again these unsettled and unsettling questions. Such efforts bring us to a final question about Tocqueville's presence in contemporary intellectual debates: has he—against all odds—become a postmodern author?

A Postmodern Tocqueville?

I have been discussing certain attempts among contemporary French theorists to explore the question of the normative foundations of modern democracy by a turn to Tocqueville. Of course these concerns about the contested nature of democratic foundations are not merely French. They are the preoccupations of postmodern or 'late-modern' thinkers of various nationalities and persuasions. It may be useful, therefore, to conclude this discussion of Tocqueville's ability to bring to public consciousness the dilemmas of democracy at the turn of the new century by touching briefly on his fate among American 'postmodernist' political theorists.

In America, political theorists influenced by Nietszche and Heidegger (as well as by Foucault and Derrida) have put forth their own versions of democratic politics 'in a world without intrinsic design', an 'agonistic' arena where ironic interrogation allegedly stirs things up, prevents closure, shifts the frame, enlarges debates, and guards against the lure of newly repressive naturalisms that erase or demonize the other.[74] But Tocqueville has rarely been taken up as an inspiring guide in this context. Because of his reputation in America as the theorist of liberal democratic hegemony, his appropriation by many social conservatives, and his own anxious political erasures—gender and class, and to some extent race—he has largely figured as an opponent for those who explore these themes. Yet even here he exhibits a certain power to elicit thought and to be transformed from establishment theorist to provocateur.

Tocqueville has recently appeared as the subject of several sustained and sympathetic readings in the distinctive idiom of American postmodernism.[75] A deliberately 'artful' reading such as that of Mark Reinhardt, for example, focuses less on a 'republican Tocqueville' who recommends the art of association and participation than on an older 'liberal Tocqueville' who celebrates resistance to the levelling tendencies of the democratic state. Yet this is a liberal Tocqueville with an anarchic and postmodern twist.

Implicitly reading Tocqueville through the lens of Foucault, and noting the parallels between Tocqueville's image of an insidious new tutelary power and Foucault's view of the disciplinary institutions and discourses of modernity, Reinhardt draws inspiration from Tocqueville's advocacy of a pluralization of power centres and his concern for protecting individuality and diversity from 'communal suffocations'. Reinhardt understands Tocqueville to be reminding us that 'for democracy to be meaningful, it must be radically plural; it must enable heterogeneous actors to share, in many ways and many places, in exercising and challenging the power that shapes their lives, their selves'.[76] Here we have an attempt to enlist Tocquevillian insights in a struggle against not only the constricting uniformities produced by the centralized administrative state but also against the homogenizations allegedly induced by nationalism, corporate culture, and even the global political economy.

In the American context, such a radical reading of Tocqueville has to address not only his conservative religious preconceptions, as does the work of Marcel Gauchet discussed above, but also his deep resistance to any disorder generated by politicizing the triad of race, class, and gender. These particular 'sites of contestation' have played an important role in the postmodern critique of liberal political theory in America, and any postmodern appropriation of Tocqueville must confront directly his willingness to exclude social groups that arouse too great an ambivalence about social order. Unlike thinkers who manifest some sympathy for disciplinary projects involving religion, class, or family, postmodernists strenuously resist Tocqueville's indulgence of his own cultural anxieties. Reinhardt, for example, is quite sensitive to the kinds of democratic closure that I have discussed above in Chapter 4, and he argues— sensibly, I think—that these closures are not necessarily linked to some radical defect in Tocqueville's overall theory of democracy, for Tocqueville has no such consistently worked-out theory. Rather, Tocqueville's limitations result from his worries about the robust psychological profile needed to withstand democracy's toleration of difference and to take part in the fractious democratic practices of debate and contestation.[77]

Reinhardt himself wishes to transpose Tocqueville's notion of sturdy independence, a notion that Tocqueville endorses politically but rejects in some crucial social contexts, into a contemporary social and cultural register. He wishes, that is, to appropriate Tocqueville's endorsement of 'virile' freedom—the ability to react with individual courage, resourcefulness, and foresight against the imposition of outside control—to contest the regimes of race, gender, and sexuality. Here we have come full circle. The deep appreciation of unruly aristocratic premodern liberties that launched Tocqueville on his intellectual search for the conditions under which his contemporaries could resist despotism now inspires late-modern defiance of the 'disciplinary regimes of global capitalism' that allegedly threaten to enslave our own age. And why not? It is perhaps appropriately ironic for a theorist who was a master of irony that he should enter the twenty-first century hoist on his own petard: that is, used as a tool for undermining the very disciplinary structures—of markets, religious faith, and sexuality—that he himself thought would make possible modern liberty.

Tocqueville Today

In this chapter we have listened to the contemporary voices of Alexis de Tocqueville debating the historical difficulties of peacefully creating a liberal political culture, the need for secondary associations to provide the social capital for that culture, and the challenges of theorizing and practising liberal democracy in the absence of unifying moral foundations. Partly because his original voice defied historical determinisms, the hegemonic claims of the 'social', and the philosophic defence of faith, Tocqueville speaks persuasively today to many constituencies bereft of those consolations. Even those who no longer believe in the explicit guidance of history, social science, or transcendent moral truth need to act politically and to give reasons for those actions. Tocqueville's texts still live because he calls attention to certain political issues that cluster around matters of collective political judgement and choice in a world in which people disagree deeply about which principles ought to govern those choices. In the absence of such agreement, how can people act in concert to reform their societies without succumbing to violent ideological delusions or to deadening authoritarianism? How can they renew or create the moral and social solidarities that make democratic political action productive in the face of contrary forces that undermine such solidarities? How should they confront the possibility that the sense of unity underlying democratic legitimacy might be a fragile, non-renewable gift of history? These questions transcend many political differences, and Tocqueville's appeal has similarly risen above party.

Why do we still read Tocqueville today? For those of us who agree with him that 'without comparisons the mind does not know how to proceed' or who believe that people 'grasp fragments of truth, but never truth itself', his subtle efforts to combine empirical study with imaginative interpretation in the absence of any overarching or justifying metatheory must strike a sympathetic chord. His heuristic strategies are our own, and we mine his reconstructions of collective psychology and political culture for hypotheses that might produce a fresh way of seeing our own predicaments. Even Tocqueville's failures of empathy—for atheists, socialists, and those scribbling women—instruct by reminding us to distrust what seems most trustworthy in the deep structure of our own *mentalités*. Subtle tyrannies of majority opinion can, after all, 'relieve [us] of the trouble of thinking' (DAII, 691). And in the final analysis it is Tocqueville's thinking that compels. Behind the polished nineteenth-century rhetorical prose is concentrated intelligence in motion: probing a statement, adjusting it carefully, turning it on its head, getting it right. His texts resist settling into established grooves of interpretation, and continue to engage new readers because this powerful, animated, and sometimes contradictory thinking lies so close to the surface. Tocqueville, then, is ever available for conversation—both casual and profound—and the impulse to report on the intellectual exchange, to add yet again 'comme disait M. de Tocqueville', can be irresistible.

Notes

1 Tocqueville to Eugene Stoffels, Feb. 1835, quoted in James Kloppenberg, 'Life Everlasting: Tocqueville in America', *La Revue Tocqueville/The Tocqueville Review*, 17 (2) (1996), 20.

2 Jon Elster, *Political Psychology* (Cambridge: Cambridge University Press, 1993), 101.

3 A wide range of 'readings' of Tocqueville supply the materials for my discussion of contemporary appropriations of his works. With some exceptions, I have not focused here on the more scholarly secondary works on Tocqueville that have greatly informed my own reading, and to which I have referred in preceding chapters. Rather I concentrate on theorists and commentators who use Tocqueville explicitly to further various political or theoretical agendas of their own.

4 Seymour Drescher, 'Worlds Together, Worlds Apart: Tocqueville and the Franco-American Exchange', in Lloyd Kramer (ed.), *The French-American Connection: 200 Years of Cultural and Intellectual Interaction* (Chapel Hill, NC: Institut Français de Washington, 1994), 28.

5 Seymour Drescher, *Tocqueville and England* (Cambridge, Mass.: Harvard University Press, 1964), 220.

6 I have found the work of Michael Hereth particularly insightful. See his *Alexis de Tocqueville: Die Gefährdung der Freiheit in der Demokratie*, translated as *Alexis de Tocqueville: Threats to Freedom in Democracy*, trans. George Bogardus (Durham, NC: Duke University Press, 1986).

7 Françoise Melonio argues throughout *Tocqueville et les français* (Paris: Aubier, 1993) that Tocqueville is literally 'excentrique' in the French tradition. See p. 198 and *passim*.

8 On Tocqueville's reception in America, see George W. Pierson, 'On the Centenary of Tocqueville's *Democracy in America*', *Yale University Library Gazette*, 10 (2) (1935), 33–8; Lynn Marshall and Seymour Drescher, 'American Historians and Tocqueville's Democracy', *Journal of American History*, 55 (1968), 512–32; Robert Nisbet, 'Many Tocquevilles', *American Scholar*, 46 (1976), 59–75; James Schleifer, 'Tocqueville's Reputation in America', in Andrew J. Consentino (ed.), *A Passion for Liberty: Alexis de Tocqueville on Democracy and Revolution*, (Washington, DC: Library of Congress, 1989); Kloppenberg, 'Life Everlasting', 19–36.

9 Abraham S. Eisenstadt, 'Introduction', in *Reconsidering Tocqueville's 'Democracy in America'*, (New Brunswick, NJ: Rutgers University Press, 1988) 13.

10 See e.g. James Schleifer, *The Making of Tocqueville's 'Democracy in America'* (Chapel Hill: University of North Carolina Press, 1980), perhaps the most scholarly and reliable guide to *Democracy*. Schleifer carefully unravels contradictions, and compares notebooks with the finished texts to give us a picture of Tocqueville's creation of *Democracy in America*. But his fascination with Tocqueville's ability to penetrate American society, with the 'richness and profundity of his insights' (p. 274), is what sustains his own interest in Tocqueville as a subject of study.

11 Mélonio, *Tocqueville et les français*, 55–121.

12 Drescher, 'Worlds', 29.

13 Mélonio, *Tocqueville et les français*, 111.

14 Ibid. 263–9.

15 It is unsurprising, for example, that Pierre Rosanvallon's *L'État en France de 1789 à nos jours* (Paris: Éditions du Seuil, 1990) should begin with a long quotation from Tocqueville's *L'Ancien Régime* and end with

reflections on that work. For a discussion of Tocqueville's *L'Ancien Régime* in recent debates over the French Revolution, see above, pp. 228–31.

16 Raymond Aron's seminal treatment of *Democracy in America* in his *Les étapes de la pensée sociologique* (Paris: Gallimard, 1967) looks important in retrospect, but in some ways his was a voice crying in the desert. The more recent fuller appreciation of the *Democracy* dates only from the late 1970s and early 1980s. In this regard Jean-Claude Lamberti's *Tocqueville et les deux démocraties* (Paris: Presses Universitaires de France, 1983) was very influential.

17 Drescher, 'Worlds', 29.

18 Robert H. Wiebe, *Self-Rule: A Cultural History of American Democracy* (Chicago: University of Chicago Press, 1995), 42.

19 Among the obvious exceptions, of course, are works by American Tocqueville scholars such as Seymour Drescher, Melvin Richter, Roger Boesche, and Alan Kahan.

20 Cited in Schleifer, 'Tocqueville's Reputation in America', 20.

21 Ibid. 19.

22 He also inspires David Reisman's decade-defining *The Lonely Crowd* (New Haven, Conn.: Yale University Press, 1950), which examines the American sociological face of 'mass society'.

23 Rogers M. Smith, 'Response to Stevens, "Beyond Tocqueville, Please!"', *American Political Science Review*, 89 (4) (1995), 990.

24 Robert Dawidoff, *The Genteel Tradition and the Sacred Rage: High Culture vs. Democracy in Adams, James, and Santayana* (Chapel Hill: University of North Carolina Press, 1992), 1. Among the important texts on Tocqueville in American Studies, see Max Lerner, *Tocqueville and American Civilization* (New York: Harper & Row, 1969); Richard Rulard, *'De la Démocratie en Amérique* and *The Education of Henry Adams'*, *Comparative Literature Studies*, 2 (1965), 195–207.

25 For a nuanced elaboration of this theme, see Dawidoff, *The Genteel Tradition*, 1–29.

26 See above, pp. 245–7.

27 Phenomenology and structuralism, far from being intellectual alternatives to Marxism, were highly vulnerable to Marxist reworkings. Indeed, even the excitement generated by theorists like Foucault and Derrida, still percolating in American academic circles, now looks to many on the Continent less like a new awakening than the final struggle to escape from an intellectual obsession with *marxisant* political discourse. For a trenchant view of the delusions of the French avant-garde, see Tony Judt, *Past Imperfect: French Intellectuals, 1944–1956* (Berkeley: University of California Press, 1992).

28 Mélonio, *Tocqueville et les français*, 274.

29 The phrase is from Jean-Paul Sartre, quoted in Mark Lilla, 'The Legitimacy of the Liberal Age', in Lilla (ed.), *New French Thought: Political Philosophy* (Princeton, NJ: Princeton University Press, 1994), 5.

30 For a general discussion of this theme, see Tony Judt, *A Grand Illusion? An Essay on Europe* (New York: Hill & Wang, 1996).

31 On the relationship between Tocqueville and Furet, see the discussion in Mélonio, *Tocqueville et les français*, 289–94, which has shaped the view put forward here.

32 See Furet, 'Beyond the Annales', *Journal of Modern History* (winter 1987), 21.

33 See above, pp. 157–61.

34 Furet, 'Revolutionary Government', in François Furet and Mona Ozouf (eds.), *A Critical Dictionary of the French Revolution*, trans. Arthur Goldhammer (Cambridge, Mass.: Harvard University Press, 1989), 558.

35 Interpreting the French Revolution, trans. E. Forster (Cambridge: Cambridge University Press, 1981), 180.

36 Mélonio, *Tocqueville et les français*, 7.

37 Ibid. 8.

38 The American historian Isser Woloch has taken just this set of 'Tocquevillian' questions as guides to a set of detailed French historical studies, among which are *The Jacobin Legacy: The Democratic Movement under the Directory* (Princeton, NJ: Princeton University Press, 1970); *The New Regime: Transformations of the French Civic Order, 1789–1820s* (New York: W. W. Norton, 1994); and *Napoleon and His Collaborators* (forthcoming).

39 Information on these *colloques* comes from a series of conversations of the author with Françoise Mélonio, one of the participants, in the summer of 1995. Other participants in the *colloques* included François Furet, Philippe Raynaud, Pierre Grémion, Eduardo Nolla, and Claude Lefort. More recently, other scholars engaged in various aspects of the debate over the role of civil society—either in transitions to democracy or in the international arena more generally—have also used Tocqueville to 'interrogate' these issues. See e.g. Ferenc Fehér, 'Tocqueville's Missionaries: Civil Society Advocacy and the Promotion of Democracy', *World Policy Journal*, 17 (1) (2000), 9–19; Enrique Krauze, 'Mores and Democracy in Latin America', *Journal of Democracy*, 11 (1) (2000), 18–24; Adam Michnik, 'Reflections on the Collapse of Communism', ibid. 119–26; Hahm Chaibong, 'The Cultural Challenge to Individualism', ibid. 127–34; Ghia Nodia, 'The End of Revolution?', ibid. 164–71.

40 See e.g. Marvin Meyers, *The Jacksonian Persuasion: Politics and Belief* (Stanford, Calif.: Stanford University Press, 1957), 24–41, and Sean Wilentz, 'Many Democracies: On Tocqueville and Jacksonian America',

in Eisenstadt, *Reconsidering Tocqueville's 'Democracy in America'*, 207–28.

41 Robert Putnam, *Civic Traditions in Modern Italy* (Princeton, NJ: Princeton University Press, 1993), 11. Tocqueville's famous phrase 'habits of the heart' of course serves as the title of Robert Bellah's nostalgic lament for the loss of 'Tocqueville's America'. See Robert N. Bellah, Richard Madsen, William M. Sullivan, Ann Swidler, and Steven M. Tipton, *Individualism and Commitment in American Life: Readings on the Themes of Habits of the Heart* (New York: Harper & Row, 1987). For more recent works on the theme of the decline of America's moral and social capital see E. J. Dionne Jr. (ed.), *Community Works: The Revival of Civil Society in America* (Washington, DC: Brookings Institution, 1998), Robert K. Fullinwider (ed.), *Civil Society, Democracy, and Civic Renewal* (Lanham, Md.: Rowman & Littlefield, 1999); and William Galston, 'Civil Society and the "Art of Association"', *Journal of Democracy*, 11 (1) (2000), 64–70.

42 Robert Putnam's seminal article, 'Bowling Alone: America's Declining Social Capital', *Journal of Democracy*, 6 (Jan. 1995), 65–79, which begins by citing Tocqueville, succinctly articulated this argument.

43 Thus Benjamin Barber, in *Strong Democracy* (Berkeley: University of California Press, 1984), 233–6, makes his most extensive references to Tocqueville in connection with voluntary associations, participatory politics, and the necessary interactions between the two.

44 Jean L. Cohen and Andrew Arato, *Civil Society and Political Theory* (Cambridge, Mass.: MIT Press, 1994), 134.

45 Ibid. 19: 'The associations of civil society in Tocqueville's theory prepare private individuals for the exercise of public power, a task that the literary public sphere, on its own, is incapable of performing. At the same time, these associations preserve the connection of citizens to the prepolitical social networks that serve as their background. In place of the Marxian identity of man and citizen, Tocqueville thus proposes a differentiated and interdependent model of social being and citizen' (230). Indeed, Cohen and Arato refer to Tocqueville positively in long analytic treatments of Hegel, Parsons, Arendt, Gramsci, Foucault, and Habermas, though they never quote him or analyse him in his own terms.

46 Cohen and Arato's conceptual apparatus, for example, is almost entirely Hegelian. They term Hegel's conception of civil society 'the institutionally most elaborated conception from which we can still learn': ibid. 117.

47 For an extended analysis of this theme, see Nancy Rosenblum, *Membership and Morals: The Personal Uses of Pluralism in America* (Princeton, NJ: Princeton University Press, 1998).

48 See e.g. Theda Skocpol, 'The Tocqueville Problem: Civic Engagement in

American Democracy', Presidential Address for the Annual Meeting of the Social Science History Association, New Orleans, 12 Oct. 1996; Sheri Berman, 'Civil Society and Political Institutionalization', *American Behavioral Scientist*, 40 (5) (1997), 562–72; and Keith E. Whittington, 'Revisiting Tocqueville's America', *American Behavioral Scientist*, 42 (1) (1998), 21–30.

49 See e.g. ibid., which looks only at *Democracy in America*.

50 Gilles Lipovetsky, '"Changer la vie" ou l'irruption de l'individualisme transpolitique', *Pouvoirs*, 39 (1986), 91–100, trans. by L. Maguire as 'May '68, or the Rise of Transpolitical Individualism', in Lilla, *New French Thought*, 212–19.

51 Ibid. 218.

52 Ibid. 216. The most extensive elaboration of this kind of historical anthropology, also explicitly indebted to Tocqueville, can be found in the works of Louis Dumont. See e.g. *Homo Hierarchicus: The Caste System and Its Implications*, trans. Mark Sainsbury, rev. edn. (Delhi: Oxford University Press, 1998) and *Homo Aequalis* (Paris: Gallimard, 1976).

53 Lipovetsky, 'May '68', 214.

54 Rosenblum, *Membership and Morals*, 35.

55 See e.g. Jeremy Hein, 'Rights, Resources, and Membership: Civil Rights Models in France and the U.S.', *Annals, AAPSS*, 530 (1993).

56 Claude Lefort, *Écrire: à l'épreuve du politique* (Paris: Calmann Lévy, 1992), 71.

57 Peter Berkowitz, 'The Art of Association', *New Republic*, 24 June 1996, 47.

58 For examples of this socially conservative criticism in support of traditional family life, see William Kristol, 'Women's Liberation: The Relevance of Tocqueville', in Ken Masugi (ed.), *Interpreting Tocqueville's 'Democracy in America'*, (Savage, Md.: Rowman & Littlefield, 1993), 480–94, or the more nuanced Jean Bethke Elshtain, 'Women, Equality, and the Family', *Journal of Democracy*, 11 (1) (2000), 157–63.

59 I am not claiming that religion has little salience in American politics. There is ample support for the judgement that Americans profess surprising levels of belief in God and in scripture, considerably higher than those of people in other liberal democracies. See Alan Wolfe, *One Nation, After All* (New York: Penguin, 1998), 44–7. What I am claiming is that these beliefs are not easily accepted as relevant to the underlying question of which normative principles should guide American democracy. That question is more often projected onto the battlefield of constitutional interpretation or analytic philosophy.

60 Among the discussions of Tocqueville and religion that are most interesting in the context of this problematic, see Peter Augustine Lawler,

The Restless Mind: Alexis de Tocqueville on the Origin and Perpetuation of Human Liberty (Lanham, Md.: Rowman & Littlefield, 1993), and 'Democracy and Pantheism' in Masugi, *Interpreting Tocqueville's 'Democracy'*, 96–120; Ralph C. Hancock, 'The Uses and Hazards of Christianity in Tocqueville's Attempt to Save Democratic Souls', in Masugi, *Interpreting Tocqueville's 'Democracy'*, 355–66; Catherine Zuckert, 'The Role of Religion in Preserving American Liberty: Tocqueville's Analysis 150 Years Later', in P. A. Lawler and J. Alulis (eds.), *Tocqueville's Defense of Human Liberty: Current Essays* (New York: Garland, 1993); See also Joshua Mitchell, *The Fragility of Freedom: Tocqueville on Religion, Democracy, and the American Future* (Chicago: University of Chicago Press, 1995), which argues provocatively that Tocqueville's political and social thought is an elaboration of his particular version of the 'Augustinian self'.

61 Lawler and Alulis, *Tocqueville's Defense of Human Liberty*, p. xi.

62 James Caeser, *Liberal Democracy and Political Science* (Baltimore: Johns Hopkins University Press, 1990), 1–4.

63 See e.g. Masugi, *Interpreting Tocqueville's 'Democracy'* (for articles on leadership and democracy); Alan Bloom, *The Closing of the American Mind* (New York: Simon & Schuster, 1987); Ralph C. Hancock, 'Liberal Education and Moral Liberty: Tocqueville as Critic of Bloom', in Lawler and Alulis, *Tocqueville's Defense of Human Liberty* (on education and democracy); Paul O. Carrese, 'Judicial Statesmanship, the Jurisprudence of Individualism, and Tocqueville's Common Law Spirit', *Review of Politics*, 60 (3) (1998), on Tocqueville and the Constitution; see also Peter Augustine Lawler, (ed.), *Tocqueville's Political Science: Classic Essays* (New York: Garland, 1992).

64 See Daniel J. Mahoney, 'Introduction', in Mahoney and P. Seaton (eds. and trans.), *Modern Liberty and its Discontents: Pierre Manent* (Lanham Md.: Rowman & Littlefield, 1998), 18–23.

65 See Pierre Manent, *Tocqueville and the Nature of Democracy*, trans. John Waggoner (Lanham, Md.: Rowman & Littlefield, 1993), 83–107; 'Christianity and Democracy: Some Remarks on the Political History of Religion, or, on the Religious History of Modern Politics' and 'On Modern Individualism' in Mahoney and Seaton, *Modern Liberty*, 97–115, 151–9.

66 See Marcel Gauchet, 'Tocqueville' (a translation of 'Tocqueville, l'Amérique et nous', *Libre*, 7 (1980)), in Lilla, *New French Thought*, 109.

67 Ibid. 91.

68 Ibid. 101–2.

69 Ibid. 103.

70 Ibid. 109.

71 Claude Lefort, 'La question de la démocratie', in *Essais sur le politique:*

XIX–XX siècles (Paris: Éditions du Seuil, 1986), 25. For Lefort's appreciation of Tocqueville's relevance to contemporary theory, see ibid. 23 and 'Les droits de l'homme et l'État-providence', in *Essais*, 36: Tocqueville's work 'teaches us that our own questions had already appeared in the first half of the nineteenth century'.

72 Gauchet, 'Tocqueville', 109–10.

73 Michael Sandel, *Democracy's Discontent: America in Search of Public Philosophy* (Cambridge, Mass.: Belknap Press of Harvard University, 1996), 27.

74 See e.g. William Connolly, *Political Theory and Modernity* (Ithaca, NY: Cornell University Press, 1993), 190 and *passim*.

75 Readings that largely use Tocqueville as a foil for their own contrasting views are those of Stephen Schneck, 'Habits of the Head: Tocqueville's America and Jazz', *Political Theory*, 17 (4) (1989), 638–62; Stephen Schneck, 'New Readings of Tocqueville's *America*: Lessons for Democracy', *Polity*, 25 (2) (1992), 283–98; and William Connolly, 'Tocqueville, Territory, and Violence', *Theory, Culture, and Society*, 11 (1994), 19–41. A more sympathetic appropriation of Tocqueville can be found in Mark Reinhardt, *The Art of Being Free: Taking Liberties with Tocqueville, Marx, and Arendt* (Ithaca, NY: Cornell University Press, 1997). There have also been attempts to appropriate Tocqueville to analyse a postmodern aesthetic in democratic art and culture. See Paul A. Cantor, 'Postmodern Prophet: Tocqueville Visits Vegas', *Journal of Democracy*, 11 (1) (2000), 111–18.

76 Reinhardt, *Art of Being Free*, 47, 57.

77 Reinhardt disputes William Connolly's contention (in the latter's 'Tocqueville, Territory, and Violence') that Tocqueville's logic of democratic sovereignty pushes him to postulate the need for a common national identity. Reinhardt rightly recognizes that Tocqueville does not employ the sovereign 'will' as a consistent category in *Democracy in America*, and argues that Tocqueville's endorsement of democratic cultural uniformity is not logically entailed by the structure of his thought, but rather psychologically associated with quite particular social fears. Reinhardt, *Art of Being Free*, 201, n. 67. In general, Reinhardt reflects on Tocqueville with subtlety and insight. Yet the cumulative impact of successive '(re)cognitions', '(con)foundings', and 'readings (in) the gaps' tends to wear at least this reader down: ibid. 79, 87, 86.

Bibliography

Works by Tocqueville

I have cited the following readily available English translations of Tocqueville's major works in the body of the text:

AR   *The Old Regime and the French Revolution*, trans. Stuart Gilbert (Garden City, NY: Doubleday, 1955).

DAI,   *Democracy in America*, ed. Max Lerner and J.-P. Mayer, trans.
  DAII   George Lawrence (New York: Harper & Row, 1966).

S   *Recollections*, trans. George Lawrence, ed. J. P Mayer and A. P. Kerr (Garden City, NY: Doubleday, 1971).

In the notes I have cited the various editions of Tocqueville's works as follows:

OC   *Œuvres, papiers et correspondances d'Alexis de Tocqueville*. ed. J.-P. Mayer (Paris: 1951–).

OC, B   *Œeuvres complètes d'Alexis de Tocqueville*, ed. Gustave de Beaumont, 9 vols. (Paris: Michel Lévy, 1861–6).

OC, P   *Œuvres de Tocqueville*, edition Pléiade (Paris: Gallimard, 1991–).

Other English translations of Tocqueville's works

Alexis de Tocqueville's Journey in Ireland July–August 1835, ed. and trans. Emmet Larkin (Washington, DC: Catholic University of America Press, 1990).

Correspondence and Conversations of Alexis de Tocqueville with Nassau William Senior, ed. M. C. M. Simpson, 2 vols. (London: Henry S. King, 1872).

Journey to America, ed. J.-P. Mayer, trans. George Lawrence (New Haven, Conn.: Yale University Press, 1960).

Journeys to England and Ireland, ed. J.-P. Mayer, trans. George Lawrence (London: Faber and Faber; and New Haven, Conn.: Yale University Press, 1958).

The Old Regime and the Revolution, trans. Alan S. Kahan, ed. and intro. François Furet and Françoise Mélonio (Chicago: University of Chicago Press, 1998).

'Political and Social Condition of France', *London and Westminster Review*, 3 and 25 (1836), 137–69.

Selected Letters on Politics and Society, trans. James Toupin and Roger Boesche, ed. Roger Boesche (Berkeley: University of California Press, 1985).

Tocqueville and Beaumont on Social Reform, ed. and trans. Seymour Drescher (New York: Harper & Row, 1968).

The Two Tocquevilles, Father and Son: Hervé and Alexis de Tocqueville on the Coming of the French Revolution, ed. and intro. R. R. Palmer (Princeton, NJ: Princeton University Press, 1987).

Works Consulted

ALLEN, ESTHER, 'The Paradoxes of Admiration: Sarmiento, Tocqueville, and the United States', *Annals of Scholarship*, 11 (1–2) (1996), 61–81.

ANKERSMIT, F. R., *Aesthetic Politics: Political Philosophy Beyond Fact and Value* (Stanford, Calif.: Stanford University Press, 1996).

ARMSTRONG KELLY, GEORGE, *The Humane Comedy: Constant, Tocqueville, and French Liberalism* (Cambridge: Cambridge University Press, 1992).

ARON, RAYMOND, *Auguste Comte et Alexis de Tocqueville, juges de l'Angleterre* (Oxford: Clarendon Press, 1965).

—— *Dix-huit leçons sur les sociétés industrielles* (Paris: Gallimard, 1962).

—— Essai sur les libertés (Paris: Calmann-Levy, 1965).

—— *Les étapes de la pensée sociologique* (Paris: Gallimard, 1967). Published in English as *Main Currents in Sociological Thought*, 2 vols., trans. Richard Howard and Helen Weaver (New York: Doubleday Anchor, 1968).

—— 'Idées politiques et vision historique de Tocqueville', *Revue Française de Science Politique*, 3 (1960), 509–26.

BAKER, KEITH, 'The Early History of the Term "Social Science"', *Annals of Science*, 20 (1964), 211–26,

BARBER, BENJAMIN, *Strong Democracy* (Berkeley, University of California Press, 1984).

BASTID, PAUL, 'Tocqueville et la doctrine constitutionnelle', in *Alexis de Tocqueville: Livre du Centenaire, 1859–1959* (Paris: Éditions du CNRS, 1960), 45–57.

BEAUMONT, GUSTAVE DE, *Marie ou l'esclavage aux États-Unis: Tableau des mœurs américains*, 2 vols. (Paris: Gosselin, 1835); published in English as *Marie, or Slavery in the United States: A Novel of Jacksonian America*, trans. B. Chapman, introd. A. Tinnin (Stanford, Calif: Stanford University Press, 1958).

BELLAH, ROBERT N., RICHARD MADSEN, WILLIAM M. SULLIVAN, ANN SWIDLER and STEVEN M. TIPTON, *Individualism and Commitment in American Life: Readings on the Themes of Habits of the Heart* (New York: Harper & Row, 1987).

BERKOWITZ, PETER, 'The Art of Association', *New Republic* (1996), 44–49.

BERLIN, ISAIAH, 'Two Concepts of Liberty', in *Four Essays on Liberty* (London: Oxford University Press, 1969), 118–72.

BERMAN, SHERI, 'Civil Society and Political Institutionalization', *American Behavioral Scientist*, 40 (5) (1997), 562–74.

BIRNBAUM, PIERRE, *Sociologie de Tocqueville* (Paris: Presses Universitaires de France, 1970).

BLANC, LOUIS, 'De la démocratie en Amérique', *Revue Republicaine*, 5 (1836), 129–63.

BLOOM, ALAN, *The Closing of the American Mind* (New York: Simon & Schuster, 1987).

BOESCHE, ROGER, 'Tocqueville et *Le Commerce*: A Newspaper Expressing His Unusual Liberalism', *Journal of the History of Ideas*, 44 (1983).

BROGAN, HUGH, 'Alexis de Tocqueville and the Coming of the American Civil War', in *American Studies: Essays in Honour of Marcus Cunliffe* (New York: St. Martin's Press, 1991), 83–104. *Tocqueville* (London: Collins/Fontana, 1973).

BRYCE, JAMES, 'The Predictions of Hamilton and de Tocqueville', *Studies in Historical Political Science* (1887).

BURET, E., *De la misère des classes laborieuses en Angleterre et en France* (Paris: Paulin, 1840).

BURKE, PETER, 'Strengths and Weaknesses of the History of Mentalities', in *Varieties of Cultural History* (Ithaca, NY: Cornell University Press, 1997).

BURROW, J. W., *A Liberal Descent: Victorian Historians and the English Past* (Cambridge: Cambridge University Press, 1981).

CABANIS, PIERRE, *Œuvres philosophiques* (Paris: Presses Universitaires de France, 1956).

—— *Rapports du physiqe et du moral de l'homme* (Paris: Guiraudet, 1830).

CAESER, JAMES, *Liberal Democracy and Political Science* (Baltimore: Johns Hopkins University Press, 1990).

CARRESE, PAUL O., 'Judicial Statesmanship, the Jurisprudence of Individualism, and Tocqueville's Common Law Spirit', *The Review of Politics*, 60 (3) (1998).

CHARTIER, ROGER, 'Intellectual History and the History of *Mentalités*', in *Cultural History*, trans. Lydia B. Cochrane (Ithaca, NY: Cornell University Press, 1988).

CHERBULIEZ, A. E., *Étude sur les causes de la misère tant morale que physique* (Paris: Guillaumin, 1853).

CHEVALLIER, JEAN-JACQUES, *Les grandes oeuvres politiques de Machivael à nos jours* (Paris: Armand Colin, 1949).

COHEN, JEAN L. and ANDREW ARATO, *Civil Society and Political Theory* (Cambridge, Mass.: MIT Press, 1994).

CONNOLLY, WILLIAM E., *Political Theory and Modernity* (Ithaca, NY: Cornell University Press, 1993).

—— 'Tocqueville, Territory, and Violence', *Theory, Culture, and Society*, 11 (1994), 19–41.

CONSENTINO, ANDREW J., (ed.), *A Passion for Liberty: Alexis de Tocqueville on Democracy and Revolution* (Washington, DC: Library of Congress, 1989).

COTT, NANCY, *Bonds of Womanhood: Woman's Sphere in New England, 1780–1835* (New Haven, Conn.: Yale University Press, 1977).

COUSIN, VICTOR, *Justice et charité* (Paris: 1848).

DARROW, MARGARET, 'French Noblewomen and the New Domesticity, 1750–1850', *Feminist Studies*, 1 (1979), 41–65.

DAVIS, NATALIE ZEMON, *The Return of Martin Guerre* (Cambridge, Mass.: Harvard University Press, 1983).

DAWIDOFF, Robert, *The Genteel Tradition and the Sacred Rage: High Culture vs. Democracy in Adams, James, and Santayana* (Chapel Hill: University of North Carolina Press, 1992).

DE CORCELLES, FRANÇOIS, *Documens pour servir à l'histoire des conspirations des partis et des sectes* (Paris: Paulin, 1831).

DE GÉRANDO, *De la bienfaisance publique*, 2 vols. (Brussels: Havman, 1839). *Democracy in the World*, 10th anniversary edition of *Journal of Democracy* 11 (1) (2000).

DESTUTT DE TRACY, ANTOINE-LOUIS-CLAUDE. *Élémens d'idéologie*, 4 vols. (Paris: Courcier, 1817).

DIONNE, E. J. Jr (ed.), *Community Works: The Revival of Civil Society in America* (Washington, DC: Brookings Institution, 1998).

DRESCHER, SEYMOUR, *Dilemmas of Democracy: Tocqueville and Modernization* (Pittsburgh: University of Pittsburgh Press, 1968).

—— *Tocqueville and England* (Cambridge, Mass.: Harvard University Press, 1964).

—— 'Tocqueville's Two Democracies', *Journal of the History of Ideas*, 25 (2) (1964), 201–16.

—— 'Worlds Together, Worlds Apart: Tocqueville and the Franco-American Exchange', in Lloyd Kramer (ed.), *The French-American Connection: 200 Years of Cultural and Intellectual Interaction* (Chapel Hill, NC: Institut Français de Washington, 1994), 24–37.

DUMAS, JEAN-LOUIS, 'Alexis de Tocqueville ou la compréhension efficace', *Revue de Métaphysique et de Morale*, 78 (1973), 525–43.

DUMONT, LOUIS, *Homo aequalis* (Paris: Gallimard, 1976).

—— *Homo Hierarchicus: The Caste System and Its Implications*, trans. Mark Sainsbury, rev. edn. (Delhi: Oxford University Press, 1998).

EICHTAL, EUGENE DE, *Alexis de Tocqueville et la democratie libérale* (Paris: Calmann-Lévy, 1897).

EISENSTADT, ABRAHAM (ed.,) *Reconsidering Tocqueville's 'Democracy in America'* (New Brunswick, NJ: Rutgers University Press, 1988).

ELSHTAIN, JEAN BETHKE, 'Authority Figures', *New Republic*, 217 (25) (1997), 11–12.

ELSTER, JON, *Political Psychology* (Cambridge: Cambridge University Press, 1993).

ENCARNACIÓN, OMAR G., 'Tocqueville's Missionaries: Civil Society Advocacy and the Promotion of Democracy', *World Policy Journal* 17 (1) (2000), 9–19.

FAGUET, ÉMILE, *Politiques et moralistes du XIXe siècle* (Paris: Société Française d'Impression et d'Édition, 1903).

FEHÉR, FERENC, *The French Revolution and the Birth of Modernity* (Berkeley: University of California Press, 1990).

FONTANA, BIANCAMARIA, *Benjamin Constant and the Post-Revolutionary Mind* (New Haven, Conn.: Yale University Press, 1991).

FRÉGIER, H. A., *Des classes dangereuses de la population dans les grandes villes et des moyens de les rendre meilleures* (Paris: J. B. Baillière, 1840).

FULLINWIDER, ROBERT K. (ed.), *Civil Society, Democracy, and Civic Renewal* (Lanham, Md.: Rowman & Littlefield, 1999).

FURET, FRANÇOIS, 'Beyond the *Annales*', *Journal of Modern History* (1987).

—— 'Naisssance d'un paradigme: Tocqueville et le voyage en Amérique (1825–1831)', *Annales*, 39 (2) (1984), 226–39.

—— *Penser la Revolution française* (Paris: Gallimard, 1978). Published in English as *Interpreting the French Revolution*, trans. E. Forster (Cambridge: Cambridge University Press, 1981).

—— Le système conceptuel de la 'Démocratie en Amérique', preface to Tocqueville, *De la démocratie en Amérique* (Paris: Flammarion, 1981).

—— 'Tocqueville est-il un historien de la Révolution française?', *Annales*, 25 (2) (1970), 434–51.

—— and MONA OZOUF, *A Critical Dictionary of the French Revolution*, trans. Arthur Goldhammer (Cambridge, Mass.: Harvard University Press, 1989).

GARGAN, EDWARD, *Alexis de Tocqueville: The Critical Years, 1848–1851* (Washington, DC: Catholic University of America Press, 1955).

—— 'The Formation of Tocqueville's Historical Thought', *Review of Politics* (Jan. 1962), 48–61.

—— 'Tocqueville and the Problem of Historical Prognosis', *American Historical Review* (Jan. 1963), 332–45.

GIBERT, PIERRE, 'Introduction', in *Alexis de Tocqueville: égalité sociale et liberté politique* (Paris: Aubier Montaigne, 1977).

GIRARD, LOUIS, *Les libéraux français: 1814–1875* (Paris: Aubier, 1985).

GOLDSTEIN, DORIS S., 'Alexis de Tocqueville's Concept of Citizenship', *Proceedings of the American Philosophical Society*, 108 (1) (1964), 39–53.

—— 'The Religious Beliefs of Alexis de Tocqueville', *French Historical Studies*, 1 (4) (1960), 379–93.

—— *Trial of Faith: Religion and Politics in Tocqueville's Thought* (New York: Elsevier, 1975).

HEGEL, GEORG WILHELM FRIEDRICH, *Hegel's Political Writings*, ed. Z. A. Pelczynski, trans. T. M. Knox (Oxford: Clarendon Press, 1964).

—— *Lectures on the History of Philosophy*, trans. E. S. Haldane and Frances H. Simson, 3 vols. (London: Routledge & Kegan Paul, 1968).

—— *The Philosophy of History*, trans. J. Sibree (New York: Dover, 1956).

HEIN, JEREMY, 'Rights, Resources, and Membership: Civil Rights Models in France and the U.S.', *Annals, AAPSS*, 530 (1993).

HERETH, MICHAEL, *Alexis de Tocqueville*, trans. George Bogardus (Durham, NC: Duke University Press, 1986).

HERR, RICHARD, *Tocqueville and the Old Regime* (Princeton, NJ: Princeton University Press, 1962).

HEWITT, NANCY, *Women's Activism and Social Change: Rochester 1822–1872* (Ithaca, NY: Cornell University Press, 1984).

HOFFMAN, STANLEY, 'Aron et Tocqueville', *Commentaire* 8 (28–9) (1985), 200–12.

HOLMES, STEPHEN, *Benjamin Constant and the Making of Modern Liberalism* (New Haven, Conn.: Yale University Press, 1984).

HUNT, LYNN, *The Family Romance of the French Revolution* (Berkeley: University of California Press, 1993).

HUTTON, PATRICK H., 'The History of Mentalities: The New Map of Cultural History', *History and Theory* 20 (3) (1981), 237–59.

ISAMBERT, FRANÇOIS-ANDRÉ, *De la Charbonnerie au Saint-Simonisme: étude sur la jeunesse de Buchez* (Paris: Editions de Minuit, 1966) 121.

JANET, PAUL, *Histoir de la science politique dans ses rapports avec la morale*, 4th edn. (Paris: Félix Alcan, 1913).

—— *Les problèmes du XIXe siècle: la politique, la littérature, la science, la philosophie, la religion* (Paris: Michel Lévy frères, 1872).

JARDIN, ANDRÉ, *Histoire du libéralisme politique de la crise de l'absolutisme à la constitution de 1875* (Paris: Hachette, 1985).

—— *Tocqueville (1805–1859): A Biography*, trans. Lydia Davis with Robert Hemenway (London: Peter Halban, 1988).

JUDT, TONY, *A Grand Illusion? An Essay on Europe* (New York: Hill & Wang, 1996).

—— *Past Imperfect: French Intellectuals, 1944–1956* (Berkeley: University of California Press, 1992).

KAHAN, ALAN S., *Aristocratic Liberalism: The Social and Political Thought of Jacob Burckhart, John Stuart Mill, and Alexis de Tocqueville* (New York: Oxford University Press, 1992).

KELLY, GEORGE ARMSTRONG, *The Humane Comedy: Constant, Tocqueville, and French Liberalism* (Cambridge: Cambridge University Press, 1992).

KLOPPENBURG, JAMES, 'Life Everlasting: Tocqueville in America', *Tocqueville Review*, 17 (2) (1996), 19–36.

KNOX, T. M., and Z. A. PELCZYNSKI (eds.), *Hegel's Political Writings*, trans. T. M. Knox (Oxford: Clarendon Press, 1964).

LABOULAYE, ÉDOUARDDE, *L'Etat et ses limites*, 2nd edn. (Paris: Charpentier, 1863).

LADURIE, EMMANUEL LE ROY, *The Peasants of Languedoc*, trans. J. Day and G. Huppert (Urbana: University of Illinois Press, 1984).

LAMBERTI, JEAN-CLAUDE, 'De Benjamin Constant à Tocqueville', *Revue France-Forum*, 203–4 (1983), 19–26.

—— *La notion d'individualisme chez Tocqueville* (Paris: Presses Universitaires de France, 1970).

—— *Tocqueville et les deux démocraties*, (Paris: Presses Universitaires de France, 1983). Published in English as *Tocqueville and the Two Democracies*, trans. Arthur Goldhammer (Cambridge, Mass: Harvard University Press, 1989).

LANDES, JOAN, *Women and the Public Sphere in the Age of the French Revolution* (Ithaca, NY: Cornell University Press, 1988).

LASKI, HAROLD J., *The Rise of European Liberalism* (London: Allen & Unwin, 1936).

LAWLER, PETER AUGUSTINE, *The Restless Mind: Alexis de Tocqueville on the Origin and Perpetuation of Human Liberty* (Lanham, Md.: Rowman & Littlefield, 1993).

—— (ed.), *Tocqueville's Political Science: Classic Essays* (New York: Garland, 1992).

—— and J. ALULIS, (eds.), *Tocqueville's Defense of Human Liberty: Current Essays* (New York: Garland, 1993).

LEFORT, CLAUDE, *Écrire: à l'épreuve du politique* (Paris: Calmann Lévy, 1992).

—— *Essais sur le politique: XIX–XX siècles* (Paris: Éditions du Seuil, 1986).

LERNER, MAX, *Tocqueville and American Civilization* (New York: Harper & Row, 1969).

LEROY, MAXIME, *Historie des idées sociales en France, de Babeuf à Tocqueville* (Paris: Gallimard, 1962).

LILLA, MARK, (ed.), *New French Thought: Political Philosophy* (Princeton, NJ: Princeton University Press, 1994).

LIVELY, JACK, *The Social and Political Thought of Alexis Tocqueville* (Oxford: Clarendon Press, 1965).

LOGUE, JOHN, *From Philosophy to Sociology: The Evolution of French Liberalism 1870–1914* (Dekalb: Northern Illinois University Press, 1983).

MANENT, PIERRE, 'Democratic Man, Aristocratic Man, and Man Simply', trans. Daniel J. Mahoney and Paul Seaton, *Perspectives on Political Science*, 27 (2) (1998), 79–85.

—— *Modern Liberty and Its Discontents*, trans. and ed. Daniel J. Mahoney and Paul Seaton (Lanham, M.: Rowman & Littlefied, 1998).

—— *Tocqueville et la nature de la démocratie* (Paris: Julliard, 1982). Published in English as *Tocqueville and the Nature of Democracy*, trans. John Waggoner (Lanham, M.: Rowman & Littlefield, 1996).

MARSHALL, LYNN and SEYMOUR DRESCHER, 'American Historians and Tocqueville's Democracy', *Journal of American History*, 55 (1968), 512–32.

MASUGI, KEN (ed.), *Interpreting Tocqueville's 'Democracy in America'* (Savage, Md.: Rowman & Littlefield, 1993).

MAYER, J.-P., *Alexis de Tocqueville*, 2nd edn. (Paris: Gallimard, 1948).

—— *Political Thought in France from the Revolution to the Fourth Republic*, rev. edn. (London: Routledge & Kegan Paul, 1949).

MELLON, STANLEY, (ed.), *François Guizot: Historical Essays and Lectures* (Chicago: University of Chicago Press, 1972).

—— *The Political Uses of History: A Study of Historians in the French Restoration* (Stanford, Calif.: Stanford University Press, 1958).

MÉLONIO, FRANÇOISE, 'La religion selon Tocqueville', *Etudes* 360 (1) (1984), 73–88.

—— *Tocqueville et les français* (Paris: Aubier, 1993).

—— 'Tocqueville et les malheurs de la démocratie américaine (1831–1859),' *Commentaire*, 38 (1987), 381–9.

MEYERS, MARVIN, *The Jacksonian Persuasion: Politics and Belief* (Stanford, Calif.: Stanford University Press, 1957).

MILL, JOHN STUART, 'De Tocqueville on Democracy in America [II] 1840', in *Collected Works*, xviii: *Essays on Politics and Society* (Toronto: University of Toronto Press, 1977), 155–204.

—— 'On the Claims of Labour', in *Collected Works*, iv: *Essays on Economics and Society, 1824–1845* (Toronto: University of Toronto Press, 1967).

MILL, JOHN STUART, 'The Poor Laws' in *Collected Works*, xxiii: *Newspaper Writings: August 1831–October 1834* (Toronto: University of Toronto Press, 1986).

MITCHELL, JOSHUA, *The Fragility of Freedom: Tocqueville on Religion, Democracy, and the American Future* (Chicago: University of Chicago Press, 1995).

MONTESQUIEU, BARON DE, *Lettres persanes* (Paris: Garnier-Flammarion, 1964).

—— *The Spirit of the Laws*, trans. Anne Cohler, Basia Miller, and Harold Stone (Cambridge: Cambridge University Press, 1989).

MOSHER, MICHAEL A., 'The Judgmental Gaze of European Women: Gender Sexuality, and the Critique of Republican Rule', *Political Theory*, 22 (1) (1994), 25–44

MUELLER, I.-W., *John Stuart Mill and French Thought* (Urbana: University of Illinois Press, 1956).

NICOLET, CLAUDE, *L'idée républicaine en France: essai d'histoire critique* (Paris: Gallimard, 1982).

NISBET, ROBERT, 'Many Tocquevilles', *American Scholar*, 46 (1976), 59–75.

PALMER, WILLIAM, 'David Riesman, Alexis de Tocqueville and History: A Look at *The Lonely Crowd* after Forty Years', *Colby Quarterly*, 26 (1) (1990), 19–27.

—— 'Tocqueville: Colloque de Saint Cyr sur Loire', *Littérature et Nation* 7 (September 1991).

PIERSON, GEORGE WILSON, 'On the Centenary of Tocqueville's *Democracy in America*', *Yale University Library Gazette* 10 (2) (1935), 33–8.

—— 'Le 'second voyage' de Tocqueville en Amerique', in *Alexis de Tocqueville: livre du centenaire 1859–1959* (Paris: Éditions du CNRS, 1960), 71–85.

—— *Tocqueville and Beaumont in America* (New York: Oxford University Press, 1938). Reprinted 1996 (Baltimore: Johns Hopkins University Press).

—— *Tocqueville in America* (Gloucester, Mass.: Peter Smith, 1969). An abridged version of *Tocqueville and Beaumont in America*.

POGGI, GIANFRANCO, *Images of Society. Essays on Sociological Theories of Tocqueville, Marx, and Durkheim* (Stanford, Calif.: Stanford University Press, 1972).

POLIN, CLAUDE, *De la démocratie en Amérique: profil d'un œuvre* (Paris: Hatier, 1973).

PROCACCI, GIOVANNA, *Gouverner la misère: la question sociale en France, 1789–1848* (Paris: Éditions du Seuil, 1993).

PUTNAM, ROBERT, 'Bowling Alone: America's Declining Social Capital', *Journal of Democracy* (Jan. 1995).

—— *Civic Traditions in Modern Italy* (Princeton, NJ: Princeton University Press, 1993).

RAHE, PAUL, *Republics Ancient and Modern: Classical Republicanism and the American Revolution* (Chapel Hill: University of North Carolina Press, 1992).

RANDALL, JOHN HERMANN, *The Career of Philosophy*, 2 vols. (New York: Columbia University Press, 1965).

RÉDIER, ANTOINE, *Comme disait M. de Tocqueville* (Paris: Perrin, 1925).

REINHARDT, MARK, *The Art of Being Free: Taking Liberties with Tocqueville, Marx, and Arendt* (Ithaca, NY: Cornell University Press, 1997).

RÉMOND, RENÉ, *Les États-Unis devant l'opinion française, 1815–1852*, 2 vols. (Paris: Armand Colin, 1962).

—— 'Tocqueville et la démocratie en Amérique', in *Alexis de Tocqueville: Livre du Centenaire, 1859–1959*, (Paris: Éditions du CNRS, 1960), 71–86.

RÉMUSAT, CHARLES, 'De l'esprit de réaction: Royer-Collard and Tocqueville', *Revue des Deux Mondes*, 35 (1861).

—— *Essais de philosophie*, 2 vols. (Paris: J. Renouard, 1875).

—— *Mémoires de ma vie*, 5 vols. (Paris: Librairie Plon, 1958).

—— *Passé et Présent*, 2 vols. (Paris: Didier, 1857).

RICHTER, MELVIN, 'Comparative Political Analysis in Montesquieu and Tocqueville', *Comparative Politics*, 1 (2) (1969), 129–60.

—— 'Debate on Race: Tocqueville–Gobineau Correspondence', *Commentary*, 25 (1958), 151–60.

—— 'Tocqueville and French Nineteenth-Century Conceptualizations of the Two Bonapartes and Their Empires', paper delivered at the International Meeting of the Conference for the Study of Political Thought (Apr. 1999).

—— 'Tocqueville on Algeria', *Review of Politics*, 25 (1963), 362–98.

—— 'Tocqueville's Contribution to the Theory of Revolution', in Carl Friedreich (ed.), *NOMOS VIII: Revolution*, (New York: Atherton Press, 1966).

—— 'Toward a Concept of Political Legitimacy', *Political Theory*, 10 (1982), 185–214.

—— 'The Uses of Theory: Tocqueville's Adaptation of Montesquieu', in Melvin Richter (ed.), *Essays in Theory and History: An Approach to the Social Sciences* (Cambridge, Mass.: Harvard University Press, 1970).

ROGIN, MICHAEL, *Fathers and Children: Andrew Jackson and the Subjugation of the American Indian* (New York: Vintage Books, 1975).

ROSANVALLON, PIERRE, *L'État en France de 1789 à nos jours* (Paris: Éditions du Seuil, 1990).

—— *Le moment Guizot* (Paris: Gallimard, 1985).

ROSENBLUM, NANCY, 'Civil Societies: Liberalism and the Moral Uses of Pluralism', *Social Research*, 61 (3) (Fall 1994), 539–62.

—— *Membership and Morals: The Personal Uses of Pluralism in America* (Princeton, NJ: Princeton University Press, 1998).

RULARD, RICHARD, '*De la démocratie en Amérique* and *The Education of Henry Adams*', *Comparative Literature Studies*, 2 (1965), 195–207.

RYAN, MARY, *Cradle of the Middle Class: The Family in Oneida County, New York, 1790–1865* (Cambridge: Cambridge University Press, 1981).

SANDEL, MICHAEL, *Democracy's Discontent: America in Search of Public Philosophy* (Cambridge, Mass.: Belknap Press of Harvard University, 1996).

SCHLEIFER, JAMES T., *The Making of Tocqueville's 'Democracy in America'* (Chapel Hill: University of North Carolina Press, 1980).

271

SCHNECK, STEPHEN, 'Habits of the Head: Tocqueville's America and Jazz', *Political Theory*, 17 (4) (1989), 638–62.
—— 'New Readings of Tocqueville's *America*: Lessons for Democracy', *Polity*, 25 (2) (1992), 283–98.
SIEDENTOP, LARRY, *Tocqueville* (Oxford: Oxford University Press, 1994).
SISMONDI, J. C. L., 'On Landed Property', in *Political Economy and the Philosophy of Government*, trans. from *Études sur les sciences sociales* (London: John Chapman, 1847).
SKOCPOL, THEDA, 'The Tocqueville Problem: Civil Engagement in American Democracy', presidential address to the Annual Meeting of the Social Science History Association, New Orleans, 12 Oct. 1996.
SMITH, ROGERS M., 'Beyond Tocqueville, Myrdal, and Hartz: The Multiple Traditions in America', *American Political Science Review*, 87 (3) (1993), 549–66.
—— 'Response to Stevens, "Beyond Tocqueville, Please!" ', *American Political Science Review*, 89 (4) (1995), 990–5.
SPENCER, SAMIA I. (ed.), *French Women and the Age of Enlightenment* (Bloomington: Indiana University Press, 1984).
STEVENS, JACQUELINE, "Beyond Tocqueville, Please!', *American Political Science Review*, 89 (4) (1995), 987–90.
TAVENEAUX, RENÉ (ed.), *Jansénisme et politique* (Paris: Armand Colin, 1965).
—— *Passé et présent*, 2 vols, (Paris: Armand Colin, 1965).
VILLENEUVE-BARGEMONT, J.-P.-A., *Économie politique chrétienne, ou recherches sur la nature et les causes du paupérisme en France et en Europe*, 3 vols. (Paris: Paulin, 1834).
VILLERMÉ, L. R., *Tableau de l'état physique et moral des ouvriers*, 2 vols. (Paris: Jules Renouvard, 1840).
WELCH, CHERYL B, 'Liberalism and Social Rights', in C. Welch and M. Milgate, (eds.), *Critical Issues in Social Thought* (London: Academic Press, 1989), 173–9.
—— *Liberty and Utility: The French Idéologues and the Transformation of Liberalism* (New York: Columbia University Press, 1984).
WHITE, HAYDEN, *The Historical Imagination in Nineteenth-Century Europe* (Baltimore: Johns Hopkins University Press, 1973).
WHITTINGTON, KEITH, 'Revisiting Tocqueville's America', *American Behavioral Scientist*, 42 (1) (1998), 21–32.
WIEBE, ROBERT H., *Self-Rule: A Cultural History of American Democracy* (Chicago: University of Chicago Press, 1995).
WINTHROP, DELBA, 'Tocqueville's American Woman and "the True Conception of Democratic Progress" ', *Political Theory*, 14 (2) (1986), 2 39–61.
WOLFE, ALAN, *One Nation, After All* (New York: Penguin, 1998).
WOLIN, SHELDON S., *The Presence of the Past: Essays on the State and the Constitution* (Baltimore: Johns Hopkins University Press, 1990).
WOLOCH, ISSER, *The Jacobin Legacy: The Democratic Movement under the Directory* (Princeton, NJ: Princeton University Press, 1970)
—— *The New Regime: Transformations of the French Civic Order, 1789–1820s* (New York: W. W. Norton, 1994)

ZEITLIN, IRVING M., *Liberty, Equality, and Revolution in Alexis de Tocqueville* (Boston: Little Brown, 1971).

ZETTERBAUM, MARVIN, *Tocqueville and the Problem of Democracy* (Stanford, Calif.: Stanford University Press, 1967).

—— 'Tocqueville: Neutrality and the Use of History', *American Political Science Review* (1964), 611–21.

Index

religion
  as antidote to individualism
    243–4
  avoiding anarchy and impotence
    248–9
  democracy 88, 95–101, 178–85,
    246
  intellect 184, 246
  and liberty 178
  as natural 170
  patriotism 180–2
  and progress 183–5
  and reason 34–42
  revolution 176, 182–3
  Tocqueville's personal beliefs
    178–80
  see also beliefs; Catholicism;
    Christianity; Islam; morality;
    Protestantism
Rémusat, Charles de 35, 36, 37–8,
  48n61
republican regimes 33
  women's role 205
republicanism 248–9
Restoration 20
Revolution
  (1789) 4, 24, 157–61
  effect of 39–40
  equality and constricted liberty
    125–7, 230
  irreligion and Terror 248
  Old Regime, crisis of 142–9
  rising expectations as cause
    146–7
  Terror and attitude to rights 14
  (1830) 10, 38, 107
  (1848) 111, 175–6, 215n50,
    216n56
  American 60, 107
    impact on France 88
  centralization 148
  danger to democracy 106–12,
    175
  definition 107
  excesses of 175–8
  Furet on 228–31

liberal theory as alternative to
  228–34
morality 32–4
peasants' role in 146–7, 154
religion 176, 182–3
rights 176, 185–90
see also socialism
revolutionary ideas, crisis of
  absolutism 142–9
Richter, Melvin 113n17
rights
  and revolution 176, 185–90
  rights of man 13–15, 146
  see also natural rights
Roman Law 130
  patriarchal family 194
Rosanvallon, Pierre 28
Rousseau, Jean J. 70, 131, 170, 178
Royer-Collard, Pierre-Paul 35–6, 37,
  38
rural life, degradation of 135–7
rural transformation 154–7
  see also land; peasantry

Saint-Simon, Comte de 19, 26
Sandel, Michael 251
Santayana, William 226
Say, J.B. 16, 68
scepticism 38
Schleifer, James 57, 115n28, 119n65,
  164n38
'science sociale' 13
Second Empire 12, 229–30
Second Republic 12
self-government 38
  America 82
  juries 85–6
  liberty and equality 52–4
  and the Revolution 148
  sovereignty of the people 185–6
  threatened by centralization 79
  see also independent thought
self-interest
  and economics 68–9
  (enlightened) as necessary
    element in democracy 87–95